900
최상위
토플
VOCA

이동호
- 성균관대학교 번역–TESOL대학원 졸업
- 전 유엔아이어학원 토플강사
- 전 LinguaForum 연구소 토플개발팀장
- 현 다락원 영어출판부 토플팀장

   저서 TOEFL VOCA 2004, 100문장으로 사로잡는 Best 영어회화, 이것만 알면 네이티브와 통한다 외 다수

Michael A. Putlack
- MA in History, Tufts University, Medford, MA, USA
- Expert materials developer of TOEFL, TOEIC, and TEPS

900 최상위 토플 VOCA

지은이 이동호 · Michael A. Putlack
펴낸이 정규도
펴낸곳 (주)다락원

초판 1쇄 발행 2009년 7월 13일
초판 2쇄 발행 2010년 3월 5일

책임편집 이동호 · 황준
번역 이시은
디자인 구수정 · 윤지영 · 박소연

다락원 경기도 파주시 교하읍 문발리 509-1
내용문의 (02)736-2031 내선 300
구입문의 (02)736-2031 내선 113~114
Fax (02)732-2037
출판등록 1977년 9월 16일 제 300-1977-23호

값 13,000원

ISBN 978-89-5995-476-6 13740

http://www.darakwon.co.kr
- 다락원 홈페이지를 방문하시면 상세한 출판정보와
  함께 동영상강좌, MP3자료 등 다양한 어학 정보를
  얻으실 수 있습니다.

900
최상위
토플
VOCA

이동호 · Michael A. Putlack 지음

DARAKWON

머리말

토플(TOEFL)은 45년 이상 세계에서 가장 신뢰받는 영어능력 평가시험으로 인정받아 왔으며, 130개국 및 6,000개 이상의 대학이 채택해 세계에서 가장 널리 이용되는 시험으로 정평이 나있다. 일류 대학의 연구를 통해 개발된 토플 시험은 의사소통에 필요한 4대 언어 능력(읽기, 듣기, 쓰기, 말하기)을 수험생이 고루 갖추고 있는지를 종합적으로 평가하는 유일무이한 시험이다. 특히 한국과 같은 EFL(English as a Foreign Language)환경에 있는 학습자에게 있어 토플은 가장 좋은 영어 학습 방법 중 하나이다.

외국어로서 영어를 학습하는 국내 수험생들에게 있어 토플 고득점은 현실적으로 결코 쉬운 일이 아니다. 토플을 준비하는 수험생들이 – 어느 정도 기본 실력이 닦여져 있는 상태에서 본인이 성실하게만 준비한다면 – 120점 만점에 80~90점 대에 도달하는 것은 그리 어려운 일은 아닌 듯하다. 하지만 문제는 보다 높은 점수, 즉 자신의 TOEFL 성적을 100점 이상 얻길 바라는 수험생들은 이전의 노력 이상으로 공부를 해도 성적이 쉽게 오르지 않는다는 점이다.

토플 시험 그 자체는 영어에 대한 일반적인 의사소통능력을 테스트하는 것이지만, 자신의 성적을 고득점으로 이어가기 위해서는 보다 정확한 이해력 및 세련된 언어 표현력이 필요한 것이다. 이러한 이해력과 언어 표현력의 기반이 TOEFL 어휘임은 두말할 필요가 없다.

이 책은 위와 같은 목적으로 토플성적우수자(TOEFL Star Performer: 90점 이상의 토플고득점자)를 위해 집필하였다. 토플을 준비하면서 일종의 정체기를 맞은 수험생들, 즉 토플 성적이 안정적으로 90점 대 전후로 나오는 수험생들이 보다 더 높은 성적을 원하는 경우 학습할 수 있는 수험서인 것이다. 따라서, 본 책은 기본적인 어휘를 습득한 학생들이 자신의 현 수준을 뛰어넘기 위해 필요한, 고난도 어휘로만 구성되어 있으며, 최소한의 예문으로 목표로 삼는 최고급 토플 어휘를 가장 효과적으로 암기할 수 있는 구성을 가지고 있다.

본 책이 토플 고득점을 목표로 정진하는 학습자들에게 많은 도움이 되길 바란다.

다락원 영어출판부 토플팀장 이동호

이동호

CONTENTS

이 책의 특징

토플 최상위 900단어를 900문장으로 30일만에 끝낸다!

- ### An advanced academic vocabulary in 30 short days!
  토플성적우수자(TOEFL Star Performer: 90점 이상의 토플고득점자)에게 필요한 최상위 고급 어휘 900개를 30일만에 학습할 수 있도록 구성했다.

- ### 900 words succinctly explained
  아무리 어려운 토플 어휘라도 이해하기 쉽고 간결하게 기술된 brief definition과 동의어를 통해 의미를 명확하게 알 수 있도록 했다. 또한 토플 중상위권 학습자가 영문으로만 되어 있는 brief definition과 동의어를 통해 토플 어휘 학습을 배가시킬 수 있도록 구성했다.

- ### Precise example sentences provided
  900개의 토플 최상위 고급 어휘를 해당 단어를 이해하기에 가장 적합한 900개의 문장으로 학습할 수 있도록 구성했다. 900단어를 900문장으로 30일만에 끝낼 수 있다.

- ### Quick reference of Korean definitions included
  학습자가 주도적으로 학습할 수 있도록 단어의 뜻과 한글해석 부분을 scaffolding으로 따로 분리했다. Scaffolding은 약간의 도움만으로도 학습자가 최대의 학습효과를 얻을 수 있도록 안내하는 장치다. 따라서 학습자는 학습할 단어를 brief definition과 동의어, 예문 등을 활용해 최대한 학습하고, 그래도 모르는 부분이 있으면 scaffolding을 참조해 도움을 받을 수 있도록 했다.

- ### In alphabetical order for fast, easy reviewing
  모든 단어와 예문에는 고유번호를 알파벳순으로 부여해 학습자가 복습을 할 때 가장 빠르게 해당 단어를 참조해 볼 수 있도록 배려했다.

이 책의 구성

고유번호와 표제어

1~900까지 알파벳순으로 단어와 문장의 고유번호가 부여되어 있어, 쉽게 해당 단어를 참조해 볼 수 있다.

Brief Definition

이해하기 쉽게 간결한 영어로 해당 표제어를 설명해 토플 80~90점 대의 학습자라면 아주 편안하게 해당 표제어의 핵심을 이해할 수 있도록 했다.

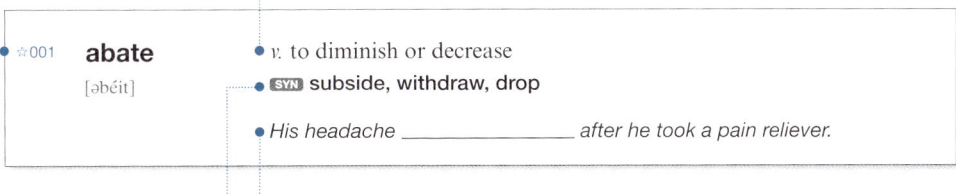

☆001 **abate**
[əbéit]

v. to diminish or decrease

SYN subside, withdraw, drop

His headache _____ after he took a pain reliever.

동의어 (synonyms)

해당 표제어와 동일한 의미를 갖는 토플 어휘를 나열했다.

예문

해당 표제어의 의미를 가장 잘 구현할 수 있는 비교적 쉬운 예문으로 구성했다. 빈칸을 두어 학습자는 해당 표제어를 직접 주어진 문맥에 맞게 활용해 보면서 어휘를 학습한다.

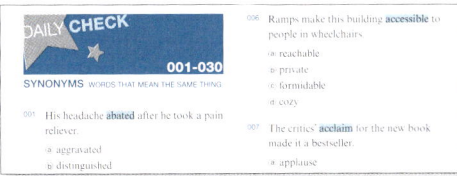

Scaffolding

약간의 도움만으로도 학습자가 최대의 학습효과를 얻을 수 있도록 안내하는 장치다. 단어의 뜻과 한글해석 부분으로 구성되어 있다.

Daily Check

1일 학습량인 30단어마다 앞에서 학습한 동일한 30개의 문장을 활용해 복습한다. 모르는 단어가 있으면 고유번호를 확인해 학습한다.

이 책의 가장 효과적인 학습방법

1   이 책은 토플 80~90점 이상의 토플상위학습자를 위한 책이다. 따라서 토플 80~90점 이상의 학습자에게 가장 큰 효과를 가져올 수 있다.

2   하루 학습할 단어는 30단어이며, 한 페이지에 6개의 표제어가 나온다. 토플상위학습자라면 6개의 표제어 중에서 2~3개는 익히 아는 단어일 가능성이 많다. 익히 아는 단어는 과감히 넘긴다.

3   모르는 단어는 brief definition과 동의어를 참조해서 해당 단어의 의미를 파악한다.

4   문장을 보면서 빈칸에 해당 단어를 채워 넣는다. 이때 시제나 어형 등에 유의한다.

5   의미파악이 모호한 경우, 해당 단어를 문장에 채워 넣고 단어의 뜻을 짐작해본다.

6   Scaffolding의 해석을 참조해 의미를 확실히 파악한다.

7   Daily Check을 통해 학습한 단어를 확인한다.

8   일주일에 한번 Daily Check을 반복하고 잊은 단어는 고유번호를 확인해 복습한다.

The more you know, the higher you score.

DAY 01

☆001 **abate**
[əbéit]

v. to diminish or decrease
SYN subside, withdraw, drop

His headache _____ after he took a pain reliever.

☆002 **abridge**
[əbrídʒ]

v. to shorten by editing
SYN shorten, cut, reduce, condense

This dictionary is an _____ version of a much larger dictionary.

☆003 **abstemious**
[əbstí:miəs]

adj. reluctant to eat or drink heavily
SYN sparing

He was so _____ that he rarely touched even a glass of wine.

☆004 **abstract**
[æbstrǽkt]

adj. not concrete or specific
SYN generalized, simplified

_____ concepts are easier to understand if you give some specific examples.

☆005 **abstruse**
[əbstrú:s]

adj. hard to understand
SYN difficult, hard

Some kinds of mathematics are so _____ that only a few people understand them.

☆006 **accessible**
[æksésəbəl]

adj. easily attained or obtained; within reach (often used in reference to public buildings)
SYN available, reachable, obtainable

Ramps make this building _____ to people in wheelchairs.

SCAFFOLDING

001 줄이다, 완화되다, 감소하다
그의 두통은 그가 진통제를 먹은 후 완화되었다abated.

002 단축하다, 요약하다, 생략하다
이 사전은 훨씬 큰 사전의 요약abridged 본이다.

003 절제하는, 금욕적인
그는 너무 금욕적abstemious이라서 와인에 손을 대는 일 조차도 거의 없었다.

004 추상적인, 관념적인
추상적인Abstract 개념은 구체적인 예를 들어 주면 더 쉽게 이해할 수 있다.

005 난해한, 심오한
어떤 종류의 수학적 계산은 너무 난해하여abstruse 몇 사람 만이 이해할 수 있다.

006 접근할 수 있는, 얻기 쉬운
경사로는 휠체어를 탄 사람들이 건물에 접근할 수accessible 있도록 해 준다.

☆007	**acclaim** [əkléim]	*n.* strongly expressed approval or acceptance; high praise (of some celebrity or public figure) **SYN** praise, applause *The critics' _____ for the new book made it a bestseller.*
☆008	**acclaim** [əkléim]	*v.* to praise someone highly, usually in public **SYN** hail, praise, applaud *The newspapers _____ the new mayor's election and wished him success.*
☆009	**accolade** [ǽkəlèid]	*n.* a good review; a highly favorable notice; a lavish expression of approval **SYN** praise *The singer received many _____ for her fine performance.*
☆010	**acknowledge** [əknálidʒ]	*v.* to take notice of something; to say that one sees or knows about a specific fact, event, or person **SYN** recognize, admit *The worker _____ that he had not done his job well.*
☆011	**acquiesce** [æ̀kwiés]	*v.* to give consent, usually by remaining silent or offering no resistance **SYN** submit, approve, go along with, offer no resistance *The company did not fire him but still _____ in his removal.*
☆012	**acrid** [ǽkrid]	*adj.* very pungent; irritating to the nose and eyes; burning (usually applied to odors) **SYN** sharp, bitter, harsh, penetrating *The _____ smell of the smoke made him hold his nose.*

DAY 01

☆013 **acrimonious**
[æ̀krəmóuniəs]

adj. expressed in angry and hostile language, with bitterness

SYN bitter, biting, sharp, nasty, acid

Their argument was so _____ that they stopped speaking to each other.

☆014 **acute**
[əkjú:t]

adj. sharp and sudden; very pointed and penetrating; extremely perceptive

SYN sharp, intense, keen, profound, pointed

The injury caused him _____ pain, but he kept walking anyway.

☆015 **adulation**
[æ̀dʒəléiʃən]

n. great admiration; intense love of and devotion to a person

SYN flattery, praise, applause

The _____ from the public made the movie actor feel very proud.

☆016 **adversary**
[ǽdvərsèri]

n. an opponent, competitor, enemy, or foe, usually in a hostile context

SYN enemy, foe, opposition

This general was the most powerful _____ the army had encountered.

☆017 **adversity**
[ædvə́:rsəti]

n. an unfavorable situation

SYN difficulty, opposition, persecution

One good thing about _____ is that it makes us stronger.

☆018 **aesthetic**
[esθétik]

adj. related to beauty

SYN beautiful

The hotel combined high technology with a strong _____ appeal.

SCAFFOLDING

013 신랄한, 독살스러운
014 격렬한, 날카로운
015 추종, 아첨
016 적, 상대편
017 불운, 역경, 재난
018 미의, 미학의, 심미적인

그들의 논쟁은 너무 신랄해서acrimonious 그들은 서로 대화하는 것을 그만뒀다.
부상은 그에게 격렬한acute 고통을 유발했지만, 그는 계속해서 걸어갔다.
대중의 추종adulation 때문에 그 영화배우는 매우 자랑스러워했다.
이 장군은 그 군대가 만났던 가장 강력한 적adversary이었다.
역경adversity의 한 가지 좋은 점은 그것이 우리를 더 강하게 만든다는 것이다.
그 호텔은 첨단 기술을 강력한 미학적aesthetic 매력과 연결시켰다.

14

☆019 **aesthetic**
[esθétik]

n. a principle of art; a system of rules or standards for recognizing and evaluating beauty

SYN beauty, taste

The painter's work was unpopular because his _____ was so crude.

☆020 **affable**
[ǽfəbəl]

adj. pleasant to talk to; agreeable; very sociable

SYN friendly, nice, personable

The _____ storekeeper told us much about the town we were visiting.

☆021 **affectation**
[æ̀fektéiʃən]

n. a display or show performed only for effect, not sincerely or honestly

SYN pretension, act, ruse, masquerade

His English accent was only an _____, for he was not English.

☆022 **affirmation**
[æ̀fərméiʃən]

n. a declaration; a statement that something is true

SYN assertion, statement

His long record of service is an _____ of his loyalty to the company.

☆023 **aggregate**
[ǽgrigèit]

n. a group or collection

SYN assemblage, composite

Some philosophies are _____ of many different ideas that have been made into unified systems of thought.

☆024 **alleviate**
[əlí:vièit]

v. to reduce or diminish

SYN relieve, lessen, reduce, assuage

He was in such pain that the doctor gave him some medicine to _____ it.

DAY 01

SCAFFOLDING

019 미의식, 미학

020 붙임성 있는, 정중한

021 가장, 뽐냄

022 확언, 단언, 긍정

023 집합(체), 총액

024 (고통을) 완화시키다, 경감하다

그 화가의 미의식aesthetic은 너무 미숙했기 때문에 그의 작품은 인기가 없었다.

그 붙임성 있는affable 가게 주인이 우리가 방문하고 있는 도시에 대해서 많은 것을 말해주었다.

그의 영어 억양은 꾸며낸 것일affectation 뿐이다. 왜냐하면 그는 영국인이 아니기 때문이다.

그의 긴 근무경력은 회사에 대한 그의 충정을 확실히 보여주는 것affirmation이다.

일부 철학적 원리들은 여러 다른 생각들이 모여 통일된 사고 체계가 된 집합체aggregates이다.

그가 너무 심한 통증을 느꼈기 때문에 의사는 그에게 그것을 경감시키는alleviate 약을 주었다.

☆025 **aloof**
[əlúːf]

adj. withdrawn; haughty; unsociable
SYN unconcerned, indifferent

Though she appeared _____ to others' problems, she really was very concerned.

☆026 **altruistic**
[æltruːístik]

adj. generous; concerned with others' welfare
SYN unselfish, generous

Some animals exhibit _____ behavior by protecting one another in times of crisis.

☆027 **amass**
[əmǽs]

v. to collect or hoard something
SYN gather, assemble, collect

He _____ a large amount of money through his dealings in land sales.

☆028 **ambiguous**
[æmbígjuəs]

adj. not specific; uncertain
SYN vague, uncertain, indeterminate

Some words in this document are so _____ that they require further explanation.

☆029 **ambivalence**
[æmbívələns]

n. uncertainty; a lack of commitment
SYN indecisiveness, uncertainty

He must overcome his _____ about the colleges and choose one or the other.

☆030 **ambivalent**
[æmbívələnt]

adj. uncertain; uncommitted
SYN indecisive, uncertain, uncommitted

These two choices are equally good, so I am _____ about them.

SCAFFOLDING

025 냉담한, 무관심한   비록 그녀가 다른 사람들의 문제에 무관심해aloof 보였지만, 사실 그녀는 매우 걱정하고 있었다.
026 이타적인   어떤 동물은 위기의 순간에 서로를 보호함으로써 이타적인altruistic 행동을 보인다.
027 쌓다, 모으다   그는 토지 매매 거래를 통해 많은 양의 돈을 모았다amassed.
028 두 가지 이상의 뜻이 있는, 모호한   이 서류에 있는 일부 단어들은 너무 모호해서ambiguous 부연설명이 필요하다.
029 상반되는 감정, 양면 가치, 주저   그는 그 대학들에 대해 주저함ambivalence을 극복하고 어느 것이든지 하나를 선택해야 한다.
030 상반되는 감정을 가진, 양면 가치적인   이 두 가지 선택사항이 모두 똑같이 좋아서 나는 한가지만 선택하기 어렵다ambivalent.

16

SYNONYMS WORDS THAT MEAN THE SAME THING

001 His headache abated after he took a pain reliever.

ⓐ aggravated
ⓑ distinguished
ⓒ subsided
ⓓ held

002 This dictionary is an abridged version of a much larger dictionary.

ⓐ prolonged
ⓑ condensed
ⓒ generated
ⓓ ameliorated

003 He was so abstemious that he rarely touched even a glass of wine.

ⓐ amiable
ⓑ sparing
ⓒ contentious
ⓓ immoderate

004 Abstract concepts are easier to understand if you give some specific examples.

ⓐ intangible
ⓑ concrete
ⓒ amicable
ⓓ precise

005 Some kinds of mathematics are so abstruse that only a few people understand them.

ⓐ derogative
ⓑ conciliatory
ⓒ congenial
ⓓ difficult

006 Ramps make this building accessible to people in wheelchairs.

ⓐ reachable
ⓑ private
ⓒ formidable
ⓓ cozy

007 The critics' acclaim for the new book made it a bestseller.

ⓐ applause
ⓑ disapproval
ⓒ popularity
ⓓ censure

008 The newspapers acclaimed the new mayor's election and wished him success.

ⓐ criticized
ⓑ added
ⓒ hailed
ⓓ emphasized

009 The singer received many accolades for her fine performance.

ⓐ foes
ⓑ awards
ⓒ articles
ⓓ criticisms

010 The worker acknowledged that he had not done his job well.

ⓐ ignored
ⓑ acquiesced
ⓒ underlined
ⓓ contended

011 The company did not fire him but still acquiesced in his removal.

ⓐ concocted
ⓑ requested
ⓒ approved
ⓓ conspired

012 The **acrid** smell of the smoke made him hold his nose.

   ⓐ bitter
   ⓑ puzzling
   ⓒ lush
   ⓓ interesting

013 Their argument was so **acrimonious** that they stopped speaking to each other.

   ⓐ friendly
   ⓑ genuine
   ⓒ prolonged
   ⓓ biting

014 The injury caused him **acute** pain, but he kept walking anyway.

   ⓐ congenital
   ⓑ intense
   ⓒ crucial
   ⓓ articulate

015 The **adulation** from the public made the movie actor feel very proud.

   ⓐ scorn
   ⓑ awareness
   ⓒ contempt
   ⓓ flattery

016 This general was the most powerful **adversary** the army had encountered.

   ⓐ enemy
   ⓑ ally
   ⓒ individual
   ⓓ leader

017 One good thing about **adversity** is that it makes us stronger.

   ⓐ fortune
   ⓑ disgust
   ⓒ difficulty
   ⓓ blessing

018 The hotel combined high technology with a strong **aesthetic** appeal.

   ⓐ metaphoric
   ⓑ sparing
   ⓒ beautiful
   ⓓ ingrained

019 The painter's work was unpopular because his **aesthetic** was so crude.

   ⓐ applause
   ⓑ taste
   ⓒ gaucheness
   ⓓ priority

020 The **affable** storekeeper told us much about the town we were visiting.

   ⓐ disagreeable
   ⓑ quiet
   ⓒ inborn
   ⓓ friendly

021 His English accent was only an **affectation**, for he was not English.

   ⓐ affection
   ⓑ pretension
   ⓒ sincerity
   ⓓ earnestness

022 His long record of service is an **affirmation** of his loyalty to the company.

   ⓐ aggregation
   ⓑ assertion
   ⓒ denial
   ⓓ solidarity

023 Some philosophies are **aggregates** of many different ideas that have been made into unified systems of thought.

   ⓐ constituencies
   ⓑ disparities
   ⓒ proportions
   ⓓ assemblages

024 He was in such pain that the doctor gave him some medicine to **alleviate** it.

  ⓐ relieve

  ⓑ distinguish

  ⓒ deplore

  ⓓ decry

025 Though she appeared **aloof** to others' problems, she really was very concerned.

  ⓐ passionate

  ⓑ unconcerned

  ⓒ ambivalent

  ⓓ uncommitted

026 Some animals exhibit **altruistic** behavior by protecting one another in times of crisis.

  ⓐ blighted

  ⓑ ambitious

  ⓒ biased

  ⓓ unselfish

027 He **amassed** a large amount of money through his dealings in land sales.

  ⓐ dispersed

  ⓑ spent

  ⓒ assembled

  ⓓ vanished

028 Some words in this document are so **ambiguous** that they require further explanation.

  ⓐ vague

  ⓑ lucid

  ⓒ distasteful

  ⓓ crystalline

029 He must overcome his **ambivalence** about the colleges and choose one or the other.

  ⓐ stability

  ⓑ indecisiveness

  ⓒ persistence

  ⓓ tenacity

030 These two choices are equally good, so I am **ambivalent** about them.

  ⓐ caustic

  ⓑ amenable

  ⓒ uncertain

  ⓓ breakeven

DAY 01

Answers

001-005 ⓒⓑⓑⓐⓓ	016-020 ⓐⓒⓒⓑⓓ
006-010 ⓐⓐⓒⓑⓑ	021-025 ⓑⓑⓓⓐⓑ
011-015 ⓒⓐⓓⓑⓓ	026-030 ⓓⓒⓐⓑⓒ

DAY 02

☆031 **ambulatory**
[ǽmbjulətɔ̀ːri]

adj. able to walk

SYN **walking, mobile**

He was in a wheelchair for a while after his accident but is
_____ now.

☆032 **ameliorate**
[əmíːljərèit]

v. to make better

SYN **improve, alleviate**

Adding fertilizer _____ the poor condition of the soil.

☆033 **amiable**
[éimiəbəl]

adj. friendly; likable; genial; personable

SYN **likable, friendly**

An _____ person usually has a lot of friends.

☆034 **amity**
[ǽməti]

n. friendship; concord

SYN **friendship, comradeship**

There was such _____ between the two men that they
remained friends for more than 60 years.

☆035 **amorphous**
[əmɔ́ːrfəs]

adj. undefined in form; shapeless

SYN **shapeless, undefined**

Through the telescope, the nebula looked like a big, _____
cloud of gas.

☆036 **ample**
[ǽmpl]

adj. enough or more than enough

SYN **abundant, plentiful, profuse, substantial, adequate, enough**

_____ free parking is available.

☆037 **anachronistic**
[ənǽkrənístik]
adj. from another time; not of this particular era

SYN outdated, old-fashioned

The automobile soon made horse-drawn vehicles seem _____.

☆038 **analogous**
[ənǽləgəs]
adj. similar in purpose, design, or function

SYN comparable, similar

A flipper on a whale is _____ to a wing on a bird.

☆039 **anarchist**
[ǽnərkist]
n. one who opposes all authority or authoritarianism

SYN anti-authoritarian

The peaceful _____ simply wanted people to live independently and to mind their own business.

☆040 **anarchy**
[ǽnərki]
n. extreme social disorder or unrest

SYN chaos, riot

When the police in the city went on strike, the result was _____ for several days.

☆041 **anecdote**
[ǽnikdòut]
n. a brief story about a person

SYN story, report

There were many funny _____ about the professor, who liked to tell amusing stories.

☆042 **animated**
[ǽnəmèitid]
adj. energetic; made to move or to appear to be in motion

SYN lively, vigorous

He became very _____ when someone asked him to discuss his most recent book.

SCAFFOLDING

037 시대에 맞지 않는, 시대 착오의   자동차는 곧 말이 끄는 차량을 시대에 뒤떨어져anachronistic 보이게 했다.

038 유사한, 닮은   고래의 지느러미는 새의 날개와 유사하다analogous.

039 무정부주의자, 반체제 반역자   그 온화한 무정부주의자anarchist는 단순히 사람들이 독립적으로 살 수 있고 자신의 일에만 신경을 쓸 수 있는 것을 원했다.

040 무정부 상태, 혼란, 무질서   그 도시에서 경찰들이 파업을 했을 때, 그 결과는 며칠 동안의 혼란anarchy이었다.

041 일화, 비화   그 교수에 대한 웃긴 일화anecdotes가 많이 있었는데, 그 교수는 재미있는 이야기 하는 것을 좋아했다.

042 생기가 있는, 활기가 넘치는   누군가 그에게 자신의 가장 최근 책에 대해 토론하고자 했을 때 그는 매우 활기가 넘쳤다animated.

DAY 02

☆043 **animosity**
[ǽnəmásəti]

n. enmity; hostile or unfriendly feeling

SYN hostility, opposition, enmity

The _____ between the two families ended when two of their children married.

☆044 **anomaly**
[ənáməli]

n. a departure from the norm; something unusual or exceptional

SYN deviation, oddity

This map of the area shows a slight _____ in gravity that indicates an ore deposit.

☆045 **anonymous**
[ənánəməs]

n. anonymity
[ǽnəníməti]

adj. unidentified; uncredited; unattributable to one specific source

SYN nameless, unidentified

The document is marked "_____," so we have no idea who the author was.

☆046 **antagonism**
[æntǽgənìzəm]

n. opposition; enmity

SYN opposition, enmity

Mutual _____ left the two countries unable to cooperate on anything.

☆047 **antediluvian**
[æntidilú:viən]

adj. very old; ancient; prehistoric; literally, "from before the flood," meaning Noah's flood

SYN ancient, antique, prehistoric

Dinosaurs were once identified simply as _____ monsters.

☆048 **antidote**
[ǽntidòut]

n. a counteragent or a cure for a poison

SYN remedy, cure, countermeasure

The _____ for the snake's venom was very rare and expensive.

SCAFFOLDING

043 원한, 증오, 적개심   두 가정 사이의 원한animosity은 그들의 자녀들이 결혼을 함으로써 끝이 났다.

044 변칙, 이례   그 지역의 이 지도는 광물 매장량을 나타내는 중량에 대한 약간의 변칙anomaly을 보여준다.

045 작자 불명의, 익명의   그 문헌은 "작자 불명anonymous"이라고 되어 있어서 우리는 작가가 누구였는지 모른다.

046 반대, 적개심, 반작용   서로에 대한 적개심antagonism은 두 나라를 어떤 것에 있어서도 서로 협력할 수 없는 상태로 놓아 두었다.

047 노아의 홍수 이전의, 구시대적인   공룡은 한 때 단순히 구시대의antediluvian 괴물로 인식되었다.

048 해독제, 해결 방법   뱀 독의 해독제antidote는 매우 희소하고 비쌌다.

☆049 **antipathy**
[æntípəθi]

n. aversion, fear, or hatred

SYN dislike, hatred

Because of _____ to flowers, he had no plants at all in his house.

☆050 **antiquated**
[æntikwèitid]

adj. obsolete; out of date

SYN old-fashioned, antique, outdated, ancient

When his _____ car broke down, he could not find the parts to fix it.

☆051 **anxiety**
[æŋzáiəti]

n. worry; unease; apprehension; fear about what may happen in the future

SYN nervousness, edginess

adj. anxious
[æŋkʃəs]

Flying caused her such _____ that she preferred to travel by train instead.

☆052 **apathy**
[ǽpəθi]

n. a lack of concern or interest

SYN indifference, unconcern

It is hard to raise money for a cause toward which there is widespread _____ .

☆053 **apocryphal**
[əpákrəfəl]

adj. untrue; imaginary; unverifiable; mythical; not supported by historical or biographical facts

SYN invented, unverifiable, untrue, mythical

Please don't believe that story because it is _____ .

☆054 **appease**
[əpíːz]

v. to bring peace and quiet

SYN soothe, calm

To _____ her angry neighbor, she sent a gift of fruit and flowers.

DAY 02

SCAFFOLDING

049 반감, 혐오, 싫은 일   그는 꽃을 매우 싫어해서antipathy 그의 집에는 식물이 하나도 없었다.

050 낡은, 시대에 뒤진   그의 낡은antiquated 차가 고장났을 때 그는 그것을 고칠 부품을 구할 수가 없었다.

051 걱정, 불안, 염원   비행기를 타는 것은 그녀에게 큰 불안감anxiety을 가져다 주었기 때문에 그녀는 대신 기차로 여행하기를 선호했다.

052 무감동, 무감정, 냉담, 무관심   사람들의 관심이 없는apathy 일을 위해 돈을 끌어 모으는 것은 어렵다.

053 저작자가 의심스러운, 가짜의   그 이야기는 위작apocryphal이니까 믿지 마라.

054 달래다, 가라앉히다, 만족시키다   그녀는 화가 난 이웃을 달래기 위해appease 과일과 꽃을 선물로 보냈다.

☆055 **apprehension**
[æ̀prihénʃən]

n. worry about the future

SYN unease, worry, fretfulness

The streets were icy, so she viewed any travel with _____.

☆056 **apprehensive**
[æ̀prihénsiv]

adj. worried about the future

SYN uneasy, worried, fretful

I'm _____ about hiking along that path because of falling rocks.

☆057 **arable**
[ǽrəbəl]

adj. suitable for farming

SYN farmable, fertile

The state has a large farming industry because it has plenty of _____ land.

☆058 **arbitrary**
[ɑ́:rbitrèri]

adj. determined by whim or circumstance

SYN capricious, irrational, random

Our budget was set by an _____ decision and does not meet our real needs.

☆059 **archaic**
[ɑ:rkéiik]

adj. out of date or fashion

SYN antiquated, old, outdated

This letter is written in such _____ language that no one today can understand it.

☆060 **ardent**
[ɑ́:rdənt]

adj. eager; passionate; committed; determined; fanatical

SYN passionate, eager, emotional

An _____ football player as a child, he became a professional when he grew up.

SCAFFOLDING

055 우려, 염려, 불안   거리는 얼음으로 덮여 있었기 때문에 그녀는 모든 움직임을 우려와apprehension 함께 바라보았다.
056 우려하는, 염려하는   나는 낙석 때문에 그 길을 따라서 걸어가는 것에 대해 걱정이 된다apprehensive.
057 경작할 수 있는, 경작에 알맞은   그 주는 경작 가능한arable 땅이 많기 때문에 거대한 농산업이 들어서있다.
058 제멋대로인, 독단적인   우리의 예산은 제 멋대로인arbitrary 결정에 의해서 세워졌고 우리의 실질적인 요구에 부합하지 않는다.
059 고풍의, 고대의   이 편지는 상당한 고대archaic의 언어로 쓰여졌기 때문에 오늘날에는 아무도 그것을 이해할 수 없다.
060 열렬한, 열심인, 격렬한   어려서부터 열렬한ardent 축구 선수였던 그는 성인이 되어서 프로 축구 선수가 되었다.

24

SYNONYMS WORDS THAT MEAN THE SAME THING

031 He was in a wheelchair for a while after his accident but is **ambulatory** now.

ⓐ disabled

ⓑ compliant

ⓒ deleterious

ⓓ mobile

032 Adding fertilizer **ameliorated** the poor condition of the soil.

ⓐ improved

ⓑ worsened

ⓒ adopted

ⓓ lapsed

033 An **amiable** person usually has a lot of friends.

ⓐ mean

ⓑ coy

ⓒ friendly

ⓓ clumsy

034 There was such **amity** between the two men that they remained friends for more than 60 years.

ⓐ comradeship

ⓑ respect

ⓒ hostility

ⓓ depravity

035 Through the telescope, the nebula looked like a big, **amorphous** cloud of gas.

ⓐ expansive

ⓑ detrimental

ⓒ shapeless

ⓓ feasible

036 **Ample** free parking is available.

ⓐ deliberate

ⓑ devious

ⓒ fertile

ⓓ profuse

037 The automobile soon made horse-drawn vehicles seem **anachronistic**.

ⓐ fell

ⓑ remote

ⓒ outdated

ⓓ viable

038 A flipper on a whale is **analogous** to a wing on a bird.

ⓐ perpendicular

ⓑ tame

ⓒ submissive

ⓓ similar

039 The peaceful **anarchist** simply wanted people to live independently and to mind their own business.

ⓐ protestor

ⓑ protagonist

ⓒ antagonist

ⓓ anti-authoritarian

040 When the police in the city went on strike, the result was **anarchy** for several days.

ⓐ order

ⓑ chaos

ⓒ discipline

ⓓ tumulus

041 There were many funny **anecdotes** about the professor, who liked to tell amusing stories.

ⓐ legends

ⓑ stories

ⓒ captions

ⓓ prescriptions

042 He became very **animated** when someone asked him to discuss his most recent book.

ⓐ still
ⓑ vigorous
ⓒ lethargic
ⓓ phlegmatic

043 The **animosity** between the two families ended when two of their children married.

ⓐ hostility
ⓑ goodwill
ⓒ affection
ⓓ rivalry

044 This map of the area shows a slight **anomaly** in gravity that indicates an ore deposit.

ⓐ deviation
ⓑ conformity
ⓒ normality
ⓓ example

045 The document is marked "**anonymous**," so we have no idea who the author was.

ⓐ taciturn
ⓑ unidentified
ⓒ unanimous
ⓓ confidential

046 Mutual **antagonism** left the two countries unable to cooperate on anything.

ⓐ troupe
ⓑ tumult
ⓒ uncertainty
ⓓ opposition

047 Dinosaurs were once identified simply as **antediluvian** monsters.

ⓐ indistinct
ⓑ prehistoric
ⓒ haughty
ⓓ prolix

048 The **antidote** for the snake's venom was very rare and expensive.

ⓐ procedure
ⓑ remedy
ⓒ tolerance
ⓓ appeasement

049 Because of his **antipathy** to flowers, he had no plants at all in his house.

ⓐ sympathy
ⓑ affinity
ⓒ enmity
ⓓ allergy

050 When his **antiquated** car broke down, he could not find the parts to fix it.

ⓐ old-fashioned
ⓑ modernized
ⓒ appreciated
ⓓ fastened

051 Flying caused her such **anxiety** that she preferred to travel by train instead.

ⓐ blight
ⓑ edginess
ⓒ inclination
ⓓ abstinence

052 It is hard to raise money for a cause toward which there is widespread **apathy**.

ⓐ zeal
ⓑ consideration
ⓒ unconcern
ⓓ ruthlessness

053 Please don't believe that story because it is **apocryphal**.

ⓐ unverifiable
ⓑ classified
ⓒ evoked
ⓓ hefty

054 To **appease** her angry neighbor, she sent a gift of fruit and flowers.

ⓐ soothe
ⓑ request
ⓒ inflame
ⓓ disrespect

055 The streets were icy, so she viewed any travel with **apprehension**.

ⓐ tranquility
ⓑ placidity
ⓒ harshness
ⓓ fretfulness

056 I'm **apprehensive** about hiking along that path because of falling rocks.

ⓐ understandable
ⓑ uneasy
ⓒ equipped
ⓓ inclined

057 The state has a large farming industry because it has plenty of **arable** land.

ⓐ barren
ⓑ flat
ⓒ void
ⓓ fertile

058 Our budget was set by an **arbitrary** decision and does not meet our real needs.

ⓐ problematic
ⓑ peaceful
ⓒ random
ⓓ sparing

059 This letter is written in such **archaic** language that no one today can understand it.

ⓐ prosaic
ⓑ outdated
ⓒ modern
ⓓ verbose

060 An **ardent** football player as a child, he became a professional when he grew up.

ⓐ apathetic
ⓑ eager
ⓒ athletic
ⓓ biased

Answers

031-035 ⓓⓐⓒⓐⓒ	046-050 ⓓⓑⓑⓒⓐ
036-040 ⓓⓒⓓⓓⓑ	051-055 ⓑⓒⓐⓐⓓ
041-045 ⓑⓑⓐⓐⓑ	056-060 ⓑⓓⓒⓑⓑ

☆061 **arid**
[ǽrid]

adj. having little or no rain; being without moisture
SYN barren, desert, dry, parched, boring, dull, tedious

An _____ climate is characterized by a high evaporation rate and very little precipitation.

☆062 **arrogance**
[ǽrəgəns]

n. extreme pride; a superior attitude
SYN haughtiness, pride

After her business succeeded, she became known for her _____, impatience, and rudeness.

☆063 **arrogant**
[ǽrəgənt]

adj. extremely proud and overbearing
SYN haughty, proud, overbearing

His _____ manners at school made him widely disliked.

☆064 **articulate**
[ɑːrtíkjəlèit]

adj. well-spoken; fluent; able to explain one's thoughts clearly
SYN eloquent, well-spoken, fluent

Being highly _____, he could explain the lessons very clearly.

☆065 **artifact**
[ɑ́ːrtəfæ̀kt]

n. an object produced by human work; a tool or craft; anything artificial
SYN tool, craft

Native American _____ tell us much about the cultures which produced them.

☆066 **artisan**
[ɑ́ːrtəzən]

n. an artist or craftsman; a skilled worker
SYN craftsman, artist

The basketmakers were skilled _____ who decorated their baskets with complex designs.

SCAFFOLDING

061 건조한, 불모의 　　　　건조한arid 기후는 높은 증발율과 적은 강우량으로 특징지어진다.

062 거만, 불손, 오만 　　　그녀는 사업이 성공하고 나서 거만arrogance하고 성급하며 무례한 사람으로 알려지게 되었다.

063 거만한, 건방진 　　　　학교에서 그의 거만한arrogant 태도는 많은 사람들이 그를 싫어하게 만들었다.

064 명료한, 발음이 똑똑한 　그는 발음이 매우 똑똑해서articulate 강의를 아주 명쾌하게 설명할 수 있었다.

065 인공물, 공예품 　　　　미국 향토 공예품들은artifacts 그것들을 만들어 낸 문화들에 대해 많은 것을 말해 준다.

066 장인, 공예가 　　　　　그 바구니 제작자들은 바구니를 복잡한 디자인으로 장식하는 숙련된 공예가들artisans이었다.

☆067 **ascendancy**
[əséndənsi]

n. a rise to higher rank or status

SYN rise, ascent, climb

During their _____, many civilizations experienced rapid population growth.

☆068 **ascetic**
[əsétik]

adj. self-denying; unwilling to indulge in luxuries or personal comforts

SYN austere, strict

The monks led extremely _____ lives and ate only dry bread and vegetables.

☆069 **aspire**
[əspáiər]

v. to hope; to aim; to have high goals

SYN hope, aim

My father _____ to be an artist but had to be content to work as an architect instead.

☆070 **assiduous**
[əsídʒuəs]

adj. hardworking; conscientious; attentive to details, deadlines, and quality of work

SYN diligent, conscientious, hardworking

Although he was an _____ worker, he never rose very high in rank at the company.

☆071 **assuage**
[əswéidʒ]

v. to relieve; to make less intense or severe

SYN soothe, relieve, cool, calm

To _____ her brother's hurt feelings, she told him everyone on the team still liked him.

☆072 **astute**
[əstjúːt]

adj. shrewd; perceptive; very intelligent

SYN clever, ingenious, perceptive

To improve the flavor of the dish, the cook thought of an _____ use for garlic.

DAY 03

SCAFFOLDING

067 우위, 우세, 권세　　많은 문명들은 패권기ascendancy 동안 급속한 인구 성장을 경험했다.
068 고행의, 금욕적인, 금욕주의의　　그 수도사들은 매우 금욕적인ascetic 삶을 살면서 마른 빵과 야채만을 먹었다.
069 열망하다, 높이 오르다　　우리 아버지는 예술가가 되는 것을 열망하셨지만aspired 대신에 건축가로서의 일에 만족해야만 했다.
070 끊임없는, 근면한　　그는 비록 열심히 일 했지만assiduous 회사에서 아주 높은 지위에 오르지는 못했다.
071 완화하다, 진정시키다, 달래다　　오빠의 상한 감정을 달래기assuage 위해서 그녀는 오빠에게 팀원 모두가 여전히 그를 좋아한다고 말했다.
072 기민한, 영리한, 독창적인　　그 요리사는 음식의 맛을 향상시키기 위해서 마늘의 독창적인astute 사용법을 생각해 냈다.

☆073 **atrophy**
[ǽtrəfi]

n. a decrease in size because of disuse

SYN wasting, deterioration, weakening

The _____ in his muscles showed that he had had little opportunity to exercise them.

☆074 **attribute**
[ətríbjuːt]

n. a trait, property, quality, or characteristic

SYN trait, characteristic, quality

Among the _____ of this species is the ability to change color.

☆075 **audacious**
[ɔːdéiʃəs]

adj. bold; brave; fearless

SYN daring, bold, risky

The soldiers carried out an _____ raid on the enemy and took many prisoners.

☆076 **augment**
[ɔːgmént]

v. to make something bigger or stronger

SYN increase, expand, strengthen

Heavy rains _____ the water supply in the reservoir.

☆077 **auspicious**
[ɔːspíʃəs]

adj. indicative of success or favorable conditions

SYN favorable, promising

The good weather seemed like an _____ time to plant a garden.

☆078 **austere**
[ɔːstíər]

adj. stern; harsh; severe; lacking in comfort or adornment

SYN severe, strict, gaunt

The family's little home looked _____ compared with the hotel we had just left.

SCAFFOLDING

073 쇠약, 감퇴
074 속성, 특질
075 대담한, 뻔뻔스러운, 무례한
076 증가시키다, 증대시키다
077 길조의, 상서로운
078 엄한, 꾸밈없는, 간결한

그의 근육 쇠약atrophy은 그가 근육을 운동시킬 기회가 거의 없었다는 것을 보여준다.
이 종의 특질attributes 중 하나는 색깔을 변화시키는 능력이다.
그 군인들은 적을 대담히audacious 급습하고 많은 포로들을 빼앗았다.
폭우는 저수지의 물 공급량을 증대시켰다augmented.
좋은 날씨는 정원에 나무를 심기에 상서로운auspicious 시간처럼 보였다.
그 가족의 작은 집은 우리가 막 떠난 호텔과 비교했을 때 검소해austere 보였다.

30

☆079 **authentic**
[ɔ:θéntik]

adj. real; genuine; confirmed; true rather than false

SYN **genuine, true, verifiable**

X-rays help us tell the difference between _____ paintings and fakes.

☆080 **authoritarian**
[əθɔ̀:rətɛ́əriən]

adj. requiring absolute obedience to orders

SYN **dictatorial, commanding**

In an _____ society, all orders must be obeyed.

☆081 **autonomous**
[ɔ:tánəməs]

adj. independent; self-governing; self-sustaining

SYN **independent, free**

The state of Texas was an _____ republic before it joined the United States.

☆082 **avarice**
[ǽvəris]

n. intense desire for money and material wealth

SYN **greed, money lust**

Molière wrote a famous play about a man who was consumed by _____.

☆083 **aversion**
[əvə́:rʒən]

n. dislike; antipathy; loathing; a desire to avoid something when at all possible

SYN **dislike, fear, distaste**

After his car accident, he had an _____ to driving.

☆084 **avert**
[əvə́:rt]

v. to prevent, deter, or turn away; to keep from happening

SYN **prevent, avoid, forestall**

The bus driver was able to _____ an accident by putting on the brakes at once.

DAY 03

SCAFFOLDING

079 믿을 만한, 진정한, 진짜의   엑스레이는 진짜authentic 그림과 모조품의 차이를 구별하는 데에 도움이 된다.
080 권위주의자, 독재주의자   독재주의authoritarian 사회에서는 반드시 모든 명령에 복종해야 한다.
081 자치적인, 독립된, 자율적인   텍사스 주는 미합중국에 합류하기 전에 자치autonomous 공화국이었다.
082 탐욕, 허욕   Molière는 탐욕avarice에 사로잡힌 한 남자에 관한 유명한 극을 썼다.
083 싫음, 혐오, 반감   그는 교통사고 후 운전에 대한 혐오감이 생겼다aversion.
084 돌리다, 비키다, 피하다   그 버스기사는 즉시 브레이크를 밟음으로써 사고를 피할 수avert 있었다.

31

☆085 **banal**
[bənǽl]

adj. boring; trite; undistinguished; unoriginal

SYN trite, familiar, boring

The drama was a _____ story of bored people seeking amusement.

☆086 **baneful**
[béinfəl]

adj. evil or causing evil

SYN damaging, deleterious, detrimental, injurious, harmful

No _____ herbs have been found so far.

☆087 **barren**
[bǽrən]

adj. lifeless; sterile; unable to support life or produce offspring

SYN unproductive, lifeless, sterile

Between the two cities was a _____ piece of land where only a few small trees grew.

☆088 **bastion**
[bǽstʃən]

n. a stronghold, source of strength, or fortified area

SYN stronghold, fortress, citadel

The castle was a _____ of strength, so everyone fled to it for safety in times of danger.

☆089 **bear**
[bɛər]

v. to carry, support, endure, survive, withstand, or uphold

SYN carry, hold, withstand

The loss of his home was more than he could _____, so he collapsed.

☆090 **beguile**
[bigáil]

v. to deceive by trickery

SYN deceive, trick

The salesman _____ the man into buying a product that did not work.

SYNONYMS WORDS THAT MEAN THE SAME THING

061 An **arid** climate is characterized by a high evaporation rate and very little precipitation.

ⓐ acid

ⓑ lush

ⓒ barren

ⓓ moist

062 After her business succeeded, she became known for her **arrogance**, impatience, and rudeness.

ⓐ recalcitrance

ⓑ prudence

ⓒ impudence

ⓓ discretion

063 His **arrogant** manners at school made him widely disliked.

ⓐ haughty

ⓑ humble

ⓒ elaborate

ⓓ discrete

064 Being highly **articulate**, he could explain the lessons very clearly.

ⓐ confounded

ⓑ eloquent

ⓒ separate

ⓓ convoluted

065 Native American **artifacts** tell us much about the cultures which produced them.

ⓐ scientists

ⓑ artists

ⓒ crafts

ⓓ politicians

066 The basketmakers were skilled **artisans** who decorated their baskets with complex designs.

ⓐ protagonists

ⓑ craftsmen

ⓒ virtuosos

ⓓ playmates

067 During their **ascendancy**, many civilizations experienced rapid population growth.

ⓐ decline

ⓑ conversion

ⓒ innovation

ⓓ rise

068 The monks led extremely **ascetic** lives and ate only dry bread and vegetables.

ⓐ indulgent

ⓑ hedonistic

ⓒ austere

ⓓ dynamic

069 My father **aspired** to be an artist but had to be content to work as an architect instead.

ⓐ repudiated

ⓑ hoped

ⓒ expired

ⓓ respired

070 Although he was an **assiduous** worker, he never rose very high in rank at the company.

ⓐ continuous

ⓑ inconsistent

ⓒ honest

ⓓ diligent

DAY 03

071 To **assuage** her brother's hurt feelings, she told him everyone on the team still liked him.

ⓐ soothe

ⓑ raise

ⓒ provoke

ⓓ aggravate

072 To improve the flavor of the dish, the cook thought of an **astute** use for garlic.

ⓐ reachable

ⓑ clever

ⓒ audacious

ⓓ overt

073 The **atrophy** in his muscles showed that he had had little opportunity to exercise them.

ⓐ weakening

ⓑ incline

ⓒ corrosion

ⓓ thrive

074 Among the **attributes** of this species is the ability to change color.

ⓐ achievements

ⓑ manners

ⓒ traits

ⓓ assignments

075 The soldiers carried out an **audacious** raid on the enemy and took many prisoners.

ⓐ daring

ⓑ polite

ⓒ virulent

ⓓ gallant

076 Heavy rains **augmented** the water supply in the reservoir.

ⓐ diminished

ⓑ increased

ⓒ restored

ⓓ dwindled

077 The good weather seemed like an **auspicious** time to plant a garden.

ⓐ audacious

ⓑ ominous

ⓒ apparent

ⓓ promising

078 The family's little home looked **austere** compared with the hotel we had just left.

ⓐ gaunt

ⓑ permissive

ⓒ luxurious

ⓓ joyous

079 X-rays help us tell the difference between **authentic** paintings and fakes.

ⓐ counterfeit

ⓑ verifiable

ⓒ faulty

ⓓ precarious

080 In an **authoritarian** society, all orders must be obeyed.

ⓐ lenient

ⓑ anarchist

ⓒ free

ⓓ dictatorial

081 The state of Texas was an **autonomous** republic before it joined the United States.

ⓐ independent

ⓑ subject

ⓒ subordinate

ⓓ deposed

082 Molière wrote a famous play about a man who was consumed by **avarice**.

ⓐ conformity

ⓑ greed

ⓒ generosity

ⓓ satisfaction

083 After his car accident, he had an **aversion** to driving.

ⓐ affectation

ⓑ dislike

ⓒ assertion

ⓓ desire

084 The bus driver was able to **avert** an accident by putting on the brakes at once.

ⓐ allow

ⓑ help

ⓒ address

ⓓ avoid

085 The drama was a **banal** story of bored people seeking amusement.

ⓐ novel

ⓑ sensible

ⓒ boring

ⓓ cognizant

086 No **baneful** herbs have been found so far.

ⓐ harmful

ⓑ onerous

ⓒ officious

ⓓ sage

087 Between the two cities was a **barren** piece of land where only a few small trees grew.

ⓐ sterile

ⓑ fertile

ⓒ contaminated

ⓓ inventive

088 The castle was a **bastion** of strength, so everyone fled to it for safety in times of danger.

ⓐ nest

ⓑ hotbed

ⓒ incubator

ⓓ stronghold

089 The loss of his home was more than he could **bear**, so he collapsed.

ⓐ withstand

ⓑ shed

ⓒ succumb

ⓓ abort

090 The salesman **beguiled** the man into buying a product that did not work.

ⓐ awakened

ⓑ enlightened

ⓒ deceived

ⓓ lured

Answers

061-065 ⓒⓒⓐⓑⓒ	076-080 ⓑⓓⓐⓑⓓ
066-070 ⓑⓓⓒⓑⓓ	081-085 ⓐⓑⓑⓓⓒ
071-075 ⓐⓑⓐⓒⓐ	086-090 ⓐⓐⓓⓐⓒ

☆091 **belie**
[bilái]

v. to describe falsely or in misleading terms

SYN misrepresent, camouflage

He behaved in a friendly way to _____ his hostile motives.

☆092 **belittle**
[bilítl]

v. to speak unkindly of someone

SYN insult, denigrate, condemn

She disliked her neighbors and used every opportunity to _____ them.

☆093 **belligerent**
[bəlídʒərənt]

adj. aggressive; hostile; inclined toward warfare or aggression

SYN warlike, hostile, threatening

The two _____ countries went to war, but it did not last long.

☆094 **benefactor**
[bénəfæktər]

n. one who helps another, especially with money

SYN supporter, donor, protector

Thanks to gifts from several _____, the clinic was able to remain open.

☆095 **benevolent**
[bənévələnt]

adj. charitable; friendly; supportive; protective

SYN friendly, kind, supportive

The government followed a _____ policy of providing food and medical aid abroad.

☆096 **benign**
[bináin]

adj. kind; gentle; harmless; neutral; unwilling or unable to harm others

SYN kind, friendly, favorable

The lake provided a _____ environment for turtles to live and breed in.

SCAFFOLDING

091 속여 나타내다, 잘못 전하다, 모순되다 그는 적대감을 감추기belie 위해서 우호적인 태도로 행동했다.

092 흠잡다, 과소평가하다 그녀는 이웃들을 싫어해서 그들을 흠잡기belittle 위한 모든 기회를 사용했다.

093 호전적인, 교전중인 전쟁을 좋아하는belligerent 두 나라는 전쟁을 일으켰지만, 그 전쟁은 오래 가지 않았다.

094 은인, 후원자 그 병원은 후원자benefactors 몇 명의 선물 덕분에 폐업을 하지 않을 수 있었다.

095 자애로운, 인정 많은, 자선을 위한 정부는 해외에 음식과 의료를 지원하는 자선benevolent 정책을 따랐다.

096 친절한, 온화한 그 호수는 거북이가 살고 번식하기에 온화한benign 환경을 제공했다.

☆097 **bequeath**
[bikwíːð]

v. to leave (as in a will); to pass something down
SYN leave, sign away

In her will, my aunt _____ her collection of antique furniture to me.

☆098 **bias**
[báiəs]

n. a prejudice or preference either toward or against something; in extreme cases, bigotry
SYN prejudice, preference

This news report shows a strong _____ in favor of the city's new policy.

☆099 **blasphemy**
[blǽsfəmi]

n. an insult to a religion
SYN irreverence

The priests considered any criticism of their religion to be _____.

☆100 **bleak**
[bliːk]

adj. gloomy; unwelcoming; inhospitable; lifeless; unpromising
SYN desolate, depressing, gloomy

The ship was wrecked on a _____ island near the Arctic Circle.

☆101 **blighted**
[bláitid]

adj. impaired; adverse; harmed by a disease or an adverse environment; seriously handicapped; usually applied to plants or land
SYN withered, shriveled

We found a _____ landscape where nothing could grow.

☆102 **blithe**
[blaið]

adj. lighthearted; happy; unburdened with concern or responsibility
SYN carefree, unconcerned, happy

The child showed a _____ acceptance of everything her parents told her.

SCAFFOLDING

097 유언으로 증여하다, (후세에) 남기다   이모는 유언을 통해서 자신이 소장하고 있던 골동품 가구들을 내게 증여했다bequeathed.
098 성향, 선입견, 편견   이 뉴스 기사는 그 도시의 새로운 정책에 찬성하는 강한 성향을bias 보여준다.
099 신성모독, 불손한 언동   성직자들은 자신들의 종교에 대한 어떠한 비판도 전부 신성모독blasphemy이라고 여겼다.
100 황량한, 삭막한, 차가운   그 배는 북극권 근처의 황량한bleak 섬에서 난파되었다.
101 마른, 시든   우리는 아무것도 자랄 수 없는 시들은blighted 풍경을 발견했다.
102 즐거운, 쾌활한, 경솔한   그 아이는 부모님이 말하는 모든 것을 기쁘게blithe 받아들였다.

☆103 **blueprint**
[blúːprìnt]

n. a detailed plan or set of guidelines; more particularly, architectural plans for a building

SYN plan, scheme, outline

This report provided a _____ for later work in the field of rocketry.

☆104 **bolster**
[bóulstər]

v. to support or reinforce; to make stronger or more resistant

SYN support, reinforce, strengthen

The speech by the general _____ morale among the soldiers.

☆105 **braggart**
[brǽgərt]

n. one who boasts to excess about his or her own accomplishments or abilities

SYN boaster, self-promoter

He boasted so much about his achievements that he became known as a _____.

☆106 **brawn**
[brɔːn]

n. muscular strength; extreme muscular development

SYN strength, might, muscularity

The man's _____ gave him the ability to lift heavy loads.

☆107 **brevity**
[brévəti]

n. shortness; conciseness; the use of very few words to express something

SYN shortness, succinctness

His speeches are known for their _____ and never last more than five minutes.

☆108 **buttress**
[bʌ́tris]

n. a solid structure built against a wall as a support

SYN support, brace

Behind the door, a pile of furniture served as a _____ against intruders.

SCAFFOLDING

103 청사진, (세밀한) 계획 　 이 보고서는 훗날의 로켓공학 분야의 일에 대한 청사진을blueprint 제시했다.

104 덧베개로 받쳐주다, 북돋우다 　 장군의 연설은 군인들 사이의 사기를 북돋아 주었다bolstered.

105 허풍선이, 호언장담가 　 그는 자신의 성공에 대해 너무 많이 자랑을 해서 허풍선이로braggart 알려지게 되었다.

106 근육, 완력 　 그 남자의 근력은brawn 그가 무거운 짐을 들 수 있게 해 주었다.

107 짧음, 간결 　 그의 연설은 간결하며brevity 5분을 넘지 않는다고 알려져 있다.

108 버팀벽, 지지물 　 문 뒤의 가구 더미는 침입자들에 대해서 버팀벽buttress의 역할을 했다.

38

☆109 **cacophonous**
[kækáfənəs]

adj. noisy; discordant in the extreme; often applied to loud, poorly played music

SYN noisy, uproarious

The band made a _____ noise as it was tuning up, but it then played beautifully.

☆110 **cajole**
[kədʒóul]

v. to appeal; to urge in a gentle way

SYN appeal, plea, push

With a friendly letter and a gift of flowers, we _____ her to sing in the concert.

☆111 **calculated**
[kǽlkjəlèitid]

adj. carefully planned; deliberate; targeted

SYN planned, deliberate

The mayor's announcement was a _____ effort to weaken his opponent and to win re-election.

☆112 **candid**
[kǽndid]

adj. sincere; honest; frank; confidential

SYN sincere, honest

My _____ opinion is that your report still needs a lot of work.

☆113 **candor**
[kǽndər]

n. honesty; frankness; confidentiality; one's undisguised opinion

SYN honesty, frankness

In a moment of _____, she told us what she really thought about the company.

☆114 **capricious**
[kəpríʃəs]

n. caprice
[kəprí:s]

adj. unpredictable; flighty; impulsive; inconsistent; unreliable

SYN unpredictable, flighty, fickle

Her problem was that she was too _____ to work steadily at one job.

DAY 04

SCAFFOLDING

109 귀에 거슬리는, 불협 화음의   밴드는 조율을 할 때 거슬리는cacophonous 소음을 냈지만 그 후 아름답게 연주했다.

110 구슬리다, 부추기다   우리는 정다운 편지와 꽃 선물로 그녀가 콘서트에서 노래를 부르도록 부추겼다cajoled.

111 계산된, 계획된   시장의 발표는 그의 적수를 꺾고 재선에서 승리하기 위한 계산된calculated 노력이었다.

112 솔직한, 숨김 없는   내 솔직한candid 생각은 너의 보고서가 아직 많이 보완되어야 한다는 것이다.

113 솔직, 허심탄회, 공평무사   그녀는 회사에 대해 그녀가 진정으로 생각하는 것에 대해 허심탄회하게candor 이야기했다.

114 변덕스러운, 불안정한   그녀의 문제는 너무 변덕스러워서capricious 한 곳에서 꾸준히 일할 수 없다는 것이었다.

39

☆115 **cardiologist**
[kàːrdiálədʒist]

n. a doctor specializing in the heart and diseases of the heart
SYN heart doctor, heart specialist

Because of his heart trouble, my father sees a _____ on a regular basis.

☆116 **carping**
[káːrpiŋ]

adj. complaining; nagging; highly critical, and persistent in being so
SYN complaining, nagging

The _____ voice of her mother made the young woman very angry.

☆117 **caustic**
[kɔ́ːstik]

adj. sarcastic; biting; intended to cause pain or harm through words
SYN sarcastic, biting

The writer was known for his _____ criticism of motion pictures.

☆118 **censorious**
[sensɔ́ːriəs]

adj. highly critical; often applied to extremely harsh or unfavorable attitudes or language
SYN critical, nasty

Her _____ attitude toward the rest of her family caused them to avoid her.

☆119 **censure**
[sénʃər]

n. strong criticism; often used in the context of official disapproval
SYN criticism, condemnation

The state's expensive programs came in for _____ from the voters who had to pay for them.

☆120 **certitude**
[sɔ́ːrtətjùːd]

n. certainty; confidence; 100 percent probability, or faith in such
SYN certainty, sureness

We can say with _____ that this software will work every time.

SCAFFOLDING

115 심장(병)학자
116 트집잡는, 잔소리가 심한
117 부식성의, 신랄한
118 지나치게 비판적인, 까다로운
119 비난, 책망, 혹평
120 확신, 확실(성)

우리 아버지는 심장에 문제가 있어서 정기적으로 심장학 의사cardiologist를 만난다.
어머니의 트집잡는carping 목소리는 그 젊은 여자를 매우 화나게 만들었다.
그 작가는 영화를 신랄하게caustic 비판하는 것으로 알려져 있었다.
나머지 가족들에 대한 그녀의 까다로운censorious 태도는 그들로 하여금 그녀를 피하도록 만들었다.
그 주의 고비용 프로그램들은 그것들에 대한 비용을 지불해야 하는 유권자들로부터 비난censure을 받았다.
우리는 이 소프트웨어가 항상 작동한다는 것을 확실히certitude 말할 수 있다.

40

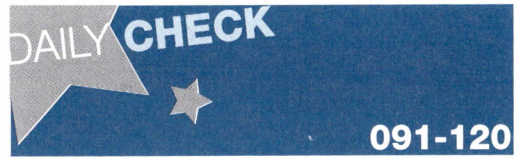
SYNONYMS WORDS THAT MEAN THE SAME THING

091 He behaved in a friendly way to **belie** his hostile motives.

ⓐ misrepresent

ⓑ exclude

ⓒ glorify

ⓓ conceive

092 She disliked her neighbors and used every opportunity to **belittle** them.

ⓐ challenge

ⓑ denigrate

ⓒ subjugate

ⓓ subside

093 The two **belligerent** countries went to war, but it did not last long.

ⓐ amiable

ⓑ warlike

ⓒ sociable

ⓓ aesthetic

094 Thanks to gifts from several **benefactors**, the clinic was able to remain open.

ⓐ vandals

ⓑ churls

ⓒ supporters

ⓓ senders

095 The government followed a **benevolent** policy of providing food and medical aid abroad.

ⓐ malevolent

ⓑ unique

ⓒ spiteful

ⓓ friendly

096 The lake provided a **benign** environment for turtles to live and breed in.

ⓐ ominous

ⓑ favorable

ⓒ disciplined

ⓓ malignant

097 In her will, my aunt **bequeathed** her collection of antique furniture to me.

ⓐ insulted

ⓑ left

ⓒ censured

ⓓ berated

098 This news report shows a strong **bias** in favor of the city's new policy.

ⓐ prejudice

ⓑ angle

ⓒ phase

ⓓ notion

099 The priests considered any criticism of their religion to be **blasphemy**.

ⓐ prattle

ⓑ oath

ⓒ irreverence

ⓓ exuberance

100 The ship was wrecked on a **bleak** island near the Arctic Circle.

ⓐ subsided

ⓑ desolate

ⓒ prevalent

ⓓ bright

101 We found a **blighted** landscape where nothing could grow.

ⓐ withered

ⓑ subjugated

ⓒ vehement

ⓓ intrinsic

DAY 04

102 The child showed a **blithe** acceptance of everything her parents told her.

    ⓐ obsolete

    ⓑ carefree

    ⓒ pretentious

    ⓓ sad

103 This report provided a **blueprint** for later work in the field of rocketry.

    ⓐ profanity

    ⓑ reverence

    ⓒ gratuity

    ⓓ scheme

104 The speech by the general **bolstered** morale among the soldiers.

    ⓐ succumbed

    ⓑ strengthened

    ⓒ weakened

    ⓓ expired

105 He boasted so much about his achievements that he became known as a **braggart**.

    ⓐ successor

    ⓑ follower

    ⓒ blast

    ⓓ boaster

106 The man's **brawn** gave him the ability to lift heavy loads.

    ⓐ weakness

    ⓑ competency

    ⓒ faculty

    ⓓ strength

107 His speeches are known for their **brevity** and never last more than five minutes.

    ⓐ coercion

    ⓑ angst

    ⓒ succinctness

    ⓓ sentiment

108 Behind the door, a pile of furniture served as a **buttress** against intruders.

    ⓐ superstructure

    ⓑ opposition

    ⓒ hindrance

    ⓓ brace

109 The band made a **cacophonous** noise as it was tuning up, but it then played beautifully.

    ⓐ radical

    ⓑ immutable

    ⓒ noisy

    ⓓ unalterable

110 With a friendly letter and a gift of flowers, we **cajoled** her to sing in the concert.

    ⓐ impaired

    ⓑ spurned

    ⓒ pushed

    ⓓ kicked

111 The mayor's announcement was a **calculated** effort to weaken his opponent and to win re-election.

    ⓐ impartial

    ⓑ planned

    ⓒ munificent

    ⓓ scant

112 My **candid** opinion is that your report still needs a lot of work.

    ⓐ iconoclastic

    ⓑ hypothetical

    ⓒ sincere

    ⓓ impecunious

113 In a moment of candor, she told us what she really thought about the company.

ⓐ honesty

ⓑ occasion

ⓒ heresy

ⓓ awkwardness

114 Her problem was that she was too capricious to work steadily at one job.

ⓐ theatrical

ⓑ unpredictable

ⓒ sparing

ⓓ sporadic

115 Because of his heart trouble, my father sees a cardiologist on a regular basis.

ⓐ pediatrician

ⓑ gynecologist

ⓒ heart doctor

ⓓ surgeon

116 The carping voice of her mother made the young woman very angry.

ⓐ impeccable

ⓑ spurious

ⓒ nagging

ⓓ cozy

117 The writer was known for his caustic criticism of motion pictures.

ⓐ incessant

ⓑ sarcastic

ⓒ stubborn

ⓓ intermittent

118 Her censorious attitude toward the rest of her family caused them to avoid her.

ⓐ critical

ⓑ assiduous

ⓒ prosaic

ⓓ rustic

119 The state's expensive programs came in for censure from the voters who had to pay for them.

ⓐ profile

ⓑ pushover

ⓒ criticism

ⓓ quandary

120 We can say with certitude that this software will work every time.

ⓐ skepticism

ⓑ certainty

ⓒ foresight

ⓓ incredulity

Answers

091-095	ⓐⓑⓑⓒⓓ	106-110	ⓓⓒⓓⓒⓒ
096-100	ⓑⓑⓐⓒⓑ	111-115	ⓑⓒⓐⓑⓒ
101-105	ⓐⓑⓓⓑⓓ	116-120	ⓒⓑⓐⓒⓑ

DAY 05

☆121 **charlatan**
[ʃáːrlətən]

n. a fraud or faker; a con artist or hoaxer; someone with fraudulent appeal or qualifications
SYN fraud, faker

The _____ deceived many people with his promises to cure their illnesses.

☆122 **circumlocution**
[sə̀ːrkəmloukjúːʃən]

n. evasive or indirect language; doubletalk
SYN evasion, digression, rambling, tautology, vagueness

He practiced _____ so well that he could speak for hours without getting to the point.

☆123 **circumspect**
[sə́ːrkəmspèkt]

adj. thinking very carefully about something before doing it because there may be risks involved
SYN careful, cautious, deliberate, guarded, prudent, vigilant

Be _____ in word and deed.

☆124 **clarify**
[klǽrəfài]

v. to make clear; to explain clearly
SYN elucidate, explain

Let me _____ several things that the textbook did not make clear.

☆125 **cliché**
[kliːʃéi]

n. an overused word or idea
SYN platitude, bromide

Some expressions are used so often that they have become _____.

☆126 **coalesce**
[kòuəlés]

v. to unite or come together into a coherent whole
SYN unite, unify

In a furnace, these elements _____ to form artificial jewels.

☆127 **coercion**
[kouə́:rʃən]

n. force, pressure, or the threat of harm (used to make someone do something against his or her will)
SYN force, pressure

_____ *may be used to make people say things they do not believe.*

☆128 **colloquial**
[kəlóukwiəl]

adj. informal; ordinary in speech; having the quality of ordinary, everyday speech
SYN informal, free

_____ *speech is more widely used than formal speech.*

☆129 **combustible**
[kəmbʌ́stəbəl]

adj. burnable; flammable; capable of catching fire
SYN burnable, flammable

To reduce fire hazards, remove _____ *material from certain areas.*

☆130 **commemorate**
[kəmémərèit]

v. to remember and acknowledge officially, as with a ceremony
SYN observe, mark, honor

A ceremony was held to _____ *the people who were killed in the war.*

☆131 **compile**
[kəmpáil]

v. to collect or gather information from various sources
SYN collect, gather

We have _____ *last quarter's sales figures.*

☆132 **complacency**
[kəmpléisnsi]

n. a happy, self-satisfied, unconcerned attitude
SYN self-satisfaction, smugness

There is little room for _____ *in this time of global economic hardship.*

SCAFFOLDING

127 강제, 강압, 탄압 정치   강압은Coercion 사람들로 하여금 자신이 믿지 않는 것을 이야기 하도록 하기 위해서 사용될 수 있다.
128 구어체의, 일상 회화의   구어체의Colloquial 말투는 격식 있는 말투보다 더 널리 사용된다.
129 가연성의, 흥분하기 쉬운   화재의 위험을 줄이기 위해 특정 지역에는 가연성combustible 물질을 두지 마라.
130 (축사, 의식으로) 기념하다, 축하하다   전쟁으로 죽은 사람들을 기리기commemorate 위한 행사가 열렸다.
131 하나로 모으다, 수집하다, 편집하다   우리는 지난 분기의 판매수치를 집계하였다compiled.
132 (부정적) 자기 만족, 만족을 주는 것   이러한 국제경제의 난황 속에서는 자기만족complacency의 여지가 거의 없다.

DAY 05

☆133 **complacent**
[kəmpléisənt]

adj. happy; unconcerned; content; unworried; unaware of any need to change
[SYN] self-satisfied, smug

There is a danger that we will become _____ when we are successful.

☆134 **complementary**
[kàmpləméntəri]

adj. supplemental; harmonious; often used in the context of colors or shapes that go well with each other
[SYN] supplementary, additional, compatible

The room was decorated in _____ colors to create a harmonious effect.

☆135 **compliance**
[kəmpláiəns]

n. obedience; conformance; submission to others' requirements or needs
[SYN] obedience, submission, subordination

The inspector found the building to be in _____ with city regulations.

☆136 **compliant**
[kəmpláiənt]

adj. obedient; submissive; responsive to others' needs, requests, or orders
[SYN] obedient, submissive, subordinate

If you are too _____ with others' wishes, you will waste much time.

☆137 **composure**
[kəmpóuʒər]

n. a calm state of mind; tranquillity
[SYN] calmness, coolness

The news that his son had been injured shook his _____ badly.

☆138 **comprehensive**
[kàmprihénsiv]

adj. wide in scope; highly inclusive
[SYN] extensive, complete

This book is a _____ survey of 20th-century literature.

---

133 자기 만족의, 개의치 않는　　우리는 성공했을 때 자기 만족에complacent 빠질 위험이 있다.
134 서로 보완하는, 보충하는　　그 방은 조화의 효과를 위해서 서로 보완하는complementary 색으로 장식되어 있었다.
135 응낙, 수락, 순종　　조사관은 그 건물이 도시 규정에 부합하다고compliance 판단했다.
136 유순한, 고분고분한　　다른 사람들의 요구에 너무 고분고분하다compliant 보면 많은 시간을 낭비하게 될 것이다.
137 침착, 평정　　그의 아들이 다쳤다는 소식은 그의 침착성composure을 심하게 흔들었다.
138 이해력 있는, 이해가 빠른, 포괄적인　　이 책은 20세기 문학의 포괄적인comprehensive 개관이다.

☆139 **compromise**   *n.* an agreement by mutual concession

[kámprəmàiz]   **SYN** settlement, agreement

The two sides in the conflict reached a _____ that ended their disagreement.

☆140 **concede**   *v.* to acknowledge, yield, or surrender

[kənsíːd]   **SYN** acknowledge, give, surrender

We must _____ that we were wrong about many things.

☆141 **conciliate**   *v.* to reconcile; to try to end a disagreement

[kənsílièit]   **SYN** appease, pacify

His duty was to _____ the people, not to provoke them.

☆142 **conciliatory**   *adj.* trying to appease others or reconcile differences

[kənsíliətɔ̀ːri]   **SYN** pleasant, reassuring

The speech was _____ in tone and expressed a willingness to compromise.

☆143 **concise**   *adj.* short; brief; succinct; compact; condensed into very few words

[kənsáis]   **SYN** short, brief, succinct

What you need to keep in mind is to be clear and _____ when you write the monthly reports.

☆144 **concur**   *v.* to agree about something; to reach an agreement or consensus

[kənkə́ːr]   **SYN** agree, acknowledge, admit, concede, recognize, accede, acquiesce

You and I _____ in our opinion of this painter's work.

DAY 05

☆145 **condense**
[kəndéns]

v. to reduce or shorten, as by editing a document; to assume a liquid state from a vaporous state

SYN shorten, reduce, edit, cut

We had to _____ our report to make it a summary of only 100 words.

☆146 **condescend**
[kàndisénd]

v. to stoop; to step down to a lower level than one's own

SYN stoop, deign

He _____ to their intellectual level in order to be understood.

☆147 **condone**
[kəndóun]

v. to excuse, pardon, or justify; to give explicit or tacit approval to an error or misdeed

SYN excuse, pardon

The governor was afraid that pardoning the prisoner would appear to _____ his crimes.

☆148 **confine**
[kənfáin]

v. to prevent something from spreading beyond a certain place or group

SYN enclose, impound, isolate, jail, sequester, limit, regulate, restrain, restrict

Would you _____ your remarks to just the facts?

☆149 **conflagration**
[kànfləgréiʃən]

n. a large fire, usually on the scale of a forest, building, or city

SYN fire, blaze

The old city hall was destroyed in a _____ that burned down much of the city.

☆150 **confluence**
[kánfluəns]

n. a convergence, joining, or coming together; usually used in the context of flowing water

SYN convergence, union

At the _____ of the two rivers was a city.

SCAFFOLDING

145 응축하다, 요약하다   우리는 보고서를 100단어만으로 요약해야condense 했다.
146 자기를 낮추다, 창피를 무릅쓰고 ~하다   그는 이해하기 쉽게 기꺼이 그들의 지적 수준에 맞춰주었다condescended.
147 용서하다, 묵과하다   정부는 죄수를 사면해 주는 것이 그의 범죄를 묵과하는condone 것으로 보일까 걱정했다.
148 제한하다, 한하다, 감금하다   발언은 사실에만 한정해confine 주시겠어요?
149 큰 화재   그 오래된 시청은 도시의 상당 부분을 태운 큰 화재conflagration로 인하여 파괴되었다.
150 합류, 집합   두 강의 합류점confluence에 한 도시가 있었다.

48

SYNONYMS WORDS THAT MEAN THE SAME THING

121 The **charlatan** deceived many people with his promises to cure their illnesses.

ⓐ honesty

ⓑ fraud

ⓒ confidence

ⓓ rebuttal

122 He practiced **circumlocution** so well that he could speak for hours without getting to the point.

ⓐ remorse

ⓑ cessation

ⓒ digression

ⓓ rancor

123 Be **circumspect** in word and deed.

ⓐ vindictive

ⓑ unremarkable

ⓒ careful

ⓓ derogative

124 Let me **clarify** several things that the textbook did not make clear.

ⓐ ornate

ⓑ recant

ⓒ repress

ⓓ elucidate

125 Some expressions are used so often that they have become **clichés**.

ⓐ idioms

ⓑ platitudes

ⓒ decorum

ⓓ diffidence

126 In a furnace, these elements **coalesce** to form artificial jewels.

ⓐ unite

ⓑ hasten

ⓒ impede

ⓓ flourish

127 **Coercion** may be used to make people say things they do not believe.

ⓐ dilemma

ⓑ haughtiness

ⓒ constraint

ⓓ force

128 **Colloquial** speech is more widely used than formal speech.

ⓐ recalcitrant

ⓑ informal

ⓒ divisive

ⓓ contrite

129 To reduce fire hazards, remove **combustible** material from certain areas.

ⓐ prominent

ⓑ flammable

ⓒ dreadful

ⓓ unruly

130 A ceremony was held to **commemorate** the people who were killed in the war.

ⓐ exploit

ⓑ honor

ⓒ usurp

ⓓ verify

131 We have **compiled** last quarter's sales figures.

ⓐ collected

ⓑ undermined

ⓒ venerated

ⓓ extorted

132 There is little room for **complacency** in this time of global economic hardship.

ⓐ amity

ⓑ discernment

ⓒ smugness

ⓓ malice

133 There is a danger that we will become **complacent** when we are successful.

ⓐ marred

ⓑ self-satisfied

ⓒ lurid

ⓓ skeptical

134 The room was decorated in **complementary** colors to create a harmonious effect.

ⓐ slight

ⓑ tangential

ⓒ noxious

ⓓ supplementary

135 The inspector found the building to be in **compliance** with city regulations.

ⓐ obedience

ⓑ prattle

ⓒ disobedience

ⓓ violatioin

136 If you are too **compliant** with others' wishes, you will waste much time.

ⓐ feasible

ⓑ submissive

ⓒ casual

ⓓ optimistic

137 The news that his son had been injured shook his **composure** badly.

ⓐ torso

ⓑ turpitude

ⓒ calmness

ⓓ awkwardness

138 This book is a **comprehensive** survey of 20th-century literature.

ⓐ unkempt

ⓑ extensive

ⓒ unsung

ⓓ superficial

139 The two sides in the conflict reached a **compromise** that ended their disagreement.

ⓐ troupe

ⓑ uproar

ⓒ settlement

ⓓ denial

140 We must **concede** that we were wrong about many things.

ⓐ extol

ⓑ acknowledge

ⓒ perpetuate

ⓓ restore

141 His duty was to **conciliate** the people, not to provoke them.

ⓐ bolster

ⓑ appease

ⓒ placate

ⓓ contemplate

142 The speech was **conciliatory** in tone and expressed a willingness to compromise.

ⓐ ostentatious

ⓑ eclectic

ⓒ pleasant

ⓓ decent

143 What you need to keep in mind is to be clear and concise when you write the monthly reports.

ⓐ polemical
ⓑ effective
ⓒ short
ⓓ brazen

144 You and I concur in our opinion of this painter's work.

ⓐ agree
ⓑ differ
ⓒ submit
ⓓ vary

145 We had to condense our report to make it a summary of only 100 words.

ⓐ enlarge
ⓑ generalize
ⓒ reduce
ⓓ unfold

146 He condescended to their intellectual level in order to be understood.

ⓐ ignored
ⓑ respected
ⓒ concerned
ⓓ deigned

147 The governor was afraid that pardoning the prisoner would appear to condone his crimes.

ⓐ recall
ⓑ excuse
ⓒ castigate
ⓓ accept

148 Would you confine your remarks to just the facts?

ⓐ expand
ⓑ release
ⓒ impede
ⓓ restrain

149 The old city hall was destroyed in a conflagration that burned down much of the city.

ⓐ pitfall
ⓑ flamboyance
ⓒ fire
ⓓ nostalgia

150 At the confluence of the two rivers was a city.

ⓐ convergence
ⓑ branch
ⓒ limb
ⓓ source

DAY 06

☆151 **confound**
[kənfáund]

v. to confuse or disrupt; often used in reference to human plans or business

SYN confuse, disrupt

The storm _____ all attempts to find survivors from the shipwreck.

☆152 **congenial**
[kəndʒíːnjəl]

adj. friendly; pleasant; harmonious and agreeable in one's relationships and dealings with others

SYN friendly, hospitable, welcoming

My mother's manner was so _____ that she had many friends.

☆153 **conjecture**
[kəndʒéktʃər]

n. a speculation, serious guess, or hypothesis put forward for testing

SYN guess, speculation

This is just _____, but I think our boss will retire soon.

☆154 **consensus**
[kənsénsəs]

n. an agreement within a group; a majority view or unanimous opinion

SYN agreement, majority view

The _____ among economists is that this new policy will not help the economy.

☆155 **consolidate**
[kənsálədèit]

v. to make or become solid or strong

SYN combine, incorporate, merge, unite, compress, concentrate

The CEO decided to _____ the two companies into one.

☆156 **conspicuous**
[kənspíkjuəs]

adj. outstanding; highly visible; in sharp contrast with the surroundings

SYN outstanding, bold, prominent

The most _____ feature of this landscape is the small volcano.

SCAFFOLDING

151 혼동하다, 당황케 하다   폭풍은 난파선으로부터 생존자들을 구하기 위한 모든 시도를 혼란스럽게 만들었다confounded.

152 마음이 맞는, 기분 좋은, 친절한   우리 어머니의 태도는 너무 친절해서congenial 그녀에게는 많은 친구들이 있다.

153 짐작, 추측, 억측   이것은 그냥 추측conjecture이지만, 곧 우리의 상사가 은퇴할 것 같다.

154 일치, 합의, 여론   경제학자들의 일치된 의견consensus은 이 새로운 정책이 경제에 보탬이 되지 않을 것이라는 것이다.

155 결합하다, 합체시키다, 공고히 하다   그 CEO는 두 회사를 하나로 합치기로consolidate 결심했다.

156 눈에 띄는, 잘 보이는, 두드러진   이 경치에서 가장 눈에 띄는conspicuous 지형물은 작은 화산이다.

☆157 **constraint**
[kənstréint]

n. a limitation, limiting factor, condition, boundary, or restriction
SYN limitation, limit, bound

The only _____ on building this system is how much money you can afford to spend on it.

☆158 **contempt**
[kəntémpt]

n. a strongly negative, condemning, or disdainful attitude
SYN scorn, disdain

He made such a big mistake that everyone else held him in _____.

☆159 **contend**
[kənténd]

v. to argue, disagree, or dispute; to fight physically over something
SYN argue, dispute

Some members of my family _____ angrily over where our next reunion should be held.

☆160 **contentious**
[kənténʃəs]

adj. quarrelsome; argumentative; divisive; controversial, when applied to a topic or issue
SYN quarrelsome, argumentative

One _____ member can make it difficult for a group to reach agreement.

☆161 **contrite**
[kəntráit]

adj. characterized by sorrow and regret for something one has done
SYN sorry, regretful

Instead of feeling _____ about his crimes, the criminal said he had done no wrong.

☆162 **contrive**
[kəntráiv]

v. to manage or succeed
SYN concoct, devise, fashion, improvise, invent

He _____ her death.

DAY 06

☆163 **converge**
[kənvə́:rdʒ]

v. to meet, come together, conjoin, or unite; often used in reference to trends or attitudes

SYN meet, unit

Two highways _____ at an intersection near my home.

☆164 **conviction**
[kənvíkʃ ə n]

n. a firm belief in something

SYN belief, persuasion

His _____ did not allow him to fight in the war.

☆165 **cordial**
[kɔ́:rdʒəl]

adj. warm and friendly; sincere; sociable

SYN sincere, friendly

Talks between the two groups were conducted in a _____ atmosphere and were productive.

☆166 **corroborate**
[kərábərèit]

v. to support with information; to make more definite

SYN support, reinforce, strengthen

We expect the results of the study to _____ our claim of harm to the environment.

☆167 **corrode**
[kəróud]

v. to destroy a metal gradually by chemical means such as rust or acid

SYN rust, dissolve, eat away, destroy

Rust had _____ the ship's hull so badly that the ship was falling apart.

☆168 **corrugated**
[kɔ́:rəgèitid]

adj. folded into a pattern of parallel ridges and grooves

SYN folded, rippled

Boxes made of _____ cardboard are able to support heavy loads without collapsing.

☆169 **corrupt**
[kərʌ́pt]

adj. characterized by immorality, greed, and depravity; often used in the context of politics
SYN immoral, depraved

n. corruption
[kərʌ́pʃən]

The official's acceptance of an expensive gift led to charges of _____ against him.

☆170 **credulity**
[krədjú:ləti]

n. extreme willingness to believe, especially on slender evidence
SYN naïveté, gullibility

The public's _____ allowed con artists to carry out many frauds.

☆171 **credulous**
[krédʒuləs]

adj. easily deceived; too ready to believe something on little or no evidence
SYN naïve, gullible

The children were so young and _____ that they could be led to believe almost anything.

☆172 **criterion**
[kraitíəriən]

n. a rule, guideline, test, or principle on which one may form an opinion
SYN rule, guideline, test

What is the _____ of beauty?

☆173 **crucial**
[krú:ʃəl]

adj. decisive; critical
SYN critical, decisive, determining, important, significant

The issue of the Palestinian state is _____ to Israel.

☆174 **cryptic**
[kríptik]

adj. thought to have a hidden meaning
SYN puzzling, mystifying, mysterious

The _____ inscription on the ancient monument has yet to be interpreted.

DAY 06

☆175 **culpable**
[kʌ́lpəbl]

adj. having guilt; deserving of blame or condemnation
SYN guilty, blameworthy

If he is _____ of a major crime, then he may go to jail.

☆176 **cursory**
[kə́:rsəri]

adj. performed in haste, without close attention or care
SYN hasty, careless, quick

We missed a lot of information in the report because we gave it only a _____ reading.

☆177 **curtail**
[kə:rtéil]

v. to curtail, cut short, or stop in the middle of something
SYN reduce, cut short, abbreviate

High fuel prices _____ the delivery of merchandise to stores.

☆178 **dearth**
[də:rθ]

n. a lack, absence, shortage, or deficiency
SYN lack, absence, shortage

Our research suffers from a _____ of information on this subject.

☆179 **debilitate**
[dibílətèit]

v. to weaken; to deplete the energy of someone or something
SYN weaken, enervate, wear out

Poor nutrition _____ the people so badly that their bodies could no longer resist infections.

☆180 **debunk**
[di:bʌ́ŋk]

v. to discredit or disprove something by analyzing its faults or weaknesses
SYN discredit, disprove, mock

Some authors have written books to _____ popular beliefs in visitors from other planets.

151 The storm **confounded** all attempts to find survivors from the shipwreck.

ⓐ cajoled

ⓑ kindled

ⓒ lauded

ⓓ disrupted

152 My mother's manner was so **congenial** that she had many friends.

ⓐ unpleasant

ⓑ friendly

ⓒ distorted

ⓓ amusing

153 This is just **conjecture**, but I think our boss will retire soon.

ⓐ lampoon

ⓑ premise

ⓒ speculation

ⓓ conclusion

154 The **consensus** among economists is that this new policy will not help the economy.

ⓐ labyrinth

ⓑ conspiracy

ⓒ majority view

ⓓ jeopardy

155 The CEO decided to **consolidate** the two companies into one.

ⓐ neglect

ⓑ combine

ⓒ placate

ⓓ strut

156 The most **conspicuous** feature of this landscape is the small volcano.

ⓐ minimal

ⓑ imperceptible

ⓒ modest

ⓓ prominent

157 The only **constraint** on building this system is how much money you can afford to spend on it.

ⓐ edge

ⓑ freedom

ⓒ limit

ⓓ autonomy

158 He made such a big mistake that everyone else held him in **contempt**.

ⓐ disdain

ⓑ lust

ⓒ respect

ⓓ admiration

159 Some members of my family **contended** angrily over where our next reunion should be held.

ⓐ pummeled

ⓑ unfolded

ⓒ argued

ⓓ derided

160 One **contentious** member can make it difficult for a group to reach agreement.

ⓐ quarrelsome

ⓑ irrational

ⓒ irreproachable

ⓓ agreeable

DAY 06

161 Instead of feeling contrite about his crimes, the criminal said he had done no wrong.

ⓐ unrepentant

ⓑ sorry

ⓒ disappointed

ⓓ remorseless

162 He contrived her death.

ⓐ usurped

ⓑ promoted

ⓒ concocted

ⓓ warranted

163 Two highways converge at an intersection near my home.

ⓐ part

ⓑ diverge

ⓒ disgorge

ⓓ meet

164 His convictions did not allow him to fight in the war.

ⓐ qualms

ⓑ indecision

ⓒ incertitude

ⓓ beliefs

165 Talks between the two groups were conducted in a cordial atmosphere and were productive.

ⓐ sincere

ⓑ distant

ⓒ acute

ⓓ aloof

166 We expect the results of the study to corroborate our claim of harm to the environment.

ⓐ placate

ⓑ eradicate

ⓒ emulate

ⓓ support

167 Rust had corroded the ship's hull so badly that the ship was falling apart.

ⓐ marred

ⓑ ameliorated

ⓒ rusted

ⓓ built up

168 Boxes made of corrugated cardboard are able to support heavy loads without collapsing.

ⓐ smoothed

ⓑ squashed

ⓒ pulverized

ⓓ folded

169 The official's acceptance of an expensive gift led to charges of corruption against him.

ⓐ morality

ⓑ embezzlement

ⓒ misappropriation

ⓓ depravity

170 The public's credulity allowed con artists to carry out many frauds.

ⓐ decency

ⓑ decorum

ⓒ gullibility

ⓓ retaliation

171 The children were so young and credulous that they could be led to believe almost anything.

ⓐ suspicious

ⓑ gullible

ⓒ wary

ⓓ prudent

172 What is the **criterion** of beauty?

ⓐ hierarchy

ⓑ rule

ⓒ excerpt

ⓓ disrepute

173 The issue of the Palestinian state is **crucial** to Israel.

ⓐ safe

ⓑ shallow

ⓒ critical

ⓓ complimentary

174 The **cryptic** inscription on the ancient monument has yet to be interpreted.

ⓐ obvious

ⓑ manifest

ⓒ puzzling

ⓓ plain

175 If he is **culpable** of a major crime, then he may go to jail.

ⓐ incorrigible

ⓑ guilty

ⓒ condensed

ⓓ innocent

176 We missed a lot of information in the report because we gave it only a **cursory** reading.

ⓐ cautious

ⓑ methodical

ⓒ hasty

ⓓ moderate

177 High fuel prices **curtailed** the delivery of merchandise to stores.

ⓐ indicted

ⓑ reduced

ⓒ expanded

ⓓ augmented

178 Our research suffers from a **dearth** of information on this subject.

ⓐ abundance

ⓑ implement

ⓒ lack

ⓓ poverty

179 Poor nutrition **debilitated** the people so badly that their bodies could no longer resist infections.

ⓐ stimulated

ⓑ invigorated

ⓒ weakened

ⓓ vitalized

180 Some authors have written books to **debunk** popular beliefs in visitors from other planets.

ⓐ conceal

ⓑ protect

ⓒ prove

ⓓ discredit

Answers

151-155 ⓓⓑⓒⓒⓑ	166-170 ⓓⓒⓓⓓⓒ
156-160 ⓓⓒⓐⓒⓐ	171-175 ⓑⓑⓒⓒⓑ
161-165 ⓑⓒⓓⓓⓐ	176-180 ⓒⓑⓒⓒⓓ

☆181 **decorum**
[dikɔ́:rəm]

n. good behavior; appropriate conduct; attention to etiquette
SYN propriety, dignity, politeness

Visitors to a courtroom are expected to observe strict _____ while court is in session.

☆182 **deference**
[défərəns]

n. submitting to the wishes, opinions, or authority of another
SYN respect, subordination, courtesy

One is expected to show _____ to people of high social rank.

☆183 **degradation**
[dègrədéiʃən]

n. a reduction in quality or moral standing
SYN shame, depravity, deterioration

His _____ was a result of substance abuse and cost him his job.

☆184 **dehydrate**
[di:háidreit]

v. to remove water from something
SYN desiccate, dry out

_____ potatoes can be stored for a long time and then prepared just by adding water.

☆185 **deleterious**
[dèlətíəriəs]

adj. causing harm, injury, or damage; having a negative or destructive effect
SYN harmful, damaging, injurious

The _____ effects of smoking include lung cancer and other lung diseases.

☆186 **deliberate**
[dilíbərət]

adj. done by intent, with awareness of the effect; planned; intended; conscious
SYN intentional, conscious, planned

This message was a _____ attempt to spread lies and rumors about an innocent person.

SCAFFOLDING

181 단정, 예의바름 — 법정에 방문하는 사람들은 재판 진행 중에 엄중한 예절decorum을 준수해야 한다.

182 복종, 존경 — 사회적으로 지위가 높은 사람에게는 존경deference을 표해야 한다.

183 좌천, 하락, 파면 — 그의 파면degradation은 약물 남용의 결과였고, 그것 때문에 그는 직업을 잃었다.

184 탈수하다, 건조시키다 — 말린Dehydrated 감자는 오랫동안 보관할 수 있고 물만 첨가하면 요리가 가능하다.

185 해로운, 유독한 — 흡연의 해로운deleterious 효과는 폐암과 다른 폐질환들을 포함한다.

186 신중한, 사려 깊은, 고의적인 — 이 메시지는 무고한 사람에 대한 거짓과 소문을 퍼뜨리기 위한 고의적인deliberate 시도였다.

☆187 **delineate**
[dilínièit]

v. to draw a picture of something; to outline, explain, or sketch something

SYN sketch, outline, depict

A skilled artist can _____ a whole landscape with only a few lines or brushstrokes.

☆188 **denounce**
[dináuns]

v. to condemn; to speak harshly of someone or something

SYN condemn, attack, decry

The voters _____ the mayor's decision as contrary to the public interest.

☆189 **deplete**
[diplíːt]

v. to consume something without replacing it; to use up

SYN use up, exhaust, consume

Hard work in the extreme heat quickly _____ his energy.

☆190 **deplore**
[diplɔ́ːr]

v. to complain or speak critically about something

SYN condemn, complain, bemoan, bewail

Newspaper editorials _____ the city's lack of concern about improving schools.

☆191 **depose**
[dipóuz]

v. to remove an official from office; often used in reference to royalty or top executives

SYN dethrone, unseat, expel, recall, remove

The country's new leader was _____ after only two months in office.

☆192 **depravity**
[diprǽvəti]

n. moral corruption; vice; immorality

SYN immorality, corruption

The emperor's reign was remembered as a collection of crimes, offenses, and _____ too awful to describe.

DAY 07

☆193 **deprecate**
[déprikèit]

v. to speak in disapproval or condemnation of something; to belittle, fault, or criticize strongly

SYN belittle, condemn

In angry language, she _____ everyone that she saw as an enemy.

☆194 **deprive**
[dipráiv]

v. to take or keep something from someone

SYN despoil, rob, bereave, dispossess, divest, remove

They _____ him of his right to a trial.

☆195 **deride**
[diráid]

v. to make fun of; to criticize in a joking or amusing way

SYN mock, lampoon, make fun of

Though critics _____ the motion picture, it became very popular and financially successful.

☆196 **derivative**
[dirívətiv]

adj. copied from, or modeled after, another work

SYN unoriginal, copied, imitated

The story was so _____ that we knew from the start how it would end.

☆197 **desecrate**
[désikrèit]

v. to ruin or violate some supposedly sacred site

SYN profane, violate, defile

The vandals were accused of _____ and robbing the chapel.

☆198 **desiccate**
[désikèit]

v. to dry or dehydrate; to remove water from something by evaporation

SYN dry, dehydrate

A month of hot, dry weather _____ the crops in the field and ruined the harvest.

SCAFFOLDING

193 반대하다, 비난하다   그녀는 성난 목소리로, 자신이 본 모든 사람들을 적이라고 비난했다deprecated.

194 박탈하다, 빼앗다, 해임시키다   그들은 그가 재판 받을 권리를 박탈했다deprived.

195 비웃다, 조롱하다   비록 비평가들은 그 영화를 비웃었지만derided, 그것은 큰 인기를 얻었고 결국 재정적으로도 성공을 거두었다.

196 끌어낸, 유도적인, 모방한   그 이야기는 너무나도 모방적이었기derivative 때문에 우리는 처음부터 그것이 어떻게 끝날지 알고 있었다.

197 신성을 더럽히다, 속되게 쓰다   반달들은 예배당을 더럽히고desecrating 약탈했다고 비난을 받았다.

198 건조시키다, 무기력하게 하다   한 달 동안의 덥고 건조한 날씨는 들의 곡식들을 마르게 했고desiccated 수확을 망쳐 놓았다.

☆199 **despondent**
[dispándənt]

adj. in despair or near despair

SYN gloomy, sad, depressed

The patient felt _____ after he was told that he had only a month to live.

☆200 **detached**
[ditǽtʃt]

adj. separate from something else; divided; independent; emotionally uninvolved; objective

SYN separate, free, uninvolved

She felt _____ from the events taking place around her; it was as if they were part of a movie she was watching.

☆201 **deter**
[ditə́:r]

v. to warn against, prevent, or discourage some action

SYN warn, prevent, discourage

The fence topped with barbed wire _____ people from trespassing on the property.

☆202 **determined**
[ditə́:rmind]

adj. highly motivated and committed to do something; steadfast; assiduous

SYN committed, motivated, focused, resolute

My mother was _____ to succeed in business, and she became a company president.

☆203 **deterrent**
[ditə́:rənt]

n. something that deters or discourages an action

SYN warning, preventative, disincentive, shield

The United States and the Soviet Union each maintained a huge nuclear _____ for many years.

☆204 **detrimental**
[dètrəméntl]

adj. harmful, destructive, counterproductive, or strongly negative in effect

SYN harmful, hurtful, destructive

Drinking too much coffee during the day can be _____ to sleeping at night.

DAY 07

SCAFFOLDING

199 의기소침한, 낙담한
환자는 한 달 밖에 살 수 없다는 소리를 듣고 나서 낙담했다 despondent.

200 독립된, 사심 없는
그녀는 자기 주위에서 일어나고 있는 일들이 마치 그녀가 보고 있는 영화의 장면들일 뿐인 것처럼 그 사건들에 대해 특별한 생각이 없었다 detached.

201 단념시키다, 방해하다
유자 철선으로 덮인 울타리는 사람들의 소유지 침입을 막았다 deterred.

202 단호한, 굳게 결심한, 확정된
우리 어머니는 업무에서 성공하기로 각오를 했고 determined, 그녀는 회사의 사장이 되었다.

203 방해물, 단념하게 하는 것
미국과 소련은 각각 오랫동안 막대한 핵 억지력 deterrent을 유지해 왔다.

204 해로운, 불리한
낮 동안 커피를 너무 많이 마시는 것은 밤에 자는 것에 방해가 될 detrimental 수 있다.

☆205 **devious**
[díːviəs]

adj. not honest, frank, or straightforward; deceitful; crooked; untrustworthy

SYN deceitful, dishonest, shifty

In the play, the duke has a _____ plan to make himself the king through lies, flattery, and violence.

☆206 **devise**
[diváiz]

v. to make, create, plan, think up, or invent something; often used in reference to finding solutions to problems

SYN make, invent, create

The policeman _____ a plan to catch the criminals he was after.

☆207 **devotion**
[divóuʃən]

n. a commitment or dedication to something; often used in the context of religion

SYN dedication, loyalty, commitment

The painter's _____ to art led him to spend years working on a single painting.

☆208 **didactic**
[daidǽktik]

adj. designed to teach something; often used to describe stories that impart lessons

SYN educational, instructional

Some writers think literature should serve a _____ purpose and teach the reader important lessons.

☆209 **diffidence**
[dífidəns]

n. the state of being shy, retiring, or timid; reluctance to call attention to oneself

SYN shyness, timidity

Some mistook his usual silence for _____, when in fact he just disliked idle talk.

☆210 **diffident**
[dífidənt]

adj. unwilling to put oneself forward or to call attention to oneself

SYN shy, timid, retiring

A _____ young woman, she never spoke unless someone spoke to her first.

SCAFFOLDING

205 구불구불한, 솔직하지 않은, 사악한
그 연극에서 공작은 거짓, 아첨, 폭력을 통해 자신을 왕으로 만들고자 하는 사악한devious 계획을 한다.

206 궁리하다, 고안하다
경찰은 그가 쫓고 있는 범죄자를 잡기 위한 계획을 고안했다devised.

207 헌신, 전념, 헌납
예술에 대한 그 화가의 헌신devotion은 그가 한 점의 그림을 그리는 데에 수년의 시간을 쏟도록 했다.

208 교훈적인, 설교적인
어떤 작가들은 문학이 교훈적인didactic 목적을 가져야 하며 독자에게 중요한 교훈을 가르쳐야 한다고 생각한다.

209 자신이 없음, 기가 죽음
어떤 사람들은 그의 평소의 침묵을 기가 죽은 것diffidence으로 오해했지만, 사실 그는 단지 무의미한 이야기를 싫어했던 것이다.

210 자신 없는, 소심한, 삼가는
그녀는 소심한diffident 여자로서 누군가 먼저 말을 걸어줄 때까지 입을 열지 않았다.

SYNONYMS WORDS THAT MEAN THE SAME THING

181 Visitors to a courtroom are expected to observe strict **decorum** while court is in session.

ⓐ depravity

ⓑ lowliness

ⓒ dignity

ⓓ aplomb

182 One is expected to show **deference** to people of high social rank.

ⓐ contempt

ⓑ respect

ⓒ derision

ⓓ aversion

183 His **degradation** was a result of substance abuse and cost him his job.

ⓐ depravity

ⓑ commitment

ⓒ treachery

ⓓ uniformity

184 **Dehydrated** potatoes can be stored for a long time and then prepared just by adding water.

ⓐ desecrated

ⓑ unkempt

ⓒ vague

ⓓ desiccated

185 The **deleterious** effects of smoking include lung cancer and other lung diseases.

ⓐ precocious

ⓑ outermost

ⓒ harmful

ⓓ wayward

186 This message was a **deliberate** attempt to spread lies and rumors about an innocent person.

ⓐ impulsive

ⓑ distant

ⓒ impecunious

ⓓ intentional

187 A skilled artist can **delineate** a whole landscape with only a few lines or brushstrokes.

ⓐ vaporize

ⓑ sketch

ⓒ depose

ⓓ overuse

188 The voters **denounced** the mayor's decision as contrary to the public interest.

ⓐ condemned

ⓑ venerated

ⓒ vented

ⓓ heeded

189 Hard work in the extreme heat quickly **depleted** his energy.

ⓐ impeded

ⓑ pondered

ⓒ saturated

ⓓ exhausted

DAY 07

190 Newspaper editorials **deplored** the city's lack of concern about improving schools.

ⓐ scrutinized

ⓑ bolstered

ⓒ complained

ⓓ deterred

191 The country's new leader was **deposed** after only two months in office.

ⓐ corrupted

ⓑ approved

ⓒ corrugated

ⓓ removed

192 The emperor's reign was remembered as a collection of crimes, offenses, and **depravities** too awful to describe.

ⓐ stratagems

ⓑ uproars

ⓒ vestiges

ⓓ immoralities

193 In angry language, she **deprecated** everyone that she saw as an enemy.

ⓐ disagreed

ⓑ approved

ⓒ compromised

ⓓ condemned

194 They **deprived** him of his right to trial.

ⓐ robbed

ⓑ thrived

ⓒ derided

ⓓ redirected

195 Though critics **derided** the motion picture, it became very popular and financially successful.

ⓐ characterized

ⓑ mocked

ⓒ digressed

ⓓ impaired

196 The story was so **derivative** that we knew from the start how it would end.

ⓐ unoriginal

ⓑ impecunious

ⓒ steadfast

ⓓ subsided

197 The vandals were accused of **desecrating** and robbing the chapel.

ⓐ precluding

ⓑ disclosing

ⓒ ebbing

ⓓ violating

198 A month of hot, dry weather **desiccated** the crops in the field and ruined the harvest.

ⓐ diminished

ⓑ dried

ⓒ invented

ⓓ imposed

199 The patient felt **despondent** after he was told that he had only a month to live.

ⓐ solemn

ⓑ elusive

ⓒ gloomy

ⓓ viable

200 She felt **detached** from the events taking place around her; it was as if they were part of a movie she was watching.

ⓐ derogated

ⓑ separated

ⓒ diffident

ⓓ prudish

201 The fence topped with barbed wire **deterred** people from trespassing on the property.

   ⓐ usurped

   ⓑ prevented

   ⓒ diffused

   ⓓ vacillated

202 My mother was **determined** to succeed in business, and she became a company president.

   ⓐ committed

   ⓑ qualified

   ⓒ refuted

   ⓓ hesitant

203 The United States and the Soviet Union each maintained a huge nuclear **deterrent** for many years.

   ⓐ quagmire

   ⓑ recluse

   ⓒ shield

   ⓓ aid

204 Drinking too much coffee during the day can be **detrimental** to sleeping at night.

   ⓐ didactic

   ⓑ servile

   ⓒ pragmatic

   ⓓ harmful

205 In the play, the duke has a **devious** plan to make himself the king through lies, flattery, and violence.

   ⓐ sinister

   ⓑ deceitful

   ⓒ forthright

   ⓓ miscellaneous

206 The policeman **devised** a plan to catch the criminals he was after.

   ⓐ created

   ⓑ solicited

   ⓒ undermined

   ⓓ vented

207 The painter's **devotion** to art led him to spend years working on a single painting.

   ⓐ apathy

   ⓑ turbulence

   ⓒ dedication

   ⓓ seclusion

208 Some writers think literature should serve a **didactic** purpose and teach the reader important lessons.

   ⓐ soporific

   ⓑ pragmatic

   ⓒ educational

   ⓓ spacious

209 Some mistook his usual silence for **diffidence**, when in fact he just disliked idle talk.

   ⓐ temerity

   ⓑ confidence

   ⓒ conviction

   ⓓ shyness

210 A **diffident** young woman, she never spoke unless someone spoke to her first.

   ⓐ prudent

   ⓑ timid

   ⓒ sparing

   ⓓ bold

Answers

181-185 ⓒⓑⓐⓓⓒ	196-200 ⓐⓓⓑⓒⓑ
186-190 ⓓⓑⓐⓓⓒ	201-205 ⓑⓐⓒⓓⓑ
191-195 ⓓⓓⓓⓐⓑ	206-210 ⓐⓒⓒⓓⓑ

☆211 **diffuse**
[difjúːz]

adj. low in concentration or density, as in the case of clouds, smoke, or fog

SYN loose, fuzzy, indistinct, unconcentrated, dispersed

The telescope showed a star surrounded by a huge, _____ cloud of gas and dust.

☆212 **digress**
[daigrés]

v. to depart briefly from an intended topic of discussion

SYN depart, deviate, wander

The author's problem is that she _____ too often from her main topic.

☆213 **digression**
[daigréʃən]

n. a brief departure, deviation, or excursion from an intended topic of discussion

SYN departure, deviation, aside

The professor's lecture was full of _____ from his topic, but those were the most interesting parts.

☆214 **dilatory**
[dílətɔ̀ːri]

adj. slow, late, or delayed; intended to delay or postpone something

SYN slow, late, tardy, lagging

Though as _____ as a turtle, the child finally arrived home from school.

☆215 **diligence**
[dílədʒəns]

n. steady, hard work; dedication to completing a project or assignment

SYN dedication, assiduity, patience, commitment

He was not as skilled as some other workers, but his _____ made him successful anyway.

☆216 **diminish**
[dəmíniʃ]

v. to make something smaller or weaker

SYN shrink, drop, reduce, decline, ebb, fall

The loss of forests has _____ the numbers of many bird species.

SCAFFOLDING

211 널리 퍼진, 흩어진 | 망원경은 크고 널리 퍼진diffuse 가스와 먼지 구름에 의해 둘러싸인 별을 보여주었다.

212 벗어나다, 빗나가다 | 그 작가의 문제는 본 주제로부터 너무 자주 벗어난다digresses는 것이다.

213 본론을 벗어남, 여담, 탈선 | 교수의 강의는 주제로부터 벗어난 것digressions으로 가득했지만, 그것들이 가장 재미있는 부분들이었다.

214 느린, 늦은, 시간을 끄는 | 그 아이는 거북이처럼 느렸지만dilatory 마침내 학교에서 집으로 도착했다.

215 근면, 부지런함 | 그는 일부 다른 노동자들보다 기술이 부족했지만, 그의 근면성diligence은 어쨌든 그가 성공할 수 있게 해주었다.

216 줄이다, 감소하다 | 삼림의 손실은 새 종류의 개수를 많이 감소시켰다diminished.

☆217 **diminution**
[dìmənjúːʃən]

n. a reduction, decrease, subtraction, decline, or deduction
SYN reduction, shrinkage, decrease

The new environmental protection laws were designed to halt the _____ of the total area of wetlands.

☆218 **discerning**
[disɔ́ːrniŋ]

n. able to perceive and understand things clearly
SYN perceptive, aware, alert, observant

She was so _____ that she immediately saw the flaw in his argument.

☆219 **discernment**
[disɔ́ːrnmənt]

n. the ability to see and understand things clearly; sound judgment; skill at critical thinking
SYN perception, awareness, sharpness

Voters with keen _____ saw that the candidate's promises were meaningless.

☆220 **disclose**
[disklóuz]

v. to reveal or release information that was previously unavailable
SYN reveal, release, publicize, announce

An official report _____ the existence of several hazardous waste sites in the county.

☆221 **discord**
[dískɔːrd]

n. any lack of harmony or unanimity in a group; in a general sense, turmoil, complaint, or rebellion
SYN dissent, disharmony, disorder, protest, disagreement

The general took advantage of the _____ among his enemies to defeat them.

☆222 **discordant**
[diskɔ́ːrdənt]

adj. out of harmony with others; often used to describe harsh or unpleasant music
SYN sour, harsh, disharmonious, unsettling, upsetting, disturbing

The conductor frowned when someone in the orchestra played a _____ note by mistake.

DAY 08

SCAFFOLDING

217 감소, 축소   전체 습지의 감소diminution를 중지시키기 위한 새로운 환경보호법이 입안되었다.
218 통찰력 있는, 총명한   그녀는 매우 총명했기discerning 때문에 그의 논쟁에서 약점을 즉시 찾아냈다.
219 인식력, 판별력   날카로운 식견discernment을 가진 유권자들은 그 후보의 약속이 의미없다는 것을 알았다.
220 드러내다, 폭로하다   한 공식 보고서는 나라에 있는 몇 개의 위험한 쓰레기 처리장의 존재를 폭로했다disclosed.
221 불화, 불일치, 불협화음   장군은 적들을 물리치기 위해 그들간의 불화discord를 이용했다.
222 일치하지 않는, 사이가 좋지 않은 지휘자는 관현악단의 누군가가 실수로 불협화음의discordant 음조를 냈을 때 눈살을 찌푸렸다.

☆223 **discrepancy**
[diskrépənsi]

n. a divergence, inconsistency, or disagreement; often applied to inconsistencies in testimony or data

SYN inconsistency, disagreement

There is a slight _____ between the testimonies of the two witnesses to the crime.

☆224 **discriminate**
[diskrímənèit]

v. to make a distinction between two things; to show prejudice or bias

SYN discern, differentiate

At this distance, it is hard to _____ between the two species of birds.

☆225 **discriminating**
[diskrímənèitiŋ]

adj. able to see small differences or make fine distinctions

SYN sensitive, selective, tasteful

A _____ reader will see the difference between the two authors at once.

☆226 **disdain**
[disdéin]

n. a feeling of contempt or low esteem; a sense that something is unimportant or inferior in quality

SYN contempt, scorn

Though critics treated the artist's work with _____, people around the world loved it.

☆227 **disinclination**
[dìsinklinéiʃən]

n. a desire to avoid doing or encountering something

SYN unwillingness, reluctance, hesitancy

Allergies have left me with a _____ to have flowers in my home.

☆228 **dismiss**
[dismís]

v. to release from employment or a meeting; to regard as unimportant or irrelevant

SYN discharge, fire, release

The teacher _____ the class when the bell rang.

---

223 불일치, 모순   그 범죄에 대한 두 목격자의 증언 사이에는 약간의 불일치discrepancy가 있다.

224 구별하다, 차별하다   이 거리에서는 두 조류를 구별하기가discriminate 어렵다.

225 구별할 수 있는, 식별력 있는, 차별적인   식별력이 있는discriminating 독자는 두 작가 사이의 차이점을 즉시 알아낼 것이다.

226 경멸하다, 멸시하다   비록 비평가들은 그 예술가의 작품을 멸시적으로disdain 대했지만, 세계 각지의 사람들은 그것을 좋아했다.

227 싫증, 마음이 안 내킴   알레르기는 나에게 집에서 꽃을 기르고 싶지 않은 마음disinclination이 생기게 했다.

228 해산시키다, 해고하다   선생님은 벨이 울리자 학급을 해산시켰다dismissed.

☆229 **disparage**
[dispǽridʒ]

v. to describe something or someone in a hostile, critical manner

SYN insult, denigrate, condemn

Reviewers _____ this author's works as inaccurate, but I like to read his books.

☆230 **disparate**
[díspərit]

adj. different in kind; unlike one another

SYN different, distinct, dissimilar

The insects look similar, but they are actually two _____ species.

☆231 **disparity**
[dispǽrəti]

n. a difference or inequality; often used in reference to statistical data, especially economic data

SYN difference, inequality

Some societies show a greater _____ in income between the upper and middle classes than other societies do.

☆232 **dispassionate**
[dispǽʃənit]

adj. unaffected by emotion or partiality

SYN emotionless, unbiased, impartial

To act as referee, we need a _____ observer of the game.

☆233 **disperse**
[dispə́:rs]

v. to cause to scatter or disassemble

SYN scatter, distribute

The morning sunlight soon _____ the fog, and then we could see clearly.

☆234 **dispose**
[dispóuz]

v. to place something in an arrangement or order

SYN arrange, array, order

The king _____ the soldiers for the battle.

DAY 08

229 얕보다, 헐뜯다 　　　　평론가들은 이 작가의 작품들이 부정확하다고 헐뜯었지만disparaged, 나는 그의 책들을 읽는 것을 좋아한다.

230 본질적으로 다른, 이종(異種)의 　그 곤충들은 비슷해 보이지만 실제로는 두 개의 다른disparate 종이다.

231 부동, 불일치, 불균형 　　　어떤 사회들은 상류층과 중산층 사이에서 다른 사회들에 비해 더 심한 소득 격차disparity를 보인다.

232 냉정한, 공정한 　　　　우리는 심판으로서의 공정한dispassionate 경기 관찰자가 필요하다.

233 흩어지게 하다, 분산시키다 　아침의 햇빛은 곧 안개를 흩뜨렸고dispersed, 그때 우리는 선명하게 볼 수 있었다.

234 배치하다, 처리하다 　　그 왕은 그 병사들을 전장에 배치했다disposed.

☆235 **disputatious**
[dìspjutéiʃəs]

adj. inclined to dispute or argue
SYN argumentative, quarrelsome, contentious

One _____ person at a meeting can delay it with a needless argument.

☆236 **disseminate**
[disémənèit]

v. to distribute something; often used in reference to information or news
SYN spread, scatter, distribute

The Internet _____ the news around the world within minutes.

☆237 **dissent**
[disént]

n. a disagreement or difference of opinion; in many cases, a minority opinion opposed to that of a majority
SYN disagreement, argument

A society needs a certain amount of _____ to remain healthy by correcting errors.

☆238 **distant**
[dístənt]

adj. removed from one another in space or time
SYN far, remote, separate

The new telescope made it possible to see _____ objects much more clearly.

☆239 **distend**
[disténd]

v. to cause to expand or swell
SYN swell, bulge

An X-ray showed a _____ spot on a blood vessel that might require surgery.

☆240 **distinguish**
[distíŋgwiʃ]

v. to tell things apart; to perceive differences in size, quality, or other attributes
SYN differentiate, discern, discriminate

It is easy to _____ between these two minerals because they look so different.

235 논쟁적인, 논쟁을 좋아하는   회의에서 논쟁을 좋아하는disputatious 한 사람이 쓸데없는 논쟁으로 회의를 지연시킬 수 있다.
236 흩뿌리다, 퍼뜨리다   인터넷은 몇 분 만에 그 소식을 전세계적으로 퍼뜨렸다disseminated.
237 의견 차이, 불찬성   사회는 잘못을 고쳐가며 건강하게 유지되기 위해서 일정량의 의견 차이dissent를 필요로 한다.
238 먼, 아득한   그 새로운 망원경은 먼 거리의distant 물체를 훨씬 더 명확하게 보는 것을 가능하게 해 주었다.
239 넓히다, 과장하다   엑스레이는 수술이 필요할지도 모르는 혈관의 확장된distended 부분을 보여주었다.
240 구별하다, 분간하다   이 두 광물은 너무나도 달라 보여서 구별하기가distinguish 쉽다.

211 The telescope showed a star surrounded by a huge, **diffuse** cloud of gas and dust.

ⓐ monotonous

ⓑ fuzzy

ⓒ mercurial

ⓓ voluntary

212 The author's problem is that she **digresses** too often from her main topic.

ⓐ divulges

ⓑ stays

ⓒ focuses

ⓓ wanders

213 The professor's lecture was full of **digressions** from his topic, but those were the most interesting parts.

ⓐ levity

ⓑ deviations

ⓒ enticements

ⓓ languid

214 Though as **dilatory** as a turtle, the child finally arrived home from school.

ⓐ diligent

ⓑ honest

ⓒ prompt

ⓓ slow

215 He was not as skilled as some other workers, but his **diligence** made him successful anyway.

ⓐ assiduity

ⓑ sloth

ⓒ inconsistency

ⓓ incongruity

216 The loss of forests has **diminished** the numbers of many bird species.

ⓐ razed

ⓑ rambled

ⓒ quelled

ⓓ reduced

217 The new environmental protection laws were designed to halt the **diminution** of the total area of wetlands.

ⓐ rebuttal

ⓑ augment

ⓒ rancor

ⓓ shrinkage

218 She was so **discerning** that she immediately saw the flaw in his argument.

ⓐ saccharine

ⓑ bulged

ⓒ ravenous

ⓓ perceptive

219 Voters with keen **discernment** saw that the candidate's promises were meaningless.

ⓐ misunderstanding

ⓑ distortion

ⓒ wrench

ⓓ sharpness

220 An official report **disclosed** the existence of several hazardous waste sites in the county.

ⓐ announced

ⓑ mitigated

ⓒ concealed

ⓓ removed

DAY 08

221 The general took advantage of the **discord** among his enemies to defeat them.

ⓐ apprehension

ⓑ accord

ⓒ disorder

ⓓ harmony

222 The conductor frowned when someone in the orchestra played a **discordant** note by mistake.

ⓐ comical

ⓑ playful

ⓒ disharmonious

ⓓ straight

223 There is a slight **discrepancy** between the testimonies of the two witnesses to the crime.

ⓐ agreement

ⓑ protrusion

ⓒ disturbance

ⓓ inconsistency

224 At this distance, it is hard to **discriminate** between the two species of birds.

ⓐ differentiate

ⓑ confuse

ⓒ recall

ⓓ daze

225 A **discriminating** reader will see the difference between the two authors at once.

ⓐ adaptable

ⓑ selective

ⓒ systematic

ⓓ painstaking

226 Though critics treated the artist's work with **disdain**, people around the world loved it.

ⓐ concern

ⓑ contempt

ⓒ humility

ⓓ diminution

227 Allergies have left me with a **disinclination** to have flowers in my home.

ⓐ unwillingness

ⓑ aplomb

ⓒ mirth

ⓓ voluntary

228 The teacher **dismissed** the class when the bell rang.

ⓐ revered

ⓑ released

ⓒ venerated

ⓓ satiated

229 Reviewers **disparage** this author's works as inaccurate, but I like to read his books.

ⓐ insult

ⓑ rescind

ⓒ hold

ⓓ overwhelm

230 The insects look similar, but they are actually two **disparate** species.

ⓐ similar

ⓑ disturbing

ⓒ distinct

ⓓ parallel

231 Some societies show a greater **disparity** in income between the upper and middle classes than other societies do.

ⓐ similarity

ⓑ proportion

ⓒ compound

ⓓ inequality

232 To act as referee, we need a **dispassionate** observer of the game.

ⓐ selective

ⓑ shabby

ⓒ impartial

ⓓ picky

233 The morning sunlight soon **dispersed** the fog, and then we could see clearly.

ⓐ imposed

ⓑ scattered

ⓒ embellished

ⓓ revised

234 The king **disposed** the soldiers for the battle.

ⓐ exposed

ⓑ arranged

ⓒ seduced

ⓓ allured

235 One **disputatious** person at a meeting can delay it with a needless argument.

ⓐ agreeable

ⓑ impregnable

ⓒ argumentative

ⓓ congenial

236 The Internet **disseminated** the news around the world within minutes.

ⓐ assembled

ⓑ gathered

ⓒ divulged

ⓓ spread

237 A society needs a certain amount of **dissent** to remain healthy by correcting errors.

ⓐ assent

ⓑ disagreement

ⓒ duplicity

ⓓ sanction

238 The new telescope made it possible to see **distant** objects much more clearly.

ⓐ meticulous

ⓑ remote

ⓒ outgoing

ⓓ divergent

239 An X-ray showed a **distended** spot on a blood vessel that might require surgery.

ⓐ shrunk

ⓑ recoiled

ⓒ feeble

ⓓ bulging

240 It is easy to **distinguish** between these two minerals because they look so different.

ⓐ overlook

ⓑ deceive

ⓒ discriminate

ⓓ defame

DAY 08

☆241 **divergent**
[divə́:rdʒənt]

adj. differing or becoming different; separating or pulling apart
SYN different, irregular, unlike

This organization has strict rules and does not permit _____ opinions.

☆242 **diverse**
[divə́:rs]

adj. different; dissimilar; showing differences in kind or character
SYN different, dissimilar, unlike, varying

Letters to the editor usually express _____ opinions.

☆243 **divert**
[divə́:rt]

v. to change the direction or destination of something
SYN deflect, redirect, reroute

Engineers _____ the course of the river so that it took a different route.

☆244 **divulge**
[divʌ́ldʒ]

v. to make something known
SYN disclose, impart, relate, reveal, acknowledge, admit

The families called on President Clinton to push Pyongyang to _____ more information about the fate of their missing kin.

☆245 **docile**
[dásəl]

adj. easy to manage or control
SYN manageable, obedient, pliant, submissive, teachable

The suspect was apparently dexterous in hiding his true identity behind his _____ appearance.

☆246 **doctrine**
[dáktrin]

n. a principle, guideline, policy, or teaching, or set of such
SYN principle, policy, teaching

Often, changes in political _____ reflect changes in leadership.

SCAFFOLDING

241 다른, 갈라지는, 발산하는 — 이 조직에는 엄격한 규율이 있고 이견을divergent 허용하지 않는다.

242 다른 종류의, 다양한 — 편집장에게 보내는 편지들은 보통 다양한diverse 의견들을 표현한다.

243 딴 데로 돌리다, 전환하다 — 기술자들은 그 강의 흐름을 딴 데로 전환하여diverted 다른 루트로 통하게 했다.

244 비밀을 누설하다, 밝히다, 공표하다 — 가족들은 클린턴 대통령에게 평양에 압력을 넣어 그들의 실종된 친척들의 생사에 대한 더 많은 정보를 공표하도록divulge 할 것을 요구했다.

245 다루기 쉬운, 유순한 — 용의자는 그의 유순한docile 외면 뒤에 진정한 정체성을 숨기는데 분명히 재주가 있는 것 같았다.

246 주의, 이론, 교리 — 종종 정치 이론docrines의 변화들은 지도층의 변화들을 반영한다.

☆247 **document**
[dάkjəmənt]

n. a record of important information
SYN paper, record, file

A birth certificate is a _____ that officially records the time and place of one's birth.

☆248 **dogmatic**
[dɔ(:)gmǽtik]

adj. strictly according to a rule, dogma, or policy
SYN strict, rigid, doctrinaire

Many religions have _____ rules about what may and may not be done.

☆249 **drone**
[droun]

n. an individual who does no work or has no apparent job; a steady noise, usually low in pitch
SYN idler, slacker, buzz, hum

In a beehive, there are worker bees, and there are _____, which are much less active.

☆250 **dubious**
[djú:biəs]

adj. of questionable importance, value, or accuracy
SYN questionable, uncertain, unreliable

His claim to have worked abroad was _____ and was not taken seriously.

☆251 **dupe**
[dju:p]

v. to deceive someone completely
SYN deceive, trick, mislead

They found that the salesman had _____ them into buying a worthless piece of land.

☆252 **duplicity**
[dju:plísəti]

n. misrepresenting something seriously to others; in many cases for personal gain
SYN trickery, dishonesty, deception, misrepresentation

His record of _____ was so well known that no one trusted him.

DAY 09

247 문서, 서류 　　　　　　　　 출생 증명서는 한 사람의 출생지와 출생시간을 공식적으로 기록하는 서류document이다.

248 교리상의, 독단적인 　　　　 많은 종교들이 무엇을 해도 되고 무엇을 하면 안되는지에 대한 교리적인dogmatic 규칙들을 가지고 있다.

249 게으름뱅이, 윙윙거리는 소리, 수벌 　 벌집에는 일벌도 있고 훨씬 덜 활동적인 수벌drones도 있다.

250 수상한, 의심스러운 　　　　 그가 해외에서 일 했다는 주장은 의심스러웠기dubious 때문에 심각하게 받아들여지지 않았다.

251 속이다 　　　　　　　　　 그들은 그 판매원이 가치 없는 땅을 사도록 속였다는duped 것을 알아냈다.

252 표리부동, 일구이언 　　　　 그의 일구이언duplicity에 대한 기록은 너무나도 잘 알려져 있어서 누구도 그를 믿지 않는다.

☆253 **durable**
[djúərəbəl]

adj. of sturdy construction; capable of heavy use over a long period
SYN tough, rugged, stout, long-lasting

Some leather artifacts are so _____ that they have survived for thousands of years.

☆254 **dwindle**
[dwíndl]

v. to shrink in size
SYN curtail, decrease, lessen, reduce

Facility investment is expected to shrink by 18 percent and private consumption to _____ by 2.6 percent.

☆255 **ebullient**
[ibʌ́ljənt]

adj. joyful and enthusiastic, as if at a party or other celebration
SYN outgoing, merry, joyful

His _____ manner reminded people of a cheerleader performing at a game.

☆256 **eccentric**
[ikséntrik]

adj. highly unusual or idiosyncratic
SYN odd, strange, abnormal, unusual

The professor was known for his _____ behavior, such as singing in the classroom.

☆257 **eclectic**
[ekléktik]

adj. using material from a variety of sources
SYN mixed, varied, heterogeneous

This composer has an _____ style and mixes many kinds of music into his work.

☆258 **edify**
[édəfài]

v. to teach or instruct; to impart information or a lesson
SYN teach, instruct, inform

A fable is written to _____ readers through the use of a moral at the end of the story.

SCAFFOLDING

253 영속성 있는, 튼튼한   어떤 인조 가죽은 영속성이 너무 강해서durable 수천 년 동안 남아 있다.

254 줄다, 작아지다, 축소되다   설비 투자는 18%, 가계 소비는 2.6%로 떨어질dwindle 것으로 예상된다.

255 용솟음치는, 열광적인   그의 열광적인ebullient 태도는 사람들에게 경기에서 상연하는 치어리더를 연상시켰다.

256 별난, 괴상한   그 교수는 교실에서 노래를 부르는 등의 괴상한eccentric 행동을 하는 것으로 알려져 있다.

257 폭넓은, 절충적인   이 작곡가는 폭넓은eclectic 스타일을 가지고 있으며 많은 종류의 음악을 혼합하여 작품을 만든다.

258 신념을 기르다, 교화하다   우화는 이야기의 결말에서 교훈을 통하여 독자들을 교환하기 위해edify 쓰여진다.

☆259 **efface**
[iféis]

v. to rub out, wipe out, hide, conceal, or remove from sight; often used in the context of a self-effacing person
SYN hide, conceal, erase

The criminal made a great effort to _____ all evidence of his crime.

☆260 **effectual**
[iféktʃuəl]

adj. adequate or sufficient for a given purpose
SYN adequate, effective

The new software gave us an _____ way to collect the data we needed.

☆261 **effervescence**
[èfərvésns]

n. the quality or action of releasing gas as bubbles from a solution; a cheerful, joyful personality or manner
SYN foaminess, bubbliness, ebullience

The _____ of soda water has made it a popular beverage.

☆262 **effervescent**
[èfərvésnt]

adj. characterized by releasing large amounts of bubbles or foam; very cheerful, outgoing, or joyful
SYN foamy, bubbly, ebullient, joyful

Her _____ personality made her very successful as a salesperson because she made the products appealing.

☆263 **egotistical**
[ì:gətístikəl]

adj. self-centered to an extreme; concerned only with oneself and one's own interests
SYN self-centered, conceited

His _____ manner made him unsuccessful as a team player.

☆264 **elaborate**
[ilǽbərət]

adj. complex; executed in great detail
SYN intricate, complex, ornate

The museum displayed an _____ carving that showed hundreds of animals.

DAY 09

SCAFFOLDING

259 지워 없애다   그 범죄자는 자신의 범죄에 대한 모든 증거를 없애버리기efface 위해서 많은 노력을 기울였다.

260 효과적인, 유효한, 충분한   그 새로운 소프트웨어는 우리에게 필요한 데이터를 수집할 수 있는 효과적인effectual 방법을 제공해 주었다.

261 거품이 남, 흥분, 활기   탄산수의 거품effervescence으로 그 음료수는 인기를 얻었다.

262 거품이 나는, 흥분한, 활기 있는   그녀의 활기찬effervescent 성격은 그녀를 판매원으로서 매우 성공적으로 만들어 주었다. 왜냐하면 그녀는 상품을 매력적으로 보이게 했기 때문이다.

263 자기의 일만 하는, 자기 중심의   그의 자기중심적egotistical 태도는 그가 팀원으로서 성공적이지 못하도록 만들었다.

264 공들인, 복잡한, 정교한   그 박물관은 수백 마리의 동물들을 보여주는 화려한elaborate 조각들을 전시했다.

☆265 **elated**
[iléitid]

adj. extremely happy
SYN overjoyed, delighted

My sister _____ when she was accepted to the university of her choice.

☆266 **elegance**
[éligəns]

adj. refined in appearance and style
SYN grace, beauty

That car became known as an example of _____ in automobile design.

☆267 **elegy**
[élədʒi]

n. a song for or about a dead person; a sad song
SYN lament, threnody

Her _____ for her deceased mother was sung at a concert.

☆268 **elicit**
[ilísit]

v. to draw out; to evoke; to bring out
SYN evoke, provoke

We hope this survey will _____ responses from a lot of people.

☆269 **eloquence**
[éləkwəns]

adj. eloquent
[éləkwənt]

n. the ability to talk or write in vivid, stirring language
SYN articulateness, expressiveness

Those supporters still consider the _____ president their hero.

☆270 **elucidate**
[ilú:sədèit]

v. to make things clear; to explain clearly
SYN clarify, explain

The professor's lecture _____ the contents of the reading.

SYNONYMS WORDS THAT MEAN THE SAME THING

241 This organization has strict rules and does not permit **divergent** opinions.

ⓐ obnoxious

ⓑ colloquial

ⓒ different

ⓓ baneful

242 Letters to the editor usually express **diverse** opinions.

ⓐ dissimilar

ⓑ limited

ⓒ finite

ⓓ narrow

243 Engineers **diverted** the course of the river so that it took a different route.

ⓐ bored

ⓑ redirected

ⓒ pierced

ⓓ bereaved

244 The families called on President Clinton to push Pyongyang to **divulge** more information about the fate of their missing kin.

ⓐ vindicate

ⓑ utter

ⓒ meddle

ⓓ disclose

245 The suspect was apparently dexterous in hiding his true identity behind his **docile** appearance.

ⓐ voluble

ⓑ spacious

ⓒ rebellious

ⓓ submissive

246 Often, changes in political **doctrines** reflect changes in leadership.

ⓐ factors

ⓑ principles

ⓒ options

ⓓ questions

247 A birth certificate is a **document** that officially records the time and place of one's birth.

ⓐ remission

ⓑ file

ⓒ hedge

ⓓ profile

248 Many religions have **dogmatic** rules about what may and may not be done.

ⓐ doctrinaire

ⓑ sparing

ⓒ haggard

ⓓ gregarious

249 In a beehive, there are worker bees, and there are **drones**, which are much less active.

ⓐ doubters

ⓑ foliages

ⓒ gluttons

ⓓ idlers

250 His claim to have worked abroad was **dubious** and was not taken seriously.

ⓐ docile

ⓑ questionable

ⓒ meticulous

ⓓ grave

251 They found that the salesman had **duped** them into buying a worthless piece of land.

ⓐ conceived

ⓑ distended

ⓒ subjugated

ⓓ deceived

252 His record of **duplicity** was so well known that no one trusted him.

ⓐ reticence

ⓑ deception

ⓒ surmise

ⓓ dissent

253 Some leather artifacts are so **durable** that they have survived for thousands of years.

ⓐ flimsy

ⓑ temporary

ⓒ paltry

ⓓ long-lasting

254 Facility investment is expected to shrink by 18 percent and private consumption to **dwindle** by 2.6 percent.

ⓐ decrease

ⓑ emend

ⓒ soften

ⓓ gauge

255 His **ebullient** manner reminded people of a cheerleader performing at a game.

ⓐ fertile

ⓑ joyful

ⓒ morose

ⓓ vile

256 The professor was known for his **eccentric** behavior, such as singing in the classroom.

ⓐ irregular

ⓑ particular

ⓒ abnormal

ⓓ docile

257 This composer has an **eclectic** style and mixes many kinds of music into his work.

ⓐ luxuriant

ⓑ mixed

ⓒ pliant

ⓓ dexterous

258 A fable is written to **edify** readers through the use of a moral at the end of the story.

ⓐ instruct

ⓑ dupe

ⓒ induct

ⓓ subdue

259 The criminal made a great effort to **efface** all evidence of his crime.

ⓐ amend

ⓑ rescind

ⓒ reproduce

ⓓ conceal

260 The new software gave us an **effectual** way to collect the data we needed.

ⓐ saccharine

ⓑ residual

ⓒ adequate

ⓓ spurious

261 The **effervescence** of soda water has made it a popular beverage.

  ⓐ disparity
  ⓑ foaminess
  ⓒ duplicity
  ⓓ elegance

262 Her **effervescent** personality made her very successful as a salesperson because she made the products appealing.

  ⓐ overjoyed
  ⓑ ebullient
  ⓒ slothful
  ⓓ esoteric

263 His **egotistical** manner made him unsuccessful as a team player.

  ⓐ overt
  ⓑ loathsome
  ⓒ luminous
  ⓓ self-centered

264 The museum displayed an **elaborate** carving that showed hundreds of animals.

  ⓐ ornate
  ⓑ resourceful
  ⓒ spontaneous
  ⓓ glum

265 My sister was **elated** when she was accepted to the university of her choice.

  ⓐ shocked
  ⓑ assuaged
  ⓒ delighted
  ⓓ consoled

266 That car became known as an example of **elegance** in automobile design.

  ⓐ lament
  ⓑ ascendancy
  ⓒ grace
  ⓓ apprehension

267 Her **elegy** for her deceased mother was sung at a concert.

  ⓐ resolution
  ⓑ affidavit
  ⓒ lament
  ⓓ stanza

268 We hope this survey will **elicit** responses from a lot of people.

  ⓐ aggravate
  ⓑ obscure
  ⓒ evoke
  ⓓ placate

269 Those supporters still consider the **eloquent** president their hero.

  ⓐ rough
  ⓑ articulate
  ⓒ pointless
  ⓓ coarse

270 The professor's lecture **elucidated** the contents of the reading.

  ⓐ swore
  ⓑ withdrew
  ⓒ condensed
  ⓓ explained

Answers

241-245 ⓒⓐⓑⓓⓓ	256-260 ⓒⓑⓐⓓⓒ
246-250 ⓑⓑⓐⓓⓑ	261-265 ⓑⓑⓓⓐⓒ
251-255 ⓓⓑⓓⓐⓑ	266-270 ⓒⓒⓒⓑⓓ

☆271 **elusive**
[ilúːsiv]

adj. extremely difficult to capture, define, or specify

SYN evasive, slippery, uncatchable, vague, undefined, ambiguous

An _____ bird species, the woodpecker was not seen again for 100 years.

☆272 **emaciated**
[iméiʃièitid]

adj. extremely thin, as if near starvation

SYN gaunt, wasted, thin, skeletal

By the time he was rescued, the crash survivor was _____ and weak.

☆273 **embellish**
[imbéliʃ]

v. to adorn; to decorate; to expand or add detail, as to a story

SYN color, decorate, dress up, elaborate, ornament

Everyone who heard the story _____ it with an extra detail or quotation.

☆274 **embrace**
[imbréis]

v. to hug, hold, or take in one's arms

SYN hug, hold

My mother _____ the whole family as we came to visit her.

☆275 **emend**
[iménd]

v. to alter, amend, edit, revise, or prepare a new version of something

SYN amend, redo, revise, rewrite

The need to _____ our inaccurate report required us to spend an extra day rewriting it.

☆276 **emulate**
[émjulèit]

v. to use as a model; to copy; to aim to equal someone

SYN copy, imitate

As a child, he wanted to _____ the heroes he saw in movies.

SCAFFOLDING

271 붙잡기 어려운, 피하는, 달아나는   붙잡기 어려운elusive 조류인 딱따구리는 100년 동안 다시 보이지 않았다.

272 수척한, 여윈, 메마른   충돌사고의 생존자가 구조되었을 당시 그는 수척하고emaciated 연약한 상태였다.

273 꾸미다, 장식하다   그 이야기를 들은 모든 사람들은 추가적인 세부 설명과 인용을 통해 그 이야기를 장식했다embellished.

274 껴안다, 받아들이다   어머니는 우리가 어머니를 방문하러 오자 가족 전체를 껴안아 주셨다embraced.

275 교정하다, 수정하다   부정확한 보고서를 수정할emend 필요가 있었기 때문에 우리는 이를 다시 쓰는데 하루가 더 필요했다.

276 경쟁하다, 모방하다   그는 어렸을 때 영화에서 본 주인공들을 따라하고emulate 싶었다.

| ☆277 | **endorse**
[indɔ́ːrs] | *v.* to sign (a document such as a bank check); to approve (an action, candidate, or cause)
SYN sign, approve, authenticate, support |
| | | *The governor has _____ our candidate in the upcoming election.* |

| ☆278 | **endurance**
[indjúərəns] | *n.* the ability to withstand stress or difficult times
SYN stamina, persistence, longevity |
| | | *Famed for its _____, the old car ran for 50 years.* |

| ☆279 | **engender**
[indʒéndər] | *v.* to produce, generate, or give life to something
SYN produce, originate, procreate |
| | | *The song _____ great protests from some people who thought it insulted them.* |

| ☆280 | **enhance**
[inhǽns] | *v.* to make something better, bigger, or more advanced
SYN advance, improve, increase |
| | | *A little cinnamon would _____ the flavor of this food.* |

| ☆281 | **enigma**
[əníɡmə] | *n.* something highly mysterious or ambiguous
SYN mystery, puzzle, riddle |
| | | *The _____ of Egyptian writing was solved through the discovery of the Rosetta stone.* |

| ☆282 | **enlighten**
[inláitn] | *v.* to teach, explain, or provide understanding
SYN teach, instruct, inform |
| | | *The camp is aimed to _____ youths talented in science through discussions and dialogs with top scholars.* |

DAY 10

SCAFFOLDING

277 승인하다   주지사는 다가오는 선거에 우리의 후보자 진출을 승인했다endorsed.

278 지구력, 내구성, 인내력   내구성endurance이 강하기로 유명한 그 차는 50년을 달렸다.

279 생기게 하다, 일으키다   그 노래는 그것이 자기들을 모욕한다고 생각하는 사람들에 의해 큰 항의를 불러 일으켰다engendered.

280 높이다, 강화하다   약간의 계피는 이 음식의 맛을 높일 것이다enhance.

281 수수께끼, 불가사의한 일   이집트 문자의 수수께끼enigma는 Rosetta 돌의 발견을 통해서 풀렸다.

282 계몽하다, 설명하다, 가르치다   그 캠프는 유수한 학자들과의 토론과 대화를 통해 과학에 재능이 있는 젊은이들을 가르치는enlighten 데에 목표를 두었다.

☆283 **enmity**
[énməti]

n. intense dislike; hatred; opposition

SYN animosity, hatred

The _____ between the two nations brought them close to war.

☆284 **enthrall**
[inθrɔ́ːl]

v. to hold someone's interest completely

SYN fascinate, transfix

The first broadcast of the television show _____ the children.

☆285 **entice**
[intáis]

v. to tempt or persuade

SYN beguile, induce, lure, tempt, allure, attract, fascinate, seduce

They are attempting to _____ a North Korean female worker to defect to the South.

☆286 **ephemeral**
[ifémərəl]

adj. existing only for a very brief period

SYN brief, short-lived, temporary

The actress found that her fame was only an _____ phenomenon.

☆287 **equanimity**
[ìːkwəníməti]

n. a calm and confident attitude

SYN aplomb, composure, coolness

No amount of bad news could shake his _____ and optimism.

☆288 **equitable**
[ékwətəbəl]

adj. fair to both parties in a dispute

SYN fair, evenhanded, impartial

An _____ settlement left each claimant with half of the disputed property.

SCAFFOLDING

283 적의, 원한 | 두 나라 간의 원한enmity은 두 나라 사이에 전쟁을 가져왔다.
284 마음을 사로잡다 | 그 티비 쇼의 첫 방영은 아이들의 마음을 사로잡았다enthralled.
285 꾀다, 유혹하다, 부추기다 | 그들은 북한 여성 노동자들을 부추겨entice 남한으로 전향시키려 노력했다.
286 하루뿐인, 순식간의 | 그 여배우는 그녀의 명성이 단지 일시적인ephemeral 현상일 뿐이라는 것을 알았다.
287 평정, 침착, 균형 | 아무리 많은 나쁜 소식들도 그의 평정equanimity과 낙천적 성격을 흔들 수는 없었다.
288 공평한, 정당한 | 공평한equitable 해결로 각각의 청구자는 논란이 되는 재산의 절반씩을 받았다.

☆289 **equivocal**
[ikwívəkəl]

adj. open to interpretation in more than one way

SYN ambiguous, uncommitted, uncertain, doubtful

The candidate's statement on the issue was _____ and did not clarify his views.

☆290 **eradicate**
[irǽdəkèit]

v. to get rid of something completely

SYN abolish, annihilate, eliminate, exterminate

The National Assembly is seeking to _____ social ills.

☆291 **erratic**
[irǽtik]

adj. not regular or consistent; wavering; unpredictable

SYN wandering, uneven, uncertain

The radio signal was so _____ that we could not discern its message.

☆292 **erroneous**
[iróuniəs]

adj. in error; inaccurate; false

SYN mistaken, incorrect, wrong

The newspaper published a correction after printing an _____ news story.

☆293 **erudite**
[érʃudàit]

adj. learned or scholarly; usually used in reference to academics and their work

SYN learned, scholarly

This book is an _____ commentary on the history plays of Shakespeare.

☆294 **esoteric**
[èsətérik]

adj. capable of being understood only by a few

SYN abstruse, profound

Despite its _____ nature, the scientist's work was widely publicized.

DAY 10

☆295 **essential**
[isénʃəl]

adj. necessary for existence; indispensable

SYN necessary, vital

The presence of liquid water is _____ to life as we know it.

☆296 **ethical**
[éθikəl]

adj. in accordance with a set of principles for proper conduct

SYN correct, proper, right, virtuous

The doctors refused to perform the operation because they thought it was not _____.

☆297 **eulogy**
[júːlədʒi]

n. praise, in many cases for someone who has just died

SYN applause, praise

In the play, Mark Antony delivers his _____ for the dead Julius Caesar.

☆298 **euphemism**
[júːfəmìzəm]

n. a kind or soft expression used in place of something harsh or unpleasant

SYN ambiguity, equivocation, hedge

In certain cases, "questionable" serves as a _____ for "unlawful" or "criminal."

☆299 **euphony**
[júːfəni]

n. pleasant sound, especially in music

SYN harmony, sweetness

The songs of birds added _____ to the atmosphere at the resort.

☆300 **evanescent**
[èvənésənt]

adj. of very brief duration; fleeting

SYN ephemeral, short-lived, temporary

These clouds are _____ phenomena and can be studied only for very short intervals.

SCAFFOLDING

295 본질적인, 필수의   물의 존재는 우리가 알고 있듯이 생명에 있어서 필수적이다essential.

296 윤리적인, 도덕적인   의사들은 그 수술이 윤리적이지ethical 않다고 생각했기 때문에 그 수술을 하기를 거절했다.

297 찬사, 칭찬, 송덕문   연극에서 Mark Antony는 죽은 Julius Caesar를 위한 송덕문eulogy을 읽는다.

298 완곡어법, 완곡어구   어떤 경우에는 '미심쩍은'이라는 단어가 '불법의' 또는 '범죄의'라는 단어의 완곡어구euphemism역할을 하기도 한다.

299 듣기 좋은 음조   새들의 지저귐은 휴양지의 분위기에 듣기 좋은 음조euphony를 더해 주었다.

300 사라져 가는, 순간의   이 구름들은 순간적인evanescent 현상이라서 단지 매우 짧은 시간 동안에만 연구될 수 있다.

SYNONYMS WORDS THAT MEAN THE SAME THING

271 An **elusive** bird species, the woodpecker was not seen again for 100 years.

ⓐ flimsy

ⓑ distended

ⓒ evasive

ⓓ abstemious

272 By the time he was rescued, the crash survivor was **emaciated** and weak.

ⓐ residual

ⓑ acrid

ⓒ abstract

ⓓ thin

273 Everyone who heard the story **embellished** it with an extra detail or quotation.

ⓐ polished

ⓑ perpetuated

ⓒ placated

ⓓ adorned

274 My mother **embraced** the whole family as we came to visit her.

ⓐ tabled

ⓑ surpassed

ⓒ hugged

ⓓ intervened

275 The need to **emend** our inaccurate report required us to spend an extra day rewriting it.

ⓐ splinter

ⓑ amend

ⓒ intimidate

ⓓ lure

276 As a child, he wanted to **emulate** the heroes he saw in movies.

ⓐ meander

ⓑ imitate

ⓒ preclude

ⓓ entreat

277 The governor has **endorsed** our candidate in the upcoming election.

ⓐ supported

ⓑ sought

ⓒ sued

ⓓ denounced

278 Famed for its **endurance**, the old car ran for 50 years.

ⓐ instability

ⓑ weakness

ⓒ equanimity

ⓓ longevity

279 The song **engendered** great protests from some people who thought it insulted them.

ⓐ spurned

ⓑ contended

ⓒ generated

ⓓ curtailed

280 A little cinnamon would **enhance** the flavor of this food.

ⓐ improve

ⓑ perish

ⓒ abridge

ⓓ spurn

281 The **enigma** of Egyptian writing was solved through the discovery of the Rosetta stone.

ⓐ fragment

ⓑ elegy

ⓒ splinter

ⓓ mystery

DAY 10

282 The camp is aimed to **enlighten** youths talented in science through discussions and dialogs with top scholars.

ⓐ instruct

ⓑ confuse

ⓒ research

ⓓ portray

283 The **enmity** between the two nations brought them close to war.

ⓐ goodwill

ⓑ deterrence

ⓒ stalemate

ⓓ animosity

284 The first broadcast of the television show **enthralled** the children.

ⓐ endangered

ⓑ fascinated

ⓒ alleviated

ⓓ heeded

285 They are allegedly attempting to **entice** a North Korean female worker to defect to the South.

ⓐ repel

ⓑ locate

ⓒ lure

ⓓ identify

286 The actress found that her fame was only an **ephemeral** phenomenon.

ⓐ immediate

ⓑ insolvent

ⓒ temporary

ⓓ pervasive

287 No amount of bad news could shake his **equanimity** and optimism.

ⓐ awkwardness

ⓑ aplomb

ⓒ doubt

ⓓ insecurity

288 An **equitable** settlement left each claimant with half of the disputed property.

ⓐ threadbare

ⓑ evenhanded

ⓒ impregnable

ⓓ lurid

289 The candidate's statement on the issue was **equivocal** and did not clarify his views.

ⓐ arable

ⓑ congruous

ⓒ somber

ⓓ ambiguous

290 The National Assembly is seeking to **eradicate** social ills.

ⓐ annihilate

ⓑ establish

ⓒ initiate

ⓓ validate

291 The radio signal was so **erratic** that we could not discern its message.

ⓐ consistent

ⓑ industrial

ⓒ archaic

ⓓ uneven

292 The newspaper published a correction after printing an **erroneous** news story.

ⓐ accurate

ⓑ scandalous

ⓒ incorrect

ⓓ authentic

293 This book is an **erudite** commentary on the history plays of Shakespeare.

ⓐ illiterate

ⓑ common

ⓒ physical

ⓓ scholarly

294 Despite its **esoteric** nature, the scientist's work was widely publicized.

ⓐ public

ⓑ ardent

ⓒ bankrupt

ⓓ abstruse

295 The presence of liquid water is **essential** to life as we know it.

ⓐ superfluous

ⓑ accessory

ⓒ auxiliary

ⓓ vital

296 The doctors refused to perform the operation because they thought it was not **ethical**.

ⓐ proper

ⓑ vile

ⓒ immoral

ⓓ permitted

297 In the play, Mark Antony delivers his **eulogy** for the dead Julius Caesar.

ⓐ derision

ⓑ praise

ⓒ opinion

ⓓ analysis

298 In certain cases, "questionable" serves as a **euphemism** for "unlawful" or "criminal."

ⓐ truth

ⓑ fiction

ⓒ confrontation

ⓓ equivocation

299 The songs of birds added **euphony** to the atmosphere at the resort.

ⓐ sweetness

ⓑ cacophony

ⓒ discord

ⓓ remembrance

300 These clouds are **evanescent** phenomena and can be studied only for very short intervals.

ⓐ eternal

ⓑ intriguing

ⓒ abiding

ⓓ short-lived

DAY 10

☆301 **exacerbate**

[igzǽsərbèit]

v. to make something worse; to increase the harshness or severity of a situation

SYN worsen, intensify

We did not speak for fear that we would _____ the already tense situation.

☆302 **exalt**

[igzɔ́:lt]

v. to glorify, praise, or raise in standing

SYN elevate, glorify, praise

The press _____ the winners of the games as heroes.

☆303 **excerpt**

[éksə:rpt]

n. a passage taken from a longer written work or speech

SYN extract, sample, quotation

This article quotes an _____ from the prime minister's statement.

☆304 **execute**

[éksikjù:t]

v. to perform or carry out an action; in certain cases, to carry out an official sentence of death

SYN perform, do, kill

Opponents of capital punishment think the government should not _____ anyone for any crime.

☆305 **exemplary**

[igzémpləri]

adj. worthy of emulation; extremely good

SYN commendable, admirable, outstanding, excellent, model

This recording is an _____ performance of the song we will play at the concert.

☆306 **exemplify**

[igzémpləfài]

v. to serve as an example of something

SYN epitomize, illustrate, represent

The housecat _____ felines, which all have the same basic body structure.

SCAFFOLDING

301 악화시키다, 격화시키다   우리는 이미 긴장된 상황을 더욱 악화시킬exacerbate 수 있으리라는 두려움에 아무 말도 하지 않았다.

302 높이다, 칭찬하다   언론은 그 경기의 승리자들을 영웅이라고 칭찬했다exalted.

303 발췌, 인용   이 기사는 국무총리의 진술로부터 발췌한 것excerpt을 인용했다.

304 실행하다, 사형에 처하다   사형제도의 반대자들은 정부가 범죄 때문에 누군가를 사형하는execute 일이 없어야 한다고 생각한다.

305 모범적인, 훌륭한   이 녹음은 우리가 콘서트에서 할 노래의 모범이 되는exemplary 연주이다.

306 예시하다, 예증하다   집괭이는 모두가 똑같은 기본 신체 구조를 가지고 있는 고양이과의 좋은 예가 된다exemplifies.

☆307 **exhaustive**
[igzɔ́:stiv]

adj. covering all sources; treating a subject in its entirety
 SYN complete, comprehensive, extensive, thorough

This article is an _____ study of recent research in our field of study.

☆308 **exhilarating**
[igzílərèitiŋ]

adj. invigorating; restorative of energy or vigor
 SYN energizing, refreshing, strengthening

Some people find skiing to be an _____ experience.

☆309 **exonerate**
[igzánərèit]

v. to relieve of blame or responsibility
 SYN acquit, justify

The investigation _____ the captain of blame for the loss of his ship.

☆310 **exotic**
[igzátik]

adj. alien; from a foreign country or distant place; usually used in a positive sense
 SYN alien, foreign

The botanical garden was full of _____ plants from around the world.

☆311 **expedient**
[ikspí:diənt]

adj. suitable to one's purpose
 SYN appropriate, convenient

To meet the needs of our business, it was _____ to buy a new computer.

☆312 **expedite**
[ékspədàit]

v. to make something easier for someone else
 SYN assist, ease, help, facilitate

The new tax policy is supposed to _____ the formation of new businesses.

DAY 11

☆313 **explicit**
[iksplísit]

adj. expressed clearly; in unmistakable language

SYN clear, exact, precise, plain, unambiguous

The CEO left _____ instructions that he was not to be interrupted except in case of an emergency.

☆314 **exploit**
[iksplɔ́it]

v. to utilize or take advantage of something or someone in either a positive or a negative sense; to manipulate or control someone to one's own advantage (usually used in a negative sense)

SYN employ, use, abuse, manipulate

The goal of the company's management was to _____ the divisions among the workers to the fullest.

☆315 **expunge**
[ikspʌ́ndʒ]

v. to erase, obliterate, remove, or strike out; often used in reference to removing errors from a record

SYN delete, erase, undo

The government gave orders to _____ all references to the criminal from public records.

☆316 **extensive**
[iksténsiv]

adj. covering a wide area; incorporating many sources; broad in scope

SYN big, broad, comprehensive, inclusive, large, wide

The storm dropped heavy rain over an _____ area and caused much flooding.

☆317 **extirpate**
[ékstərpèit]

v. to destroy completely

SYN destroy

The king dedicated himself to _____ illiteracy.

☆318 **extol**
[ikstóul]

v. to celebrate, glorify, praise, or render honor to someone or something

SYN celebrate, honor, praise

Music critics _____ the singer's performance as one of the finest in history.

SCAFFOLDING

313 명확한, 명시적인, 솔직한 — CEO는 긴급 상황일 때를 제외하고는 자기를 방해하지 말라는 명확한explicit 지침을 남겼다.

314 개척하다, 개발하다, (부당하게) 이용하다 — 그 회사 관리의 목표는 직원들 사이의 분열을 최대한으로 이용하는exploit 것이었다.

315 지우다, 파괴하다, 멸종시키다 — 정부는 그 범죄에 대한 모든 언급을 공식적인 기록에서 삭제하라는expunge 명령을 내렸다.

316 광범위한, 포괄적인 — 그 폭풍은 광대한extensive 지역에 폭우를 내리게 했고 많은 홍수를 야기시켰다.

317 근절시키다, 박멸하다, 구조하다 — 그 왕은 문맹을 근절시키는데extirpating 헌신했다.

318 크게 칭찬하다 — 음악 평론가들은 그 가수의 솜씨를 역사상 가장 좋은 것 중의 하나라고 칭찬했다extolled.

☆319 **extraneous**
[ikstréiniəs]

adj. beyond a given boundary; alien; foreign; extrinsic; outside

SYN alien, foreign, outside

The law's effect on popular culture is an _____ consideration and need not concern us here.

☆320 **extreme**
[ikstrí:m]

adj. to the highest degree or farthest extent; at the limit

SYN farthest, outermost, utmost

At _____ temperatures, ordinary materials may take on extraordinary properties.

☆321 **extricate**
[ékstrəkèit]

v. to free someone or something from a difficulty, problem, snare, or trap

SYN clear, free, release

The thief tried to _____ himself from the trap that the police had set for him.

☆322 **exuberance**
[igʒú:bərəns]

n. great energy, enthusiasm, joy, or vigor

SYN enthusiasm, joy, vivacity

The musicians performed the piece with an _____ that made the audience smile.

☆323 **facilitate**
[fəsílətèit]

v. to make something easier; to assist or help with something

SYN assist, ease, expedite, help

We think an explanation of the plant's structure will _____ understanding of its ecology.

☆324 **fallacious**
[fəléiʃəs]

adj. based on a fallacy or error; misleading; faulty in reasoning or conclusions

SYN wrong, erroneous, deceptive, misleading

Though he appears sincere, his argument is _____ and should be corrected.

SCAFFOLDING

319 비본질적인, 관계가 없는, 외래의   그 법이 대중문화에 미치는 영향은 비본질적인extraneous 문제이고 여기에 있는 우리가 그것을 걱정할 필요는 없다.

320 극도의, 과격한, 맨 끝의   극심한extreme 온도에서 보통의 물질이 색다른 자질을 가지게 될지도 모른다.

321 구해내다, 해방시키다   도둑은 경찰이 그를 위해 놓아둔 덫에서 빠져 나오려고extricate 애를 썼다.

322 풍부, 윤택   그 음악가들은 악곡을 풍부하게exuberance 연주하여 청중들을 미소 짓게 만들었다.

323 용이하게 하다, 촉진하다   우리는 그 식물의 구조에 대한 설명이 그것의 생태에 대한 이해를 촉진시킬facilitate 것이라고 생각한다.

324 그릇된, 남을 현혹시키는   비록 그가 진실해 보이지만, 그의 주장은 그릇된 것이고fallacious 바로잡아야 한다.

☆325 **fallow**
[fǽlou]

adj. plowed but not seeded; not active or in use; resting before reuse
SYN idle, inactive

It is a common practice in agriculture to let certain fields lie _____ for a season.

☆326 **falter**
[fɔ́:ltər]

v. to move unsteadily; to stumble
SYN hesitate, quaver, vacillate, waver, halt, stammer

She _____ in her speech.

☆327 **fanaticism**
[fənǽtəsìzəm]

n. zeal beyond rationality; often used in the context of extreme religious belief
SYN insanity, zeal

Certain religious sects known for their _____ have become highly influential for brief periods and then declined.

☆328 **fanatic**
[fənǽtik]

n. someone who holds extreme beliefs and, in many cases, seeks to impose them on others
SYN zealot, extremist

Unless checked by rationality, strong beliefs may lead a person to become a _____.

☆329 **fastidious**
[fæstídiəs]

adj. extremely attentive to detail; hard to please
SYN careful, picky, exacting, meticulous, conscientious

Some people are so _____ about their meals that they will eat only a very few foods.

☆330 **fathom**
[fǽðəm]

v. to comprehend or understand; often used in the context of understanding things on a deep level
SYN comprehend, understand, grasp

This branch of mathematics is so advanced that it is hard to _____.

SCAFFOLDING

325 묵히고 있는, 휴경중인   특정 땅들을 한 계절 동안 쉬게fallow 해 주는 것은 농업에 있어서 일반적인 일이다.
326 움찔하다, 망설이다   그녀는 더듬으며faltered 말했다.
327 열광, 광신   광신적이라고fanaticism 알려져 있는 어떤 종교 분파들은 짧은 기간 동안 매우 영향력이 있었지만 곧 쇠퇴했다.
328 광신자, 열광자   합리적으로 점검되지 않은 강한 믿음은 사람을 광신자fanatic가 되게 만든다.
329 까다로운, 세심한, 꼼꼼한   어떤 사람들은 식사에 대해 너무 까다로워서fastidious 단 몇 가지의 음식만을 먹을 것이다.
330 추측하다, 이해하다, 수심을 재다   이 수학 분야는 너무 진보된 것이어서 이해하기fathom가 어렵다.

96

SYNONYMS WORDS THAT MEAN THE SAME THING

301 We did not speak for fear that we would **exacerbate** the already tense situation.

ⓐ squander

ⓑ reproach

ⓒ worsen

ⓓ relieve

302 The press **exalted** the winners of the games as heroes.

ⓐ glorified

ⓑ discussed

ⓒ debased

ⓓ remanded

303 This article quotes an **excerpt** from the prime minister's statement.

ⓐ extension

ⓑ fanatic

ⓒ resignation

ⓓ extract

304 Opponents of capital punishment think the government should not **execute** anyone for any crime.

ⓐ kill

ⓑ entice

ⓒ revive

ⓓ extend

305 This recording is an **exemplary** performance of the song we will play at the concert.

ⓐ contemptible

ⓑ ordinary

ⓒ celestial

ⓓ model

306 The housecat **exemplifies** felines, which all have the same basic body structure.

ⓐ excludes

ⓑ narrates

ⓒ renders

ⓓ represents

307 This article is an **exhaustive** study of recent research in our field of study.

ⓐ cursory

ⓑ comprehensive

ⓒ casual

ⓓ desultory

308 Some people find skiing to be an **exhilarating** experience.

ⓐ dampen

ⓑ intriguing

ⓒ refreshing

ⓓ discouraging

309 The investigation **exonerated** the captain of blame for the loss of his ship.

ⓐ increased

ⓑ acquited

ⓒ enshrined

ⓓ blamed

310 The botanical garden was full of **exotic** plants from around the world.

ⓐ native

ⓑ ordinary

ⓒ temporary

ⓓ alien

311 To meet the needs of our business, it was **expedient** to buy a new computer.

ⓐ impractical

ⓑ appropriate

ⓒ harmful

ⓓ purposeful

DAY 11

312 The new tax policy is supposed to **expedite** the formation of new businesses.

ⓐ hinder

ⓑ ease

ⓒ seduce

ⓓ retard

313 The CEO left **explicit** instructions that he was not to be interrupted except in case of an emergency.

ⓐ insolent

ⓑ clear

ⓒ ambiguous

ⓓ reserved

314 The goal of the company's management was to **exploit** the divisions among the workers to the fullest.

ⓐ dismiss

ⓑ oust

ⓒ utilize

ⓓ repudiate

315 The government gave orders to **expunge** all references to the criminal from public records.

ⓐ retain

ⓑ delete

ⓒ encourage

ⓓ bequeath

316 The storm dropped heavy rain over an **extensive** area and caused much flooding.

ⓐ broad

ⓑ narrow

ⓒ arid

ⓓ brief

317 The king dedicated himself to **extirpating** illiteracy.

ⓐ saving

ⓑ destroying

ⓒ sparing

ⓓ discussing

318 Music critics **extolled** the singer's performance as one of the finest in history.

ⓐ praised

ⓑ censured

ⓒ announced

ⓓ denounced

319 The law's effect on popular culture is an **extraneous** consideration and need not concern us here.

ⓐ pertinent

ⓑ outside

ⓒ inherent

ⓓ intrinsic

320 At **extreme** temperatures, ordinary materials may take on extraordinary properties.

ⓐ moderate

ⓑ outermost

ⓒ conservative

ⓓ nearest

321 The thief tried to **extricate** himself from the trap that the police had set for him.

ⓐ entangle

ⓑ release

ⓒ maintain

ⓓ keep

322 The musicians performed the piece with an exuberance that made the audience smile.

ⓐ skillfulness

ⓑ apathy

ⓒ vivacity

ⓓ inattention

323 We think an explanation of the plant's structure will facilitate understanding of its ecology.

ⓐ hinder

ⓑ complicate

ⓒ delineate

ⓓ assist

324 Though he appears sincere, his argument is fallacious and should be corrected.

ⓐ wrong

ⓑ correct

ⓒ perceptive

ⓓ original

325 It is a common practice in agriculture to let certain fields lie fallow for a season.

ⓐ cultivated

ⓑ mobile

ⓒ portable

ⓓ inactive

326 She faltered in her speech.

ⓐ acted

ⓑ confronted

ⓒ defied

ⓓ wavered

327 Certain religious sects known for their fanaticism have become highly influential for brief periods and then declined.

ⓐ moderation

ⓑ zeal

ⓒ coherence

ⓓ lucidity

328 Unless checked by rationality, strong beliefs may lead a person to become a fanatic.

ⓐ misanthrope

ⓑ vulgarian

ⓒ glutton

ⓓ zealot

329 Some people are so fastidious about their meals that they will eat only a very few foods.

ⓐ extreme

ⓑ conjectural

ⓒ picky

ⓓ radical

330 This branch of mathematics is so advanced that it is hard to fathom.

ⓐ estimate

ⓑ explain

ⓒ release

ⓓ grasp

DAY 11

☆331	**feasible** [fíːzəbəl]	*adj.* capable of being done; within one's reach or potential **SYN** possible, practical *This project is economically _____ but would violate many environmental regulations.*
☆332	**fecund** [fíːkənd]	*adj.* fruitful; richly productive **SYN** fertile, productive, prolific, blooming, flourishing *He has a _____ imagination.*
☆333	**feeble** [fíːbəl]	*adj.* lacking strength; weak **SYN** decrepit, fragile, frail, weak, debilitated *His _____ attempt at humor failed to raise a laugh.*
☆334	**fell** [fel]	*adj.* sinister; evil; malignant; cruel; inhuman; lethal, deadly, or highly destructive **SYN** cruel, deadly, sinister *The knight was killed by a _____ blow from his opponent's sword.*
☆335	**fertile** [fɔ́ːrtl]	*adj.* capable of reproduction; highly productive **SYN** productive, prolific *The soil in the valley was so _____ that the farms there were highly productive.*
☆336	**fervor** [fɔ́ːrvər]	*n.* great emotional intensity or enthusiasm **SYN** eagerness, enthusiasm, intensity, passion, zeal *She brought such _____ to her work that everyone around her became enthusiastic, too.*

SCAFFOLDING

331	그럴싸한, 있음직한	이 프로젝트는 경제적으로는 그럴싸하지만feasible 많은 환경 규제들을 위반할 것이다.
332	다산의, 비옥한, 풍성한	그는 풍부한fecund 상상력을 지녔다.
333	연약한, 힘없는, 박약한	유머를 써보려던 그의 어설픈feeble 시도는 웃음을 자아내지 못했다.
334	잔인한, 사나운, 무시무시한	그 기사는 적수가 들고 있는 검의 잔인한fell 일진으로 죽임을 당했다.
335	기름진, 비옥한, 다산의	그 계곡의 토양은 너무나도 비옥해서fertile 그곳의 농장들은 매우 생산적이었다.
336	열렬, 열정, 열성	그녀는 자신의 일에 대단한 열정fervor을 보였기 때문에 주위의 모든 사람들도 열정적이 되었다.

☆337 **fickle**
[fíkəl]

adj. given to sudden and unpredictable change; usually used in regard to behavior and personal attachments

SYN changeable, erratic, unpredictable, unstable

She was known for her _____ behavior and seemed to have a new set of friends every week.

☆338 **fitful**
[fítfəl]

adj. irregular or sporadic in activity; happening only now and then or in fits and starts

SYN intermittent, irregular, sporadic

The summer was long and dry, and it was relieved only by brief and _____ periods of rain.

☆339 **flagrant**
[fléigrənt]

adj. bold and highly offensive to accepted standards of taste, decency, or legality

SYN outrageous, scandalous, shameless, shocking

The robber's _____ violations of the law made him one of the most hunted men in the country.

☆340 **florid**
[flɔ́(:)rid]

adj. infused with red; often used to describe someone with a reddish complexion

SYN red, rosy, ruddy, flushed

Working outside on a cold day gave his face a _____ color.

☆341 **flourish**
[flə́:riʃ]

v. to grow vigorously; to do very well; to become prosperous

SYN thrive, prosper, succeed

The mild climate and rich soil provided an environment where crops could _____.

☆342 **flower**
[fláuər]

v. to develop flowers; to come to fruition or reach maturity; to produce desirable results

SYN bloom, blossom, develop, unfold, prosper

Artists and their work _____ in the supportive environment that the city provided.

DAY 12

SCAFFOLDING

337 변하기 쉬운, 변덕스러운, 불안한　　그녀는 변덕스러운fickle 행동을 한다고 알려져 있었으며 매주 새로운 무리의 친구들을 사귀는 것 같았다.

338 변하기 쉬운, 단속적인　　여름은 길고 더웠으며, 단속적으로fitful 비가 내리는 짧은 기간 동안만 좀 덜할 뿐이었다.

339 명백한, 악명 높은, 극악한　　그 강도의 극악한flagrant 위법 행위들 때문에 그는 나라에서 가장 쫓기는 사람이 되었다.

340 불그레한, 화려한, 화사한　　추운 날 밖에서 일을 했기 때문에 그의 얼굴은 빨갛게florid 되었다.

341 번영하다, 무성하게 자라다　　온화한 기후와 비옥한 토양은 곡물이 무성하게 자랄flourish 수 있는 환경을 제공했다.

342 꽃이 피다, 성숙하다, 번영하다　　예술가들과 그들의 작품은 도시가 제공한 지지적 환경에서 꽃이 폈다flowered.

☆343 **fluctuate**
[flʌ́ktʃuèit]

v. to vary in amount, value, level, etc.; to rise and fall

SYN alternate, change, oscillate, shift

Exchange rates _____ from year to year.

☆344 **foliage**
[fóuliidʒ]

n. the green leaves on a tree or plant

SYN foliation, leafage, leaves

Mt. Seorak is noted for the glorious tints of its autumn _____.

☆345 **foolhardy**
[fú:lhɑ̀:rdi]

adj. reckless; highly incautious; often used to describe acceptance of excessive risk in some behavior

SYN reckless, heedless, incautious, ill-advised, risky

Some investments are considered so _____ that no one would even consider them.

☆346 **formal**
[fɔ́:rməl]

adj. done according to forms, rules, or conventions; often used to describe ceremonies or official events

SYN ceremonious, polite, reserved, rigid, conventional, strict, codified

Because the letter was addressed to a high official, it had to be written in _____ language.

☆347 **fortuitous**
[fɔːrtjúːətəs]

adj. happening by or owing to chance; sometimes used to describe unexpected and unplanned, but welcome, events

SYN accidental, inadvertent, fortunate

A _____ change in the weather allowed us to have an easy, pleasant trip.

☆348 **frivolous**
[frívələs]

adj. not worth serious notice; pointless; without serious purpose or substantial content

SYN insignificant, trivial, insubstantial, lightweight

The novel is a _____ story about two friends who go to a party.

SCAFFOLDING

343 오르다, 변동하다 　　　환율은 매해 변한다fluctuate.
344 잎, 군엽 　　　설악산은 가을 단풍foliage으로 유명하다.
345 무모한, 터무니없는 　　　어떤 투자들은 너무 무모하게 보여서foolhardy 어느 누구도 그것들을 생각조차 하지 않으려고 했다.
346 형식적인, 공식적인 　　　그 편지는 높은 공무원 앞으로 보내는 것이었기 때문에 공식적인formal 언어로 쓰여져야만 했다.
347 뜻밖의, 우연의, 행운의 　　　뜻밖의fortuitous 날씨 변화는 우리가 편안하고 쾌적한 여행을 할 수 있도록 해 주었다.
348 천박한, 사소한, 불성실한 　　　그 소설은 파티에 가는 두 친구에 관한 사소한frivolous 이야기이다.

☆349 **frugality**
[fru:gǽləti]

n. economy or thrift when used in a positive sense; cheapness, miserliness, or parsimony when used in a negative sense
SYN economy, thrift, cheapness, parsimony

That man practices such _____ that he uses each tea bag twice.

☆350 **furtive**
[fə́:rtiv]

adj. stealthy; secret; deliberately hidden from view
SYN stealthy, secret, hidden, concealed, covert

The army spent a month in _____ preparation for an attack on a neighboring country.

☆351 **garrulous**
[gǽrələs]

adj. too talkative; given to overlong and pointless speech
SYN talkative, wordy

The _____ passenger beside us did not stop talking for the whole journey.

☆352 **gauge**
[geidʒ]

v. to measure something accurately
SYN calculate, calibrate, compute, estimate, measure

These are precision instruments which can _____ the diameter to a fraction of a millimeter.

☆353 **gaunt**
[gɔ:nt]

adj. extremely and unnaturally thin
SYN haggard, lean, skinny, emaciated, wasted, bony

His long illness left him so _____ that he resembled a skeleton.

☆354 **glacial**
[gléiʃəl]

adj. of or related to glaciers; extremely cold or icy; very slow
SYN cold, icy, wintry, slow, gradual

_____ action carved deep valleys in the landscape.

DAY 12

SCAFFOLDING

349 검소, 절약　　　　　　　　　그 남자는 매우 검소해서frugality 한 개의 티백을 두 번씩 사용한다.

350 은밀한, 수상한　　　　　　　군대는 인접 국가를 공격하기 위해 한 달 동안 은밀한furtive 준비를 했다.

351 잘 지껄이는, 말 많은, 장황한　우리 옆에 있는 말 많은garrulous 승객은 여행 내내 말 하는 것을 멈추지 않았다.

352 측정하다, 판단하다　　　　　이것들은 1밀리미터의 몇 분의 1의 직경까지 측정할gauge 수 있는 정밀기구이다.

353 몹시 여윈, 수척한　　　　　오래된 질병은 그를 몹시 여위게gaunt 해서 그는 해골처럼 보였다.

354 얼음의, 빙하의, 차가운　　　빙하Glacial 운동은 그 땅에 깊은 계곡을 만들었다.

☆355 **glutton**
[glʌ́tn]

n. a person who eats to excess
SYN gourmand, (slang) pig, hog, chowhound

A _____ may consume 10,000 kilocalories or more of food each day.

☆356 **gratify**
[grǽtəfài]

v. to give great pleasure; to satisfy
SYN please, delight, gladden, satisfy, indulge

Her success as an author _____ her but did not bring her wealth.

☆357 **gratuitous**
[grətjú:ətəs]

adj. given without charge; unearned or undeserved; superfluous; pointless; unnecessary
SYN free, unearned, unnecessary

The movie was so filled with _____ action scenes that it barely had a plot.

☆358 **gravity**
[grǽvəti]

n. mutual attraction between two masses; a serious or solemn manner or attitude; great importance
SYN attraction, pull, solemnity, seriousness, importance, significance

A joke is not appropriate considering the _____ of this subject.

☆359 **gregarious**
[grigέəriəs]

adj. sociable; talkative; fond of being with company
SYN sociable, outgoing

A _____ person, he loved conversation and was rarely seen alone.

☆360 **guile**
[gail]

n. treacherous cleverness; a deceitful and untrustworthy attitude or behavior
SYN trickery, deceit, cunning, dishonesty, sneakiness

Because of his reputation for _____, he was neither liked nor trusted by anyone.

SCAFFOLDING

355 대식가, 폭식가
356 만족시키다, 기쁘게 하다
357 무료의, 불필요한
358 중력, 인력, 중대성, 진지함
359 떼지어 사는, 사교적인
360 교활, 꾀, 술책

대식가glutton는 음식을 통해 하루에 만 킬로칼로리 또는 그 이상을 섭취할지도 모른다.
작가로서 그녀의 성공은 그녀를 기쁘게 했지만gratified 부를 가져다 주지는 못했다.
그 영화는 너무 불필요한gratuitous 액션 장면들로 가득 차서 줄거리가 거의 없었다.
이 주제의 중대성gravity을 고려하면 농담은 적절치 못하다.
그는 사교적인gregarious 사람으로서 대화를 좋아했고 혼자 있는 것을 거의 보지 못 했다.
그는 교활하기로guile 유명했기 때문에 어느 누구도 그를 좋아하거나 신뢰하지 않았다.

331 This project is economically **feasible** but would violate many environmental regulations.

   ⓐ tangential

   ⓑ possible

   ⓒ conceptual

   ⓓ attentive

332 He has a **fecund** imagination.

   ⓐ infamous

   ⓑ fertile

   ⓒ paltry

   ⓓ fragile

333 His **feeble** attempt at humor failed to raise a laugh.

   ⓐ paltry

   ⓑ weak

   ⓒ strong

   ⓓ healthy

334 The knight was killed by a **fell** blow from his opponent's sword.

   ⓐ constructive

   ⓑ sinister

   ⓒ harmless

   ⓓ beneficial

335 The soil in the valley was so **fertile** that the farms there were highly productive.

   ⓐ barren

   ⓑ sparing

   ⓒ acidic

   ⓓ productive

336 She brought such **fervor** to her work that everyone around her became enthusiastic, too.

   ⓐ apathy

   ⓑ inattention

   ⓒ loathness

   ⓓ enthusiasm

337 She was known for her **fickle** behavior and seemed to have a new set of friends every week.

   ⓐ stable

   ⓑ plausible

   ⓒ erratic

   ⓓ capacious

338 The summer was long and dry, and it was relieved only by brief and **fitful** periods of rain.

   ⓐ sound

   ⓑ continuous

   ⓒ intermittent

   ⓓ sturdy

339 The robber's **flagrant** violations of the law made him one of the most hunted men in the country.

   ⓐ unkempt

   ⓑ transparent

   ⓒ grum

   ⓓ scandalous

340 Working outside on a cold day gave his face a **florid** color.

   ⓐ pale

   ⓑ gloomy

   ⓒ brash

   ⓓ flushed

DAY 12

341　The mild climate and rich soil provided an environment where crops could **flourish**.

ⓐ mock

ⓑ inspire

ⓒ animate

ⓓ prosper

342　Artists and their work **flowered** in the supportive environment that the city provided.

ⓐ satiated

ⓑ raved

ⓒ subsided

ⓓ prospered

343　Exchange rates **fluctuate** from year to year.

ⓐ persist

ⓑ oscillate

ⓒ linger

ⓓ decrease

344　Mt. Seorak is noted for the glorious tints of its autumn **foliage**.

ⓐ branches

ⓑ roots

ⓒ bushes

ⓓ leafage

345　Some investments are considered so **foolhardy** that no one would even consider them.

ⓐ vigilant

ⓑ wary

ⓒ discreet

ⓓ reckless

346　Because the letter was addressed to a high official, it had to be written in **formal** language.

ⓐ casual

ⓑ illegal

ⓒ unusual

ⓓ codified

347　A **fortuitous** change in the weather allowed us to have an easy, pleasant trip.

ⓐ fortunate

ⓑ esoteric

ⓒ intentional

ⓓ unlucky

348　The novel is a **frivolous** story about two friends who go to a party.

ⓐ insubstantial

ⓑ innumerable

ⓒ lofty

ⓓ thorough

349　That man practices such **frugality** that he uses each tea bag twice.

ⓐ opulence

ⓑ fortune

ⓒ insanity

ⓓ thrift

350　The army spent a month in **furtive** preparation for an attack on a neighboring country.

ⓐ forthright

ⓑ intensive

ⓒ covert

ⓓ manifest

351 The **garrulous** passenger beside us did not stop talking for the whole journey.

ⓐ willful

ⓑ gregarious

ⓒ annoyed

ⓓ talkative

352 These are precision instruments which can **gauge** the diameter to a fraction of a millimeter.

ⓐ verify

ⓑ deride

ⓒ calculate

ⓓ trespass

353 His long illness left him so **gaunt** that he resembled a skeleton.

ⓐ plump

ⓑ fleshy

ⓒ lucid

ⓓ skinny

354 **Glacial** action carved deep valleys in the landscape.

ⓐ hierarchical

ⓑ icy

ⓒ incarnated

ⓓ infant

355 A **glutton** may consume 10,000 kilocalories or more of food each day.

ⓐ vulgariant

ⓑ dieter

ⓒ philanthropist

ⓓ pig

356 Her success as an author **gratified** her but did not bring her wealth.

ⓐ differed

ⓑ stratified

ⓒ gladdened

ⓓ vindicated

357 The movie was so filled with **gratuitous** action scenes that it barely had a plot.

ⓐ unnecessary

ⓑ critical

ⓒ innocuous

ⓓ pious

358 A joke is not appropriate considering the **gravity** of this subject.

ⓐ theme

ⓑ force

ⓒ motif

ⓓ significance

359 A **gregarious** person, he loved conversation and was rarely seen alone.

ⓐ amendable

ⓑ sociable

ⓒ reserved

ⓓ edible

360 Because of his reputation for **guile**, he was neither liked nor trusted by anyone.

ⓐ treachery

ⓑ gullibility

ⓒ hypocrisy

ⓓ trickery

Answers

331-335 ⓑⓑⓑⓑⓓ	346-350 ⓓⓐⓐⓓⓒ
336-340 ⓓⓒⓒⓓⓓ	351-355 ⓓⓒⓓⓑⓓ
341-345 ⓓⓓⓑⓓⓓ	356-360 ⓒⓐⓓⓑⓓ

☆361 **gullible**
[gʌ́ləbəl]

adj. easily deceived; too ready to believe something on little or no evidence

SYN credulous, naïve

A con artist seeks a _____ person who may be tricked into giving him money.

☆362 **hackneyed**
[hǽknid]

adj. too familiar because of overuse

SYN trite, overused

The speech was so full of _____ expressions that nothing in it was fresh or interesting.

☆363 **hamper**
[hǽmpər]

v. to limit or hinder the operation of something

SYN restrict, impede, interfere

Heavy rain _____ efforts to reach the people stranded by the flood.

☆364 **hangar**
[hǽŋər]

n. a shelter for storing aircraft

SYN shed, shelter, barn

Before the airplane could fly again, mechanics had to repair it in the _____.

☆365 **hardy**
[há:rdi]

adj. very bold, tough, or enduring

SYN brave, bold, tough, rugged

Beagles are a _____ and resilient breed.

☆366 **harness**
[há:rnis]

v. to use a natural force to produce useful power

SYN use, utilize, exploit

Turkey plans to _____ the waters of the Tigris and Euphrates rivers to produce hydro-electric power.

SCAFFOLDING

361 잘 속는   사기꾼은 그에게 속아서 돈을 줄 가능성이 있는 잘 속는gullible 사람을 찾는다.

362 낡아 빠진, 진부한   그 연설은 진부한hackneyed 표현들로 가득 차서 신선하거나 재미있는 것이 아무것도 없었다.

363 훼방하다, 방해가 되다   폭우는 홍수에 의해 고립된 사람들에게 다가가기 위한 노력에 방해가 되었다hampered.

364 격납고   정비사들은 비행기가 다시 뜨기 전에 격납고hangar에서 비행기를 정비해야만 했다.

365 단련된, 튼튼한   비글은 튼튼하고hardy 발랄한 종이다.

366 자연력을 동력으로 이용하다   터키는 수력발전을 위해 티그리스와 유프라테스 강의 물을 이용할harness 계획이다.

☆367 **harsh**
[hɑːrʃ]

adj. unpleasantly strong; heavy, severe, or strict
SYN rough, severe, strong, strict

_____ measures were needed to discourage crime, and therefore many criminals were sent to jail.

☆368 **hasten**
[héisn]

v. to accelerate; to increase the rate or velocity of something
SYN accelerate, hurry, speed

Because time was short, we _____ to the hospital.

☆369 **haughtiness**
[hɔ́ːtinis]

n. an arrogant and overbearing attitude
SYN arrogance, pride

Her _____ was her unpleasant way of compensating for her feelings of inadequacy.

☆370 **hedonist**
[híːdənist]

n. someone whose life is devoted to seeking pleasure
SYN epicure, rake

He was a _____ in his youth, always looking for new sources of fun.

☆371 **hedonistic**
[hìːdənístik]

adj. dedicated to seeking pleasure and luxury
SYN epicurean, sybaritic

When his income fell sharply, he had to abandon his _____ lifestyle.

☆372 **heed**
[hiːd]

v. to listen or pay close attention to something; to take a lesson or message to heart; to obey instructions or orders
SYN listen, mark, note, notice, obey

The children _____ the warning that their parents gave them.

DAY 13

☆373 **heresy**
[hérəsi]

n. a strongly dissenting and disapproved opinion; a challenge to dogma

SYN dissent, nonconformity

To challenge the prevailing opinion among scientists was considered _____.

☆374 **hierarchy**
[háiərɑ̀ːrki]

n. a structure of authority, system of rank, or chain or command

SYN government, administration, rank

Some societies have rigid _____ with clearly defined levels of authority.

☆375 **hindrance**
[híndrəns]

n. anything that impedes or interferes with a task or process

SYN obstacle, block, problem, interference

Although the heat was a _____ to working outdoors, it did not stop all labor from happening.

☆376 **homogeneous**
[hòumədʒíːniəs]

adj. uniform in texture, composition, or quality

SYN uniform, unvarying

Blending the ingredients by machine guaranteed a _____ and reliable mixture.

☆377 **hopeless**
[hóuplis]

adj. beyond hope, repair, or cure; in despair

SYN impossible, incurable, forlorn, despondent

The doctors considered his case _____ and could find no cure for his illness.

☆378 **hue**
[hjuː]

n. a color; a tint

SYN cast, color, shade, tint

His face took on an unhealthy whitish _____.

SCAFFOLDING

373 이단, 이설, 반대론   과학자들 사이에서 일반적인 의견에 도전하는 것은 이설heresy로 간주되었다.

374 계층제, 계층   어떤 과학자들은 권위의 정도에 대해 명백히 정의된 엄격한 계층제hierarchies를 가지고 있다.

375 방해, 장애, 사고   비록 더위가 밖에서 일하는 데에 장애hindrance가 되긴 했지만 모든 노동을 막지는 못했다.

376 동종의, 동일성의   기계에 의한 성분 혼합은 동질의homogeneous 믿을 수 있는 혼합물을 보증했다.

377 절망적인, 어찌할 수 없는   의사들은 그의 경우를 절망적으로hopeless 생각했고, 그의 질병에 대한 치료법을 찾지 못했다.

378 색조, 빛깔, 경향 특색   그의 얼굴은 건강하지 못한 희끄무레한 색조hue를 띠고 있었다.

☆379 **humility**
[hju:míləti]

n. a lowly condition; a low or modest opinion of oneself
SYN modesty, lowliness, self-abasement

Poverty imposed a sense of _____ on the people who lost their jobs.

☆380 **hyperbole**
[haipə́:rbəlì:]

n. great and intentional exaggeration
SYN exaggeration, extravagance

In a moment of _____, a reviewer called the book "The greatest novel ever."

☆381 **hypocrisy**
[hipákrəsi]

n. a double standard of behavior; insincerity; a discrepancy between what one believes and what one practices
SYN insincerity, deceit, duplicity

When found doing things he condemned others for doing, he became known for his _____.

☆382 **hypocritical**
[hìpəkrítikəl]

adj. characterized by hypocrisy or a double standard
SYN insincere, deceitful, duplicitous

It is _____ to do things that you criticize other people for doing.

☆383 **hypothetical**
[hàipəθétikəl]

adj. conjectured or proposed but not yet proven or disproven
SYN conjectural, suggested, imaginary, conditional

This situation is purely _____ and does not reflect anything in real life.

☆384 **iconoclastic**
[aikànəklǽstik]

adj. radical; strongly opposed to accepted opinion or practice
SYN revolutionary, radical, dissenting

The physicist took an _____ view of the "big bang" theory of the universe's origin.

DAY 13

SCAFFOLDING

379 겸손, 비하   빈곤은 직업을 잃은 사람들에게 비하적인humility 느낌을 갖게 해 주었다.

380 과장(법), 과장 표현   한 평론가는 과장법hyperbole으로 그 책을 '역대 최고의 소설'이라고 불렀다.

381 위선, 위선 행위   그가 나무라던 다른 사람들의 행동을 그가 직접 하는 것이 발견되었을 때 그는 위선hypocrisy자로 알려지게 되었다.

382 위선의, 위선(자)적인   당신이 비판하는 다른 사람들의 행동을 당신이 직접 하는 것은 위선적이다hypocritical.

383 가설의, 가설에 근거한   그 상황은 순전히 가설에 근거한hypothetical 것이고 실생활의 어떠한 것도 반영하지 않는다.

384 성상 파괴주의의, 인습 타파의   그 물리학자는 우주의 기원에 대한 '빅뱅' 이론의 인습 타파적iconoclastic 관점을 채택했다.

☆385 **idiom**
[ídiəm]

n. a figure of speech; a highly specific expression
SYN colloquialism, expression

Many English verb _____ are hard to understand at first and must be memorized one by one.

☆386 **idiosyncrasy**
[ìdiəsíŋkrəsi]

n. a unique quality or behavior
SYN quirk, uniqueness, oddity

One of my mother's _____ is that she always carries an umbrella.

☆387 **ignominy**
[ígnəmìni]

n. a state of disgrace, defeat, humiliation, discredit, failure, or low esteem
SYN disgrace, humiliation, dishonor

After losing his high-paying job, he had to live in relative _____ and poverty.

☆388 **illicit**
[ilísit]

adj. against the law; officially forbidden
SYN illegal, unlawful, criminal

For years, he engaged in many _____ activities, such as smuggling, without getting caught.

☆389 **illusory**
[ilú:səri]

adj. falsely perceived; apparent but having no basis in reality
SYN fake, imagined, unreal

The safety of the village proved _____ when a flood swept it away.

☆390 **immutable**
[immjú:təbəl]

adj. changeless; incapable of change or modification; permanent
SYN changeless, constant, permanent, unchanging, unalterable

This law of physics is _____ throughout the known universe.

SYNONYMS WORDS THAT MEAN THE SAME THING

361 A con artist seeks a **gullible** person who may be tricked into giving him money.

ⓐ vile

ⓑ credulous

ⓒ peevish

ⓓ skeptical

362 The speech was so full of **hackneyed** expressions that nothing in it was fresh or interesting.

ⓐ fresh

ⓑ overused

ⓒ exhausted

ⓓ beguiled

363 Heavy rain **hampered** efforts to reach the people stranded by the flood.

ⓐ helped

ⓑ dispersed

ⓒ impeded

ⓓ controlled

364 Before the airplane could fly again, mechanics had to repair it in the **hangar**.

ⓐ shed

ⓑ drawer

ⓒ freezer

ⓓ runway

365 Beagles are a **hardy** and resilient breed.

ⓐ rotund

ⓑ satirical

ⓒ robust

ⓓ painstaking

366 Turkey plans to **harness** the waters of the Tigris and Euphrates rivers to produce hydro-electric power.

ⓐ pry

ⓑ exploit

ⓒ rescind

ⓓ subjugate

367 **Harsh** measures were needed to discourage crime, and therefore many criminals were sent to jail.

ⓐ spry

ⓑ inadvertent

ⓒ cordial

ⓓ severe

368 Because time was short, we **hastened** to the hospital.

ⓐ hindered

ⓑ hurried

ⓒ thrilled

ⓓ rejuvenated

369 Her **haughtiness** was her unpleasant way of compensating for her feelings of inadequacy.

ⓐ humility

ⓑ humbleness

ⓒ heftiness

ⓓ arrogance

370 He was a **hedonist** in his youth, always looking for new sources of fun.

ⓐ puritan

ⓑ sensualist

ⓒ ascetic

ⓓ hermit

DAY 13

371 When his income fell sharply, he had to abandon his **hedonistic** lifestyle.

ⓐ wayward

ⓑ attentive

ⓒ sybaritic

ⓓ rash

372 The children **heeded** the warning that their parents gave them.

ⓐ hindered

ⓑ obeyed

ⓒ repeated

ⓓ ignored

373 To challenge the prevailing opinion among scientists was considered **heresy**.

ⓐ profanity

ⓑ dissent

ⓒ convenience

ⓓ convergence

374 Some societies have rigid **hierarchies** with clearly defined levels of authority.

ⓐ disorganization

ⓑ ranks

ⓒ equality

ⓓ impartiality

375 Although the heat was a **hindrance** to working outdoors, it did not stop all labor from happening.

ⓐ vileness

ⓑ venom

ⓒ continuation

ⓓ obstacle

376 Blending the ingredients by machine guaranteed a **homogeneous** and reliable mixture.

ⓐ diverse

ⓑ inexorable

ⓒ unvarying

ⓓ peripheral

377 The doctors considered his case **hopeless** and could find no cure for his illness.

ⓐ trifling

ⓑ forlorn

ⓒ bustling

ⓓ impractical

378 His face took on an unhealthy whitish **hue**.

ⓐ color

ⓑ summon

ⓒ trickery

ⓓ importance

379 Poverty imposed a sense of **humility** on the people who lost their jobs.

ⓐ endurance

ⓑ lowliness

ⓒ arrogance

ⓓ pomposity

380 In a moment of **hyperbole**, a reviewer called the book "The greatest novel ever."

ⓐ understatement

ⓑ exaggeration

ⓒ rhetoric

ⓓ eloquence

381 When found doing things he condemned others for doing, he became known for his **hypocrisy**.

ⓐ duplicity

ⓑ diligence

ⓒ dependency

ⓓ sincerity

382 It is **hypocritical** to do things that you criticize other people for doing.

ⓐ honest

ⓑ generous

ⓒ sparing

ⓓ deceitful

383 This situation is purely **hypothetical** and does not reflect anything in real life.

ⓐ retentive

ⓑ solemn

ⓒ conjectural

ⓓ willful

384 The physicist took an **iconoclastic** view of the "big bang" theory of the universe's origin.

ⓐ revolutionary

ⓑ joyful

ⓒ tenacious

ⓓ unsung

385 Many English verb **idioms** are hard to understand at first and must be memorized one by one.

ⓐ sequences

ⓑ strata

ⓒ hues

ⓓ expressions

386 One of my mother's **idiosyncrasies** is that she always carries an umbrella.

ⓐ eccentricities

ⓑ elation

ⓒ stanzas

ⓓ typicality

387 After losing his high-paying job, he had to live in relative **ignominy** and poverty.

ⓐ honor

ⓑ disgrace

ⓒ permanence

ⓓ euphoria

388 For years, he engaged in many **illicit** activities, such as smuggling, without getting caught.

ⓐ mercurial

ⓑ unlawful

ⓒ authorized

ⓓ mercenary

389 The safety of the village proved **illusory** when a flood swept it away.

ⓐ substantial

ⓑ real

ⓒ sluggish

ⓓ fake

390 This law of physics is **immutable** throughout the known universe.

ⓐ variable

ⓑ insatiable

ⓒ unalterable

ⓓ stout

☆391 **impair**
[impέər]
v. to make worse; to damage, weaken, or reduce
SYN harm, injure, damage

Poor nutrition _____ his body's ability to resist infection.

☆392 **impartial**
[impáːrʃəl]
adj. not biased or prejudiced
SYN fair, just, unbiased

The judge was famous for being _____ and for making fair and just decisions.

☆393 **impeccable**
[impékəbəl]
adj. without mistake, fault, or flaw; correct in every way
SYN ideal, perfect, flawless, faultless

She was known for her _____ manners and for always knowing how to behave.

☆394 **impecunious**
[ìmpikjúːniəs]
adj. poor; without money or resources
SYN poor, penniless, impoverished, bankrupt, destitute

The failure of his business left him _____ for a while, but he did not give up hope.

☆395 **impede**
[impíːd]
v. to obstruct or stand in the way of someone or something
SYN block, hinder, oppose, stall, resist, obstruct

The army found that muddy roads _____ its progress across the country.

☆396 **implausible**
[implɔ́ːzəbəl]
adj. appearing false, untrue, or unbelievable
SYN unbelievable, unlikely, improbable, incredible

The theory failed because it was based on an _____ set of assumptions.

SCAFFOLDING

391 감하다, 약화시키다, 손상시키다   영양 결핍은 감염에 대한 그의 신체 저항력을 약화시켰다impaired.

392 치우치지 않은, 공평한   그 심판은 한 쪽으로 치우치지 않으며 공정하고impartial 올바른 판단을 내리는 것으로 유명하다.

393 결점이 없는, 죄를 범하지 않은   그녀는 흠 없는impeccable 매너를 가졌고 항상 어떻게 행동해야 할지를 아는 사람이라고 알려져 있었다.

394 가난한, 무일푼의   그의 사업 실패는 한동안 그를 무일푼으로impecunious 만들었지만 그는 희망을 버리지 않았다.

395 방해하다, 훼방놓다   군대는 질퍽한 도로가 그 나라를 건너서 전진하는 것에 방해가 된다impeded는 것을 알았다.

396 받아들이기 어려운, 믿기지 않는   그 이론은 받아들이기 어려운implausible 억측에 기초하고 있었기 때문에 실패했다.

☆397 **implement**
[ímpləmənt]

n. a tool, utensil, or other object used to perform a task
SYN tool, utensil

Kitchen _____ like pots and pans have changed little over thousands of years.

☆398 **impose**
[impóuz]

v. to place or put upon; to subject; to mandate or order; often used in the context of placing fines, regulations, or duties upon a person
SYN subject, inflict

The government _____ fines on companies that violate the environmental protection regulations.

☆399 **impregnable**
[imprégnəbəl]

adj. impossible to conquer, defeat, or breach
SYN impenetrable, unconquerable, unbeatable, undefeatable

A heavy concrete cover made the shelter _____ against attack from the air.

☆400 **impudence**
[ímpjudəns]

n. effrontery; disrespect; insult
SYN disrespect, insolence, rudeness

The children acted with such _____ that they were suspended from school.

☆401 **impulsive**
[impʌ́lsiv]

adj. given to acting quickly and without caution or deliberation; often used to describe the behavior of young children
SYN hasty, impetuous, quick

People in love may act in _____ ways because their feelings overcome their caution.

☆402 **inadvertent**
[ìnədvə́:rtənt]

adj. happening by accident; without conscious intent or plan
SYN accidental, unintentional, unplanned

The _____ result of introducing the new species was to disrupt the ecosystem.

DAY 14

397 도구, 용구, 수단   냄비나 후라이팬과 같은 주방 도구들implements은 수천 년 동안 거의 바뀌지 않았다.

398 (의무, 벌, 세금을) 지우다, 강요하다   정부는 환경 보호 규칙을 위반하는 회사들에 대해 벌금을 부과한다imposes.

399 난공불락의, 견고한, 확고한   무거운 콘크리트 덮개는 그 대피호를 공중으로부터의 공격에 대항할 수 있도록 견고하게impregnable 해 주었다.

400 뻔뻔스러움, 무례, 건방짐   그 아이들은 너무나 건방지게impudence 행동했기 때문에 학교에서 정학을 당했다.

401 충동적인, 추진력 있는   사랑에 빠져 있는 사람들은 감정이 주의를 넘어서기 때문에 충동적인impulsive 방법으로 행동할지도 모른다.

402 우연의, 의도하지 않은, 부주의한   새로운 종을 들여온 것이 의도하지 않은inadvertent 결과로 생태계를 파괴했다.

☆403 **inadvertently**

[ìnədvə́:rtəntli]

adv. by accident; without conscious intent or plan

SYN accidentally, unintentionally

When she opened the door, she _____ let in a mosquito.

☆404 **inane**

[inéin]

adj. lacking in purpose, meaning, or relevance

SYN pointless, irrelevant, useless, empty

The song became popular even though its lyrics were considered _____.

☆405 **inapt**

[inǽpt]

adj. not apt or appropriate

SYN unsuitable, improper, incompatible, unfit

The other remarkable issue is the clumsy and _____ responses by the new Korean government.

☆406 **incessant**

[insésənt]

adj. without stop, pause, or interruption; often used to describe a noise or a conversation

SYN constant, ceaseless, nonstop, endless, unceasing, never-ending, uninterrupted

The _____ noise from the building site across the street made it hard to concentrate on work.

☆407 **incidental**

[ìnsədéntl]

adj. fortuitous; happening without being planned

SYN casual, chance

In addition to our budgeted expenses, we had a few _____ expenses on our trip.

☆408 **incisive**

[insáisiv]

adj. sharp; direct; biting; cutting; penetrating; often used in reference to speech or commentary

SYN keen, sharp, penetrating, sarcastic

This TV announcer is known for his _____ comments on the day's news.

☆409 **incite**
[insáit]

v. to provoke, encourage, or set into action; often used in reference to provoking discussion, turmoil, or violence

SYN induce, instigate, provoke, start

The criminals were convicted of _____ a riot and were sent to jail.

☆410 **inclusive**
[inklú:siv]

adj. including a great amount of information or a large number of individuals; comprehensive; broad in scope

SYN comprehensive, overall, general

The test will cover information in chapters 2 and 3 of your text, from pages 65 to 130 _____.

☆411 **incoherent**
[ìnkoʊhíərənt]

adj. consisting of unconnected or unrelated parts so as to be meaningless as a whole; often used to describe meaningless messages

SYN disjointed, jumbled, loose, scrambled, unconnected, uncoordinated

Interference made the radio message _____ and impossible to understand.

☆412 **incongruous**
[inkάŋgruəs]

adj. out of place; inappropriate; inconsistent; not in harmony

SYN inappropriate, inconsistent

His noisy behavior made him _____ in the library.

☆413 **inconsequential**
[inkὰnsikwénʃəl]

adj. of no importance or consequence

SYN unimportant, insignificant

The article was so _____ that it was not even listed in the annual index.

☆414 **incontrovertible**
[ìnkɑntrəvə́:rtəbəl]

adj. beyond doubt, question, or refutation

SYN indisputable, unquestionable, certain

Scientists presented _____ evidence that the theory was correct, so it became a law.

DAY 14

SCAFFOLDING

409 자극하다, 격려하다, 유발하다   그 범죄자들은 폭동을 유발한inciting 것으로 죄가 입증되어 감옥에 갔다.

410 포함한, 모든 것을 포함한, 포괄적인   그 시험은 교과서 2과와 3과, 65 페이지부터 130 페이지까지의 내용을 범위로 한다inclusive.

411 모순된, 조리가 닿지 않는, 흐트러진   라디오 메시지는 혼선 때문에 흐트러져incoherent 알아듣기가 어려웠다.

412 일관성이 없는, 모순된, 어울리지 않는   그는 요란한 행동 때문에 도서관에 어울리지 않았다incongruous.

413 중요하지 않은, 이치에 맞지 않는   그 기사는 너무 이치에 맞지 않아서inconsequential 연보의 목차에 실리지도 않았다.

414 논쟁의 여지가 없는, 부정할 수 없는   과학자들은 그 이론이 옳다는 부정할 수 없는incontrovertible 증거를 제시했고, 그래서 그 이론은 법칙이 되었다.

119

☆415 **incorrigible**

[inkɔ́:ridʒəbəl]

adj. beyond hope of correction, recovery, or repair; often used to refer to persistent, undesirable behavior

SYN hopeless, irreparable

One of the students was expelled from school for what seemed _____ misbehavior.

☆416 **indefatigable**

[ìndifǽtigəbəl]

adj. tireless; extremely persistent; capable of working long hours without fatigue

SYN diligent, tireless, untiring, unwearying

The cook was _____ in trying to make a perfect cake.

☆417 **indict**

[indáit]

v. to charge someone with a crime or other offense

SYN arraign, charge, incriminate

The evidence in his letters sufficed to _____ him for conspiracy.

☆418 **indifferent**

[indífərənt]

adj. not interested in or concerned about something

SYN aloof, apathetic, uncaring, unconcerned

My father is _____ to sports and never watches football on television.

☆419 **indigenous**

[indídʒənəs]

adj. (said of plants or animals) belonging naturally to or occurring naturally in a country or area; native

SYN endemic, local, native, inborn

The _____ population was virtually exterminated by the settlers.

☆420 **indiscriminate**

[ìndiskrímənit]

adj. done without care, selectivity, priority, or order

SYN careless, assorted, haphazard, miscellaneous

The building was an _____ mixture of architectural styles and was without order or coherence.

415 구제할 길 없는, 고쳐지지 않는   그 학생들 중 한 명은 고칠 수 없어 보이는incorrigible 나쁜 품행으로 인하여 학교에서 퇴학당했다.

416 지치지 않는, 끈기 있는   요리사는 완벽한 케익을 만들기 위해서 끊기 있게indefatigable 노력했다.

417 기소하다, 고발하다, 비난하다   그의 편지에 나타난 증거들은 그를 음모죄로 고발하기에indict 충분했다.

418 무관심한, 중요치 않은   우리 아버지는 스포츠에 관심이 없어서indifferent 티비로 축구를 보는 일이 절대로 없다.

419 토착의, 원산의, 자생의, 타고난   토착indigenous 주민들은 정착인들에 의해 사실상 몰살되었다.

420 분별없는, 마구잡이의   그 건물은 무분별한indiscriminate 건축 스타일의 조합물로 순서나 일관성이 없었다.

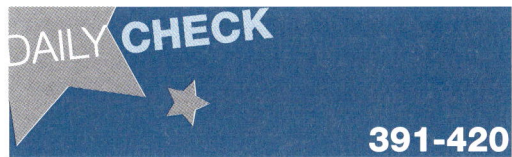

SYNONYMS WORDS THAT MEAN THE SAME THING

391 Poor nutrition **impaired** his body's ability to resist infection.

ⓐ precluded

ⓑ harmed

ⓒ improved

ⓓ enriched

392 The judge was famous for being **impartial** and for making fair and just decisions.

ⓐ unbiased

ⓑ zealous

ⓒ slanted

ⓓ impassive

393 She was known for her **impeccable** manners and for always knowing how to behave.

ⓐ defective

ⓑ petite

ⓒ flawless

ⓓ individual

394 The failure of his business left him **impecunious** for a while, but he did not give up hope.

ⓐ impoverished

ⓑ reachable

ⓒ wealthy

ⓓ innocuous

395 The army found that muddy roads **impeded** its progress across the country.

ⓐ encouraged

ⓑ furthered

ⓒ stalled

ⓓ resumed

396 The theory failed because it was based on an **implausible** set of assumptions.

ⓐ tenable

ⓑ infamous

ⓒ probable

ⓓ unlikely

397 Kitchen **implements** like pots and pans have changed little over thousands of years.

ⓐ sheds

ⓑ utensils

ⓒ hangars

ⓓ complements

398 The government **imposes** fines on companies that violate the environmental protection regulations.

ⓐ ignites

ⓑ covets

ⓒ levies

ⓓ covers

399 A heavy concrete cover made the shelter **impregnable** against attack from the air.

ⓐ dissimilar

ⓑ pugnacious

ⓒ unbeatable

ⓓ feeble

400 The children acted with such **impudence** that they were suspended from school.

ⓐ rigidity

ⓑ prudence

ⓒ rudeness

ⓓ endurance

401 People in love may act in **impulsive** ways because their feelings overcome their caution.

ⓐ spontaneous

ⓑ seasoned

ⓒ fitful

ⓓ zany

402 The **inadvertent** result of introducing the new species was to disrupt the ecosystem.

ⓐ voluntary

ⓑ checkered

ⓒ obdurate

ⓓ unplanned

403 When she opened the door, she **inadvertently** let in a mosquito.

ⓐ deliberately

ⓑ accidently

ⓒ purportedly

ⓓ overtly

404 The song became popular even though its lyrics were considered **inane**.

ⓐ sharp

ⓑ interesting

ⓒ pointless

ⓓ significant

405 The other remarkable issue is the clumsy and **inapt** responses by the new Korean government.

ⓐ improper

ⓑ rational

ⓒ regarded

ⓓ tangential

406 The **incessant** noise from the building site across the street made it hard to concentrate on work.

ⓐ sporadic

ⓑ erratic

ⓒ ceaseless

ⓓ scattered

407 In addition to our budgeted expenses, we had a few incidental expenses on our trip.

ⓐ vital

ⓑ logical

ⓒ deliberate

ⓓ chance

408 This TV announcer is known for his **incisive** comments on the day's news.

ⓐ indirect

ⓑ superficial

ⓒ penetrating

ⓓ intuitive

409 The criminals were convicted of **inciting** a riot and were sent to jail.

ⓐ discouraging

ⓑ squelching

ⓒ imitating

ⓓ provoking

410 The test will cover information in chapters 2 and 3 of your text, from pages 65 to 130 **inclusive**.

ⓐ partial

ⓑ comprehensive

ⓒ exclusive

ⓓ precise

411 Interference made the radio message **incoherent** and impossible to understand.

ⓐ clear

ⓑ lithe

ⓒ inexorable

ⓓ jumbled

412 His noisy behavior made him **incongruous** in the library.

ⓐ discrete

ⓑ ardent

ⓒ inappropriate

ⓓ contentious

413 The article was so **inconsequential** that it was not even listed in the annual index.

ⓐ significant

ⓑ pivotal

ⓒ unimportant

ⓓ educational

414 Scientists presented **incontrovertible** evidence that the theory was correct, so it became a law.

ⓐ unproven

ⓑ sage

ⓒ articulate

ⓓ indisputable

415 One of the students was expelled from school for what seemed **incorrigible** misbehavior.

ⓐ miscellaneous

ⓑ arid

ⓒ eloquent

ⓓ irreparable

416 The cook was **indefatigable** in trying to make a perfect cake.

ⓐ halfhearted

ⓑ ordinal

ⓒ tireless

ⓓ listless

417 The evidence in his letters sufficed to **indict** him for conspiracy.

ⓐ exonerate

ⓑ denote

ⓒ corroborate

ⓓ incriminate

418 My father is **indifferent** to sports and never watches football on television.

ⓐ aloof

ⓑ fastidious

ⓒ extraneous

ⓓ unambiguous

419 The **indigenous** population was virtually exterminated by the settlers.

ⓐ native

ⓑ epidemic

ⓒ pandemic

ⓓ epistemic

420 The building was an **indiscriminate** mixture of architectural styles and was without order or coherence.

ⓐ meticulous

ⓑ fallow

ⓒ slothful

ⓓ careless

Answers

391-395 ⓑⓐⓒⓐⓒ	406-410 ⓒⓓⓒⓓⓑ
396-400 ⓓⓑⓒⓒⓒ	411-415 ⓓⓒⓒⓓⓓ
401-405 ⓐⓓⓑⓒⓐ	416-420 ⓒⓓⓐⓐⓓ

☆421 **indolence**
[índələns]

n. laziness; sloth; habitual and willful inactivity

SYN laziness, sloth

Unwilling to work, he passed his days in _____, taking long naps and watching television.

☆422 **indolent**
[índələnt]

adj. characterized by indolence

SYN lazy, slothful

An _____ person is unlikely to have a successful career.

☆423 **induce**
[indjúːs]

v. to make something occur; to cause a reaction or response

SYN cause, produce, stimulate

The light from the rising sun _____ the plant to open its leaves.

☆424 **indulgent**
[indʌ́ldʒənt]

adj. allowing someone a wide range of behavior

SYN lenient, permissive, tolerant, lax, soft

She grew up with _____ parents who rarely disciplined her.

☆425 **ineffable**
[inéfəbəl]

adj. beyond description; incapable of being put into words

SYN indescribable, inexpressible

In a dream, she experienced an _____ sense of peace and happiness.

☆426 **inept**
[inépt]

adj. awkward; done without, or not having, skill

SYN awkward, clumsy, gauche, incompetent, ungainly

I've never heard anyone so _____ at making speeches.

SCAFFOLDING

421 게으름, 나태   그는 일을 하기 싫어서 여러 날을 낮잠과 티비 시청으로 게으르게indolence 보냈다.

422 게으른, 나태한   게으른indolent 사람은 성공적인 생애를 보내지 못할 가능성이 높다.

423 권유하다, 야기하다   떠오르는 태양은 식물이 잎을 열도록 해 준다induced.

424 멋대로 하게 하는, 관대한   그녀는 벌을 거의 주지 않는 관대한indulgent 부모님 밑에서 자랐다.

425 말로 표현할 수 없는   그녀는 꿈 속에서 말로 표현할 수 없는ineffable 평화와 행복을 경험했다.

426 부적당한, 무능력, 서투른   나는 그렇게 연설에 서투른inept 사람을 본적이 없다.

☆427 **inert**
[inə́:rt]

adj. not reactive or responsive; motionless

SYN immobile, inactive, nonreactive, unmoving

Helium is an _____ gas that does not react with other elements.

☆428 **inevitable**
[inévitəbəl]

adj. incapable of being stopped or averted; certain to happen

SYN unavoidable, unstoppable, unalterable

After so many years of neglect, it was _____ that his health should deteriorate.

☆429 **inexorable**
[inéksərəbəl]

adj. incapable of being changed or averted by argument or plea; beyond sympathy, pity, or mercy

SYN unchangeable, unalterable, unyielding, cruel, merciless, relentless

The soldiers faced an _____ enemy: the severe cold, which struck hard and would not yield.

☆430 **infamous**
[ínfəməs]

adj. having an extremely bad reputation

SYN notorious, villainous

An _____ criminal, the outlaw spread fear throughout the state until he was caught.

☆431 **ingenious**
[indʒíːnjəs]

adj. showing cleverness, inventiveness, and resourcefulness

SYN clever, inventive, resourceful

The first electronic computers were _____ machines that used vacuum tubes to perform calculations.

☆432 **inherent**
[inhíərənt]

adj. basic and essential to something and inseparable from its nature

SYN innate, native

Though useful, this method of analysis has a few _____ flaws.

DAY 15

SCAFFOLDING

427 둔한, 활발하지 못한   헬륨은 다른 요소들에 반응하지 않는 비활성inert 기체이다.

428 피할 수 없는, 부득이한   수 년간 간과해 온 후에 그의 건강이 악화되는 것은 피할 수 없었다inevitable.

429 냉혹한, 굽힐 수 없는   군인들은 냉혹한inexorable 적을 만났다. 그것은 그들을 강타해서 절대 물러서지 않을 것 같았던 추위였다.

430 수치스러운, 악명 높은   한 악명 높은infamous 범죄자였던 그 상습범은 잡힐 때까지 주 전역에 공포를 퍼뜨렸다.

431 재간 있는, 영리한, 정교한   처음의 전자 컴퓨터는 연산을 수행하기 위해 진공관을 사용하는 정교한ingenious 기계였다.

432 타고난, 고유의, 본래부터의   이 분석 방법은 비록 유용하긴 하지만 몇 가지 고유의inherent 결점이 있다.

☆433 **inhibit**
[inhíbit]

v. to block, check, discourage, hinder, prevent, or restrain

SYN hinder, restrain

The drug was supposed to _____ the desire to smoke cigarettes.

☆434 **innate**
[inéit]

adj. present in someone from birth; often used to describe inborn abilities

SYN inherent, inborn

The child seemed to have an _____ love of music and began singing at a very early age.

☆435 **innocuous**
[inákju:əs]

adj. unlikely to cause offense or harm

SYN harmless, inoffensive

No one could object to such an _____ little painting.

☆436 **innovate**
[ínəvèit]

v. to make unprecedented changes in something; to introduce new features or approaches

SYN introduce, change, revamp, renew

Companies that wish to _____ must understand that change brings risks with it.

☆437 **innovation**
[ìnəvéiʃən]

n. the introduction of something new, fresh, or unprecedented

SYN change, renewal, renovation, originality

The steam engine was an _____ in technology, and it transformed society.

☆438 **innumerable**
[injú:mərəbəl]

adj. too numerous to count

SYN countless, numberless

There are _____ leaves on trees in this forest.

SCAFFOLDING

433 억제하다, 금하다   이 약은 담배를 피우고 싶은 욕구를 억제시켜 주도록inhibit 되어 있었다.

434 타고난, 고유의, 본질적인   그 아이는 음악에 대해 타고난innate 애정이 있어 보였고 매우 어린 나이에 노래를 시작했다.

435 해가 없는, 악의 없는   누구도 그런 악의 없는innocuous 조그마한 그림을 싫어할 수 없었다.

436 혁신하다, 도입하다   혁신을innovate 원하는 회사들은 변화가 위험을 동반한다는 것을 이해해야 한다.

437 혁신, 쇄신   증기 기관은 기술의 혁신innovation이었고, 그것은 사회를 바꾸어 놓았다.

438 무수한, 엄청난   이 숲의 나무들에는 무수한innumerable 잎이 있다.

☆439	**inquisitive** [inkwízətiv]	*adj.* eager to investigate and acquire new knowledge; in a negative sense, snoopy, nosy, or prying **SYN** curious, interested, prying *A research scientist needs to have an _____ mind.*
☆440	**insipid** [insípid]	*adj.* without taste, interest, or distinction **SYN** bland, innocuous, lackluster, uninteresting *The author made her story so inoffensive that it became _____ instead.*
☆441	**insolvent** [insάlvənt]	*adj.* completely unable to pay one's debts **SYN** bankrupt, destitute, impoverished, penniless, impecunious *It is pointless to try collecting money from an _____ person.*
☆442	**inspire** [inspáiər]	*v.* to provide someone with a strong motive or feeling **SYN** animate, drive, impel, motivate, prompt *The manager's speech to the employees did not _____ them to increase their productivity.*
☆443	**instigate** [ínstəgèit]	*v.* to encourage, incite, prod, or urge someone to do something; to make some behavior happen **SYN** incite, provoke, urge *It took little effort to _____ a rebellion in the troubled country.*
☆444	**insularity** [insəlǽrəti]	*n.* detachment or isolation; similarity to an island **SYN** isolation, detachment, loneliness *The man's _____ prevented him from making friends easily.*

DAY 15

---

439 탐구적인, 꼬치꼬치 캐묻는 　연구 과학자는 탐구적인inquisitive 마음을 가져야 한다.
440 무미건조한, 지루한, 풍미가 없는 　그 작가는 이야기를 너무 악의 없는 내용으로 만들어서 그 이야기는 오히려 무미건조해졌다insipid.
441 지급 불능의, 파산한 　파산한insolvent 사람으로부터 돈을 받으려고 하는 것은 효과가 없는 일이다.
442 고무하다, 영감을 주다 　지배인이 직원들에게 한 연설은 그들의 생산성 향상을 고무시키지inspire 못했다.
443 유발시키다, 부추기다 　그 떠들썩한 나라에서 반역을 부추기는 데는instigate 노력이 별로 들지 않았다.
444 고립, 편협, 섬나라 근성 　그 남자의 편협함insularity은 그가 친구들을 쉽게 사귀는 것에 장애가 되었다.

☆445 **insuperable**
[insú:pərəbəl]

adj. impossible to overcome
SYN insurmountable, unbeatable

When an obstacle appears _____, overcoming it may simply take a long time.

☆446 **integrity**
[intégrəti]

n. an upright, virtuous, and honest character; a state of being intact, solid, and in one piece
SYN honor, virtue, solidity, intactness

She was known as a woman of great _____ and was respected by all of her colleagues.

☆447 **intensify**
[inténsəfài]

v. to increase the intensity of something; to sharpen or strengthen
SYN increase, sharpen, strengthen

To get better results, you must _____ your efforts.

☆448 **intervene**
[ìntərví:n]

v. to come between two parties in a dispute
SYN intercede, interrupt, mediate, separate

A foreign country sometimes _____ to stop a civil war in another country.

☆449 **intimidate**
[intímədèit]

v. to make someone afraid or hesitant by a show of force or threat of action
SYN daunt, deter, frighten, overawe

When threatened, a cat hisses and arches its back to _____ its opponent.

☆450 **intractable**
[intræktəbl]

adj. hard to control, direct, manage, or subdue
SYN obstinate, stubborn, unyielding

Injuries left him with seemingly _____ pain in his feet.

SCAFFOLDING

445 극복하기 어려운   장애물을 극복하기 어려워insuperable 보일 때, 그것을 극복하는 것은 단지 시간이 오래 걸리는 것뿐일지도 모른다.

446 고결, 성실, 정직, 완전, 통일성   그녀는 매우 성실한integrity 여성이라고 알려져 있었으며 모든 동료들로부터 존경을 받았다.

447 강하게 하다, 증대하다   당신은 더 좋은 결과를 얻기 위해서 노력을 증대시켜야 한다intensify.

448 사이에 들다, 방해하다   외국은 때때로 다른 나라의 문명 전쟁을 막기 위해 끼어든다intervenes.

449 겁주다, 협박하다   고양이는 위협을 받으면 적에게 겁을 주기intimidate 위해 쉬 하는 소리를 내면서 등을 둥글게 구부린다.

450 고치기 어려운, 완고한, 처치하기 힘든   부상은 그의 발에 고치기 어려워 보이는intractable 통증을 남겼다.

SYNONYMS WORDS THAT MEAN THE SAME THING

421 Unwilling to work, he passed his days in **indolence**, taking long naps and watching television.

ⓐ adulation
ⓑ solace
ⓒ laziness
ⓓ longevity

422 An **indolent** person is unlikely to have a successful career.

ⓐ irrelevant
ⓑ slothful
ⓒ insolent
ⓓ extrinsic

423 The light from the rising sun **induced** the plant to open its leaves.

ⓐ discouraged
ⓑ planned
ⓒ stimulated
ⓓ ousted

424 She grew up with **indulgent** parents who rarely disciplined her.

ⓐ permissive
ⓑ demanding
ⓒ passive
ⓓ exacting

425 In a dream, she experienced an **ineffable** sense of peace and happiness.

ⓐ indescribable
ⓑ elated
ⓒ fitful
ⓓ affable

426 I've never heard anyone so **inept** at making speeches.

ⓐ soft
ⓑ clumsy
ⓒ arable
ⓓ fake

427 Helium is an **inert** gas that does not react with other elements.

ⓐ elaborate
ⓑ spurious
ⓒ inactive
ⓓ arbitrary

428 After so many years of neglect, it was **inevitable** that his health should deteriorate.

ⓐ uncertain
ⓑ useless
ⓒ effectual
ⓓ unavoidable

429 The soldiers faced an **inexorable** enemy: the severe cold, which struck hard and would not yield.

ⓐ flexible
ⓑ relentless
ⓒ yielding
ⓓ changeable

430 An **infamous** criminal, the outlaw spread fear throughout the state until he was caught.

ⓐ notorious
ⓑ honorable
ⓒ noble
ⓓ virtuous

DAY 15

431 The first electronic computers were **ingenious** machines that used vacuum tubes to perform calculations.

ⓐ resourceful

ⓑ esoteric

ⓒ detrimental

ⓓ inept

432 Though useful, this method of analysis has a few **inherent** flaws.

ⓐ foreign

ⓑ alien

ⓒ exotic

ⓓ innate

433 The drug was supposed to **inhibit** the desire to smoke cigarettes.

ⓐ restrain

ⓑ condense

ⓒ squander

ⓓ free

434 The child seemed to have an **innate** love of music and began singing at a very early age.

ⓐ learned

ⓑ erudite

ⓒ inborn

ⓓ deliberate

435 No one could object to such an **innocuous** little painting.

ⓐ harmful

ⓑ effervescent

ⓒ willful

ⓓ inoffensive

436 Companies that wish to **innovate** must understand that change brings risks with it.

ⓐ deplete

ⓑ revamp

ⓒ undo

ⓓ recant

437 The steam engine was an **innovation** in technology, and it transformed society.

ⓐ preservation

ⓑ change

ⓒ termination

ⓓ inception

438 There are **innumerable** leaves on trees in this forest.

ⓐ stuffy

ⓑ countless

ⓒ scarce

ⓓ shabby

439 A research scientist needs to have an **inquisitive** mind.

ⓐ curious

ⓑ uninterested

ⓒ incredible

ⓓ educated

440 The author made her story so inoffensive that it became **insipid** instead.

ⓐ interesting

ⓑ lackluster

ⓒ ardent

ⓓ extended

441 It is pointless to try collecting money from an **insolvent** person.

ⓐ legal

ⓑ archaic

ⓒ wealthy

ⓓ bankrupt

442 The manager's speech to the employees did not **inspire** them to increase their productivity.

ⓐ discourage

ⓑ squelch

ⓒ conscribe

ⓓ animate

443 It took little effort to **instigate** a rebellion in the troubled country.

ⓐ upbraid

ⓑ efface

ⓒ provoke

ⓓ squander

444 The man's **insularity** prevented him from making friends easily.

ⓐ jeopardy

ⓑ equanimity

ⓒ antipathy

ⓓ isolation

445 When an obstacle appears **insuperable**, overcoming it may simply take a long time.

ⓐ wayward

ⓑ unbeatable

ⓒ dubious

ⓓ pernicious

446 She was known as a woman of great **integrity** and was respected by all of her colleagues.

ⓐ virtue

ⓑ anxiety

ⓒ indecency

ⓓ slight

447 To get better results, you must **intensify** your efforts.

ⓐ incite

ⓑ increase

ⓒ reprimand

ⓓ mediate

448 A foreign country sometimes **intervenes** to stop a civil war in another country.

ⓐ mollifies

ⓑ splinters

ⓒ arbitrates

ⓓ intercedes

449 When threatened, a cat hisses and arches its back to **intimidate** its opponent.

ⓐ embody

ⓑ attack

ⓒ bolster

ⓓ deter

450 Injuries left him with seemingly **intractable** pain in his feet.

ⓐ feeble

ⓑ cooperative

ⓒ obstinate

ⓓ zany

Answers

421-425 ⓒⓑⓒⓐⓐ	436-440 ⓑⓑⓑⓐⓑ
426-430 ⓑⓒⓓⓑⓐ	441-445 ⓓⓓⓒⓓⓑ
431-435 ⓐⓓⓐⓒⓓ	446-450 ⓐⓑⓓⓒⓒ

☆451 **intrepid**
[intrépid]

adj. extremely courageous
SYN brave, bold, fearless

Two _____ explorers set out across the continent with the goal of reaching the Pacific Ocean.

☆452 **intricate**
[íntrəkit]

adj. complex and hard to understand because of numerous interrelated parts or details
SYN complex, involved

The clockmaker built an _____ mechanism to determine a ship's longitude at sea.

☆453 **intrinsic**
[intrínsik]

adj. belonging to something or someone as an inherent and essential part of its nature
SYN inborn, indigenous, inherent, innate, natural

I bought this for 500 won, but its _____ value is at least 800 won.

☆454 **inundate**
[ínəndèit]

v. to cover with water, as in a flood; to overwhelm, as with data or messages
SYN flood, overwhelm

A flood _____ the farms along the river.

☆455 **invert**
[invə́:rt]

v. to turn upside down
SYN upend, reverse

To drain the pan, _____ it and let the water run out.

☆456 **irascible**
[irǽsəbəl]

adj. irritable; quick to anger
SYN irritable, touchy, short-tempered

The man had an _____ personality and often spoke angrily to others.

SCAFFOLDING

451 용기있는, 대담한   두 명의 용기있는intrepid 탐험가들은 태평양에 도달하는 목표를 가지고 대륙을 건너기 시작했다.

452 얽힌, 복잡한   시계 제조공은 바다에 있는 배 위치의 경도를 결정하기 위한 복잡한intricate 기계 장치를 만들었다.

453 본질적인, 고유의, 진성의   나는 이것을 500원에 샀지만, 이것의 본래intrinsic 가치는 최소 800원이다.

454 물에 잠기게 하다, 쇄도하다   홍수는 강을 따라서 있는 농장을 물에 잠기게 했다inundated.

455 거꾸로 하다, 뒤집다   프라이팬을 말리기 위해 그것을 뒤집어서invert 물이 빠지도록 해라.

456 화를 잘 내는, 성급한   그 남자는 화를 잘 내는irascible 성격이라서 종종 남들에게 화를 내며 말한다.

☆457 **ironic**
[airánik]

adj. biting; cynical; mocking; sarcastic; opposite of what one expected
SYN cynical, sarcastic, unanticipated, coincidental

His _____ tone of voice indicated that he meant the opposite of what he had said.

☆458 **irrational**
[iráʃənəl]

adj. not according to reason; guided by emotion or instinct rather than rational thought
SYN unreasonable, absurd

Her intense love for her family led to her make an _____ decision based on emotion rather than reason.

☆459 **irrelevant**
[iréləvənt]

adj. not connected with or applying to the subject in hand; not relevant
SYN beside the point, extraneous, immaterial, impertinent

What you say is _____ to the matter at hand.

☆460 **irreproachable**
[ìripróutʃəbəl]

adj. free of blame, flaw, or error; often used to describe some positive personal quality such as courtesy
SYN blameless, flawless

My sister's _____ courtesy has served her well in her work as a diplomat.

☆461 **isolated**
[áisəlèitid]

adj. cut off from contact or connection with others
SYN alone, insulated

Posted to an _____ outpost far from the nearest community, he felt very lonely.

☆462 **jeopardy**
[dʒépərdi]

n. a risk of death, injury, or loss; a dangerous situation
SYN danger, hazard, peril, risk

Robbers once hid along this highway and put travelers in _____.

DAY 16

SCAFFOLDING

457 반어적인, 비꼬는, 풍자적인   그의 반어적인ironic 어조는 그의 말이 실제로 자신이 말한 것의 반대를 의미한다는 것을 보여주었다.
458 이성을 잃은, 불합리한   가족에 대한 그녀의 강렬한 사랑은 그녀가 이성보다는 감정에 기초해서 불합리한irrational 결정을 내리게 했다.
459 부적절한, 관련이 없는   당신이 말하는 것은 당면한 문제에 관련이 없다irrelevant.
460 나무랄 데 없는   언니의 나무랄 데 없는irreproachable 예절은 외교관으로서 그녀가 업무를 수행하는 데에 좋은 역할을 했다.
461 고립된, 격리된   가장 가까운 마을로부터 상당히 멀리 떨어져 있는 고립된isolated 부대에 있어서 그는 매우 외로웠다.
462 위험, 위험성   한때 강도들이 이 고속도로를 따라 숨어서 여행객들을 위험에jeopardy 빠뜨렸다.

☆463 **jocular**
[dʒákjələr]

adj. meant to amuse
SYN jesting, joking, jolly, merry

A _____ man, my father knew countless jokes and funny stories.

☆464 **jovial**
[dʒóuviəl]

adj. joyful; very happy and outgoing
SYN exuberant, happy, jolly, merry

His _____ personality made him successful as an entertainer.

☆465 **keen**
[ki:n]

adj. eager; willing
SYN cutting, sharp, well-honed, acute, astute, bright, intelligent, shrewd, ardent, intent, observant

He has a _____ sense of hearing.

☆466 **kindle**
[kíndl]

v. to set on fire; to incite or provoke a response, usually a strong one
SYN ignite, incite, inflame, provoke

We had no idea that our remarks would _____ such an angry argument.

☆467 **knack**
[næk]

n. the ability to do something effectively and skilfully
SYN ability, aptitude, gift, penchant, skill, talent, hang, know-how

He has a _____ for repairing electronic equipment.

☆468 **labyrinth**
[lǽbərìnθ]

n. a very complex arrangement
SYN maze, tangle, web

The building is so big that its halls seem like a _____ where one can get lost easily.

☆469 **laconic**

[ləkánik]

adj. using only a few, well-chosen words

SYN brief, concise, terse

The professor was known for his _____ replies, some of them only one or two words long.

☆470 **laggard**

[lǽgərd]

adj. moving or proceeding slowly

SYN late, slow, tardy

One _____ runner crossed the finish line five minutes behind all the others.

☆471 **lament**

[ləmént]

v. to mourn or weep for someone or something; to express great sorrow

SYN deplore, grieve, weep

When her husband died, she _____ his death bitterly.

☆472 **lampoon**

[læmpúːn]

n. a sharp satire, parody, or mockery of something

SYN mockery, parody, ridicule, satire

The poem was a _____ of epic poetry and made fun of all of its traditions.

☆473 **languish**

[lǽŋgwiʃ]

v. to deteriorate or weaken; to fade or waste away

SYN deteriorate, fade, weaken, suffer

The prisoner _____ for years in jail before he died of lung disease.

☆474 **lassitude**

[lǽsitjùːd]

n. fatigue or weakness; in many cases, resulting from some external influence such as climate

SYN fatigue, laziness, lethargy

The hot, humid climate produced a _____ that made it hard for anyone to work.

DAY 16

SCAFFOLDING

469 간결한, 말수가 적은   그 교수는 간결한laconic 대답을 하는 것으로, 그 중에서도 어쩔 때는 한 두 단어의 길이로만 대답하는 것으로 알려져 있었다.

470 느린, 꾸물거리는   한 느린laggard 주자는 다른 모든 선수들보다 5분이나 뒤처져서 결승선을 밟았다.

471 비탄하다, 후회하다   그녀는 남편이 죽었을 때 그의 죽음을 쓰라리게 통탄했다lamented.

472 풍자문, 풍자시   그 시는 서사시의 풍자문lampoon이었고 그것의 모든 전통들을 조롱했다.

473 기력이 없어지다, 시들다   그 죄수는 감옥에서 몇 년에 걸쳐 기력이 없어진 후에languished 폐병으로 사망했다.

474 나른함, 권태   뜨겁고 습한 기후는 누구나 일을 하기 힘들게 하는 나른함lassitude을 만들어 냈다.

☆475 **laud**
[lɔːd]

v. to praise highly

SYN applaud, glorify, hail, honor, praise

Reviewers _____ the novelist for writing a great work of fiction.

☆476 **laudable**
[lɔ́ːdəbəl]

adj. deserving of praise or commendation

SYN commendable, excellent, praiseworthy

This book is a _____ effort to write a history of the Internet era.

☆477 **lavish**
[lǽviʃ]

adj. given in great amounts or done to excess; often used to describe extravagant spending or praise

SYN extravagant, generous, profuse

She gave her garden such _____ attention that it grew beautifully.

☆478 **lenient**
[líːniənt]

adj. not as strict as expected when punishing somebody or when making sure that rules are obeyed

SYN easygoing, indulgent, lax, permissive, merciful

The judge was far too _____ with him.

☆479 **lethargic**
[ləθɑ́ːrdʒik]

adj. lacking in energy, motivation, or alertness

SYN drowsy, indolent, lazy, slow-moving

His illness left him so _____ that he could barely walk across the room.

☆480 **lethargy**
[léθərdʒi]

n. a lack of energy, motivation, or alertness

SYN drowsiness, indolence, laziness, torpor

Partly because of poor nutrition, the country's inhabitants were known for their _____ and spent little time working.

475 칭송하다, 찬미하다, 기리다   비평가들은 그 소설가가 위대한 소설 작품을 쓴 것에 대해 칭송했다lauded.

476 칭찬할 만한, 훌륭한   이 책은 인터넷 시대의 역사에 대해 쓰기 위한 훌륭한laudable 노력이었다.

477 아낌 없는, 후한, 사치스러운   그녀는 정원에 아낌 없는lavish 관심을 쏟아서 그 정원은 아름답게 자랐다.

478 관대한, 자비로운   그 판사는 그에게 너무나 관대했다lenient.

479 혼수상태의, 졸린, 무기력한   질병이 그를 너무 무기력하게lethargic 해서 그는 방에서 제대로 걸을 수도 없었다.

480 무기력, 혼수상태   부분적으로 영양 결핍 때문에, 그 나라의 주민들은 무기력하다고lethargy 알려져 있었고 일하는 데에 별로 시간을 들이지 않았다.

SYNONYMS WORDS THAT MEAN THE SAME THING

451 Two **intrepid** explorers set out across the continent with the goal of reaching the Pacific Ocean.

ⓐ generous

ⓑ hypocritical

ⓒ hedonistic

ⓓ brave

452 The clockmaker built an **intricate** mechanism to determine a ship's longitude at sea.

ⓐ frivolous

ⓑ complex

ⓒ impregnable

ⓓ subsided

453 I bought this for 500 won, but its **intrinsic** value is at least 800 won.

ⓐ foreign

ⓑ innocuous

ⓒ inherent

ⓓ exotic

454 A flood **inundated** the farms along the river.

ⓐ impelled

ⓑ overwhelmed

ⓒ prompted

ⓓ removed

455 To drain the pan, **invert** it and let the water run out.

ⓐ uphold

ⓑ preserve

ⓒ upend

ⓓ bolster

456 The man had an **irascible** personality and often spoke angrily to others.

ⓐ easygoing

ⓑ sparing

ⓒ bland

ⓓ touchy

457 His **ironic** tone of voice indicated that he meant the opposite of what he had said.

ⓐ lurid

ⓑ formal

ⓒ sarcastic

ⓓ lackluster

458 Her intense love for her family led to her make an **irrational** decision based on emotion rather than reason.

ⓐ plain

ⓑ absurd

ⓒ fortuitous

ⓓ sane

459 What you say is **irrelevant** to the matter at hand.

ⓐ pertinent

ⓑ inherent

ⓒ extraneous

ⓓ intrinsic

460 My sister's **irreproachable** courtesy has served her well in her work as a diplomat.

ⓐ munificent

ⓑ flawless

ⓒ foolhardy

ⓓ faulty

461 Posted to an **isolated** outpost far from the nearest community, he felt very lonely.

ⓐ lonely

ⓑ polemical

ⓒ included

ⓓ contained

462 Robbers once hid along this highway and put travelers in jeopardy.

ⓐ peril

ⓑ innovation

ⓒ impudence

ⓓ guarantee

463 A jocular man, my father knew countless jokes and funny stories.

ⓐ zany

ⓑ jesting

ⓒ serious

ⓓ slight

464 His jovial personality made him successful as an entertainer.

ⓐ errant

ⓑ inoffensive

ⓒ merry

ⓓ gloomy

465 He has a keen sense of hearing.

ⓐ stuffy

ⓑ obvious

ⓒ acute

ⓓ zealous

466 We had no idea that our remarks would kindle such an angry argument.

ⓐ extinguish

ⓑ ignite

ⓒ quell

ⓓ obscure

467 He has a knack for repairing electronic equipment.

ⓐ penchant

ⓑ disinclination

ⓒ revulsion

ⓓ repugnance

468 The building is so big that its halls seem like a labyrinth where one can get lost easily.

ⓐ trail

ⓑ maze

ⓒ wake

ⓓ beeline

469 The professor was known for his laconic replies, some of them only one or two words long.

ⓐ peevish

ⓑ polemical

ⓒ flagrant

ⓓ terse

470 One laggard runner crossed the finish line five minutes behind all the others.

ⓐ ominous

ⓑ late

ⓒ lucid

ⓓ somber

471 When her husband died, she lamented his death bitterly.

ⓐ solicited

ⓑ contended

ⓒ rejoiced

ⓓ grieved

472 The poem was a lampoon of epic poetry and made fun of all of its traditions.

ⓐ laud

ⓑ determination

ⓒ laud

ⓓ satire

473 The prisoner **languished** for years in jail before he died of lung disease.

ⓐ dragged

ⓑ lingered

ⓒ suffered

ⓓ thrived

474 The hot, humid climate produced a **lassitude** that made it hard for anyone to work.

ⓐ vigor

ⓑ interest

ⓒ contempt

ⓓ fatigue

475 Reviewers **lauded** the novelist for writing a great work of fiction.

ⓐ hailed

ⓑ deprecated

ⓒ noted

ⓓ depreciate

476 This book is a **laudable** effort to write a history of the Internet era.

ⓐ lofty

ⓑ precarious

ⓒ excellent

ⓓ contemptible

477 She gave her garden such **lavish** attention that it grew beautifully.

ⓐ cryptic

ⓑ odious

ⓒ profuse

ⓓ frivolous

478 The judge was far too **lenient** with him.

ⓐ tense

ⓑ conscientious

ⓒ detrimental

ⓓ indulgent

479 His illness left him so **lethargic** that he could barely walk across the room.

ⓐ drowsy

ⓑ solemn

ⓒ chaotic

ⓓ prosaic

480 Partly because of poor nutrition, the country's inhabitants were known for their **lethargy** and spent little time working.

ⓐ vitality

ⓑ tier

ⓒ profanity

ⓓ indolence

DAY 16

Answers

451-455 ⓓⓑⓒⓑⓒ	466-470 ⓑⓐⓑⓓⓑ
456-460 ⓓⓒⓑⓒⓑ	471-475 ⓓⓓⓒⓓⓐ
461-465 ⓐⓐⓑⓒⓒ	476-480 ⓒⓒⓓⓐⓓ

☆481 **levity**
[lévəti]

n. lightness or humor; a light-hearted manner
SYN frivolity, humor, lightness

To introduce some _____ to his speech, he told a joke about his first day on the job.

☆482 **linger**
[líŋgər]

v. to wait, delay, or stay longer than planned
SYN delay, lag, remain, wait

The odors of a delicious meal _____ after the food itself was eaten.

☆483 **listless**
[lístlis]

adj. lacking in energy or motivation; suffering from indirection or unconcern
SYN indifferent, languid, tired, weary

Everyone felt so _____ because of the hot weather that no one did any work.

☆484 **lithe**
[laið]

adj. capable of bending easily; often used to describe the movement of athletes
SYN bendable, flexible, supple

The gymnast's _____ body seemed capable of endless supple movements.

☆485 **lofty**
[lɔ́ːfti]

adj. of great height or eminence
SYN high, elevated, eminent, towering

The king built a _____ castle in the mountains and spent his summers there.

☆486 **lucid**
[lúːsid]

adj. easy to understand; clearly expressed
SYN clear, understandable

The physicist wrote such a _____ description of his theory that anyone could understand it.

SCAFFOLDING

481 가벼움, 경솔, 변덕 　 그는 연설에 약간의 가벼움levity을 더하기 위해서 그의 출근 첫날에 대한 농담을 했다.

482 남아 있다, 꾸물거리다, 질질 끌다 　 그 맛있는 음식의 향은 음식을 다 먹은 후에도 남아 있었다lingered.

483 나른한, 마음이 내키지 않는, 무관심한 　 더운 날씨로 인해 모두가 나른해listless 있었기 때문에 아무도 일을 하지 않았다.

484 잘 휘는, 유연한 　 체육 교사의 유연한lithe 몸은 끝없는 유연한 동작이 가능해 보였다.

485 매우 높은, 고상한 　 왕은 산 속에 고상한lofty 성을 지었고 그곳에서 여름을 보냈다.

486 명쾌한, 맑은, 빛나는 　 그 물리학자는 그의 이론을 매우 명쾌하게lucid 설명하여 모두가 그것을 이해할 수 있었다.

☆487 **lure**
[luər]

n. an attraction, enticement, or inducement; something that attracts people

SYN attraction, enticement

The company offered a high salary as a _____ to attract the professor away from his university job.

☆488 **lurid**
[lúːrid]

adj. extremely vivid or sensational; horrid; shocking; dreadful

SYN sensational, vivid, terrible, horrible, shocking

Newspapers printed all the _____ details of the scandal on their front pages.

☆489 **luxuriant**
[lʌgʒúəriənt]

adj. extremely abundant; growing in profusion

SYN abundant, lush, productive

_____ plants completely covered the ground.

☆490 **malice**
[mǽlis]

n. a desire to do harm or to see harm done on someone

SYN animosity, enmity, malevolence

She felt such _____ toward her neighbors that she never said a kind word about them.

☆491 **malicious**
[məlíʃəs]

adj. characterized by malice; hostile; malevolent

SYN malevolent, hostile, vicious

_____ motives led one employee to spread harmful rumors about another.

☆492 **marred**
[maːrd]

adj. defaced or spoiled in appearance or appeal

SYN defaced, disfigured, spoiled, ruined

Though _____ slightly by gunfire during the war, the building remained beautiful.

DAY 17

☆493 **meager**
[mí:gər]

adj. scanty; slight; sparse; deficient in amount or number

SYN deficient, scanty, inadequate, insufficient

The poor soil and dry climate here let farms produce only _____ amounts of food.

☆494 **meander**
[miǽndər]

v. to wander; to walk or flow aimlessly or by a very indirect route

SYN wander, ramble, turn, wind

The river _____ back and forth across the plain in long bends.

☆495 **mercenary**
[mə́:rsənèri]

adj. working or produced with the aim of making money; often used to describe hired soldiers

SYN avaricious, greedy, venal

The _____ soldiers would fight only as long as they were paid well.

☆496 **mercurial**
[mə:rkjúəriəl]

adj. highly changeable; erratic; mutable; flighty

SYN changeable, erratic, mutable, volatile

Of a _____ temperament, she could be happy and enthusiastic one moment and depressed the next.

☆497 **merger**
[mə́:rdʒər]

n. the combination or joining of two separate units into one

SYN combination, union, joining

A _____ between the two big companies would make one giant corporation.

☆498 **methodical**
[məθάdikəl]

adj. working or proceeding in an organized, systematic manner

SYN systematic, orderly, painstaking

Cautious and _____ in her work, the inspector made sure that every part of the building was safe.

☆499 **meticulous**
[mətíkjələs]

adj. extremely careful about detail or adherence to rules

SYN painstaking, precise, thorough

The king's portrait was painted with such _____ care that one could see every detail in his clothing.

☆500 **mirth**
[mə:rθ]

n. amusement or rejoicing, especially when in the company of others

SYN merriment, jollity, amusement

The restaurant was a scene of _____ and singing when the wedding guests arrived.

☆501 **misanthrope**
[mísənθròup]

n. someone who dislikes other people; an ill-tempered, anti-social person

SYN grump, curmudgeon

A _____, our neighbor kept to himself and had no friends.

☆502 **miser**
[máizər]

n. a stingy person, unwilling to spend money at all

SYN cheapskate, skinflint, tightwad

The old _____ was reluctant to spend a penny more than necessary on anything.

☆503 **miserly**
[máizərli]

adj. highly unwilling to spend money; frugal to an extreme

SYN cheap, stingy, parsimonious, penny-pinching

Though wealthy, he was also so _____ that he would not pay to heat his home in winter.

☆504 **misnomer**
[misnóumər]

n. a misapplied or inappropriate name; a misnamed object

SYN misnaming

It was a _____ to call the Pacific Ocean "pacific" because it is not always peaceful.

DAY 17

SCAFFOLDING

499 꼼꼼한, 작은 일에 신경을 쓰는

500 즐거운 웃음 소리, 환희, 유쾌한 법석

501 인간을 혐오하는 사람, 염세가

502 구두쇠, 자린 고비

503 인색한, 욕심 많은

504 오칭(誤稱), 오기(誤記)

왕의 초상화는 매우 꼼꼼하게meticulous 그려졌기 때문에 누구나 그의 옷을 아주 자세히 볼 수 있었다.

그 식당은 결혼식 하객들이 도착했을 때 즐거운 웃음소리mirth와 노랫소리가 가득한 장면이었다.

우리 이웃인 한 염세가misanthrope는 혼자 지냈으며 친구가 하나도 없었다.

그 늙은 구두쇠miser는 어느 것에든지 필요 이상의 1페니라도 더 지불하는 것을 꺼렸다.

그는 비록 부유했지만 인색했기miserly 때문에 겨울에 집의 난방을 위한 비용을 쓰지 않으려고 했다.

태평양을 '태평'이라고 부르는 것은 오칭misnomer이었다. 왜냐하면 그것이 항상 태평한 것은 아니기 때문이다.

☆505 **mitigate**
[mítəgèit]

v. to reduce in severity, difficulty, or intensity

SYN alleviate, lessen, reduce, relieve, moderate

Having our own farm helped us to _____ the effects of the economic depression.

☆506 **modest**
[mádist]

adj. limited in extent or size; consistent with accepted standards of decency in dress or style; humble and self-effacing

SYN moderate, decent, humble, small, limited

The war hero was _____ about his achievements and thought he had done nothing outstanding.

☆507 **mollify**
[málifài]

v. to reduce in severity; to alleviate or mitigate; to pacify or appease

SYN appease, pacify, alleviate, soften, mitigate

The athlete's success in sports _____ his father's anger over his mediocre grades in school.

☆508 **monarch**
[mánərk]

n. the head of government in a monarchy; usually, a king or queen

SYN king, queen, ruler

As _____, the king was the highest civil authority in the country.

☆509 **monotonous**
[mənátənəs]

adj. lacking diversity or variety; boringly unvarying

SYN boring, tedious, unvarying

Playing the same songs over and over became _____ for the musicians.

☆510 **morose**
[məróus]

adj. very sad; depressed

SYN sad, glum, unhappy, depressed

A _____ man, he never laughed and very rarely even smiled.

SYNONYMS WORDS THAT MEAN THE SAME THING

481 To introduce some **levity** to his speech, he told a joke about his first day on the job.

ⓐ gravity
ⓑ bulk
ⓒ lightness
ⓓ austerity

482 The odors of a delicious meal **lingered** after the food itself was eaten.

ⓐ left
ⓑ remained
ⓒ hurried
ⓓ ended

483 Everyone felt so **listless** because of the hot weather that no one did any work.

ⓐ energetic
ⓑ interested
ⓒ languid
ⓓ industrious

484 The gymnast's **lithe** body seemed capable of endless supple movements.

ⓐ attentive
ⓑ impregnable
ⓒ flexible
ⓓ rigid

485 The king built a **lofty** castle in the mountains and spent his summers there.

ⓐ low
ⓑ towering
ⓒ base
ⓓ humble

486 The physicist wrote such a **lucid** description of his theory that anyone could understand it.

ⓐ muddled
ⓑ terse
ⓒ extended
ⓓ clear

487 The company offered a high salary as a **lure** to attract the professor away from his university job.

ⓐ repulsion
ⓑ rejection
ⓒ enticement
ⓓ levity

488 Newspapers printed all the **lurid** details of the scandal on their front pages.

ⓐ pleasant
ⓑ mild
ⓒ drab
ⓓ shocking

489 **Luxuriant** plants completely covered the ground.

ⓐ sparse
ⓑ lush
ⓒ leafy
ⓓ spotted

490 She felt such **malice** toward her neighbors that she never said a kind word about them.

ⓐ insularity
ⓑ longevity
ⓒ malevolence
ⓓ affection

DAY 17

145

491 **Malicious** motives led one employee to spread harmful rumors about another.

ⓐ kind

ⓑ conceited

ⓒ ludicrous

ⓓ vicious

492 Though **marred** slightly by gunfire during the war, the building remained beautiful.

ⓐ contrived

ⓑ enhanced

ⓒ defaced

ⓓ restored

493 The poor soil and dry climate here let farms produce only **meager** amounts of food.

ⓐ abundant

ⓑ nutritional

ⓒ stagnant

ⓓ scanty

494 The river **meandered** back and forth across the plain in long bends.

ⓐ marched

ⓑ trampled

ⓒ wandered

ⓓ strode

495 The **mercenary** soldiers would fight only as long as they were paid well.

ⓐ hireling

ⓑ fallow

ⓒ contrite

ⓓ tranquil

496 Of a **mercurial** temperament, she could be happy and enthusiastic one moment and depressed the next.

ⓐ gradual

ⓑ fallacious

ⓒ esoteric

ⓓ volatile

497 A **merger** between the two big companies would make one giant corporation.

ⓐ combination

ⓑ lure

ⓒ knack

ⓓ separation

498 Cautious and **methodical** in her work, the inspector made sure that every part of the building was safe.

ⓐ haphazard

ⓑ practical

ⓒ systematic

ⓓ ambitious

499 The king's portrait was painted with such **meticulous** care that one could see every detail in his clothing.

ⓐ careless

ⓑ impertinent

ⓒ resounding

ⓓ painstaking

500 The restaurant was a scene of **mirth** and singing when the wedding guests arrived.

ⓐ longevity

ⓑ jollity

ⓒ melancholy

ⓓ strife

501 A misanthrope, our neighbor kept to himself and had no friends.

ⓐ optimist
ⓑ drone
ⓒ stalemate
ⓓ grump

502 The old miser was reluctant to spend a penny more than necessary on anything.

ⓐ prodigal
ⓑ tightwad
ⓒ profligate
ⓓ wastrel

503 Though wealthy, he was also so miserly that he would not pay to heat his home in winter.

ⓐ charitable
ⓑ absentminded
ⓒ inured
ⓓ stingy

504 It was a misnomer to call the Pacific Ocean "pacific" because it is not always peaceful.

ⓐ exploitation
ⓑ misnaming
ⓒ duplicity
ⓓ contempt

505 Having our own farm helped us to mitigate the effects of the economic depression.

ⓐ intensify
ⓑ substantiate
ⓒ alleviate
ⓓ complement

506 The war hero was modest about his achievements and thought he had done nothing outstanding.

ⓐ extravagant
ⓑ lithe
ⓒ humble
ⓓ excessive

507 The athlete's success in sports mollified his father's anger over his mediocre grades in school.

ⓐ provoked
ⓑ softened
ⓒ ruffled
ⓓ traumatized

508 As monarch, the king was the highest civil authority in the country.

ⓐ serf
ⓑ subject
ⓒ ruler
ⓓ knight

509 Playing the same songs over and over became monotonous for the musicians.

ⓐ exciting
ⓑ tedious
ⓒ timely
ⓓ stimulating

510 A morose man, he never laughed and very rarely even smiled.

ⓐ blithe
ⓑ jovial
ⓒ seasonable
ⓓ glum

DAY 17

Answers

481-485 ⓒⓑⓒⓒⓑ	496-500 ⓓⓐⓒⓓⓑ
486-490 ⓓⓒⓓⓑⓒ	501-505 ⓓⓑⓓⓑⓒ
491-495 ⓓⓒⓓⓒⓐ	506-510 ⓒⓑⓒⓑⓓ

DAY 18

☆511 **mosaic**
[mouzéiik]

n. a pattern, design, or picture produced by assembling small pieces of stone or glass

SYN design, pattern, assemblage

The Romans commonly used _____ to decorate the floors of their homes.

☆512 **motive**
[móutiv]

n. the wish, urge, or emotion that makes a person do something

SYN urge, desire, wish, aim, goal, cause, incitement, inducement

The criminal's _____ for robbing the museum was a desire to have a famous painting in his home.

☆513 **mundane**
[mʌ́ndein]

adj. ordinary; not exceptional or special in any way

SYN ordinary, everyday, usual, unexceptional, plain

These tools were meant for _____ uses such as cooking food or grinding grain.

☆514 **munificent**
[mju:nífəsənt]

adj. generous; open-handed; lavish; free; the opposite of stingy or miserly

SYN generous, liberal, bountiful, lavish

Under the auspices of a _____ sovereign, this house was built for John Duke.

☆515 **nefarious**
[nifɛ́əriəs]

adj. evil in character or intent

SYN evil, vile, infamous

The outlaw was known for _____ deeds such as robbing banks and stealing horses.

☆516 **negate**
[nigéit]

v. to counteract or nullify; to make something nonexistent or ineffective

SYN nullify, counteract, neutralize, deny

This computer uses special software to _____ the effects of electronic interference.

SCAFFOLDING

511 모자이크 | 로마 사람들은 집의 바닥을 장식하기 위해서 흔히 모자이크mosaics를 사용했다.

512 동기, 동인, 목적 | 범죄자가 그 박물관을 털었던 동기motive는 자신의 집에 유명한 그림을 두고 싶은 욕구였다.

513 평범한, 현세의, 우주의 | 이 도구들은 음식을 요리하거나 곡식을 찧는 등의 평범한mundane 용도를 위한 것이었다.

514 인심 좋은, 후한 | 관대한munificent 통치자의 후원 하에 이 집은 죤 듀크를 위해 지어졌다.

515 극악한, 불법적인 | 그 상습범은 은행을 털거나 말을 훔치는 등의 불법적인nefarious 행동들을 한다고 알려져 있다.

516 무효로 하다, 취소하다, 부정하다 | 이 컴퓨터는 전자 방해의 효과를 없애기negate 위한 특별한 소프트웨어를 사용한다.

☆517 **negligence**
[néɡlidʒəns]

n. failure to carry out responsibilities or to show appropriate concern
SYN neglect, carelessness

The court found that the company's _____ had caused the release of pollutants.

☆518 **newfangled**
[njúːfǽŋɡəld]

adj. new; innovative; recently introduced; often considered a slang expression
SYN new, fresh, innovative

The farmer looked up and saw one of those _____ flying machines overhead.

☆519 **nimble**
[nímbəl]

adj. able to move quickly and easily
SYN agile, lively, quick, sprightly, spry, adroit, deft

She was extremely _____ on her feet.

☆520 **nonchalant**
[nànʃəláːnt]

adj. apparent unconcern or indifference
SYN casual, unconcerned, indifferent, cool

The king appeared _____ about his people's suffering and did nothing to help them.

☆521 **nostalgia**
[nɑstǽldʒiə]

n. homesickness; a longing to return to past times
SYN homesickness

It is common for adults to feel _____ about their childhood, when they think life was happier.

☆522 **notoriety**
[nòutəráiəti:]

n. an extremely bad reputation
SYN infamy, disrepute

Despite his _____ as a robber, the outlaw was courteous and well-mannered in everyday life.

DAY 18

SCAFFOLDING

517 태만, 무관심 법정은 그 회사의 태만negligence이 오염물질의 방출을 야기시켰다는 것을 알아냈다.
518 신형의, 최신의 그 농부는 머리 위로 그 신형newfangled 비행기들 중 하나를 올려다 보았다.
519 재빠른, 민첩한 그녀는 다리를 매우 민첩하게nimble 움직였다.
520 태연한, 무관심한 왕은 자기 백성들의 고통에 대해 무관심해nonchalant 보였고 그들을 돕기 위한 어떤 것도 하지 않았다.
521 향수, 옛날을 그리워함 어른들이 어린 시절에 대해 향수nostalgia를 느끼는 것은 흔한 일이다. 그들은 그 시절이 더 행복했었다고 생각한다.
522 악명, 악평 그 상습범은 강도로서의 악명notoriety에도 불구하고 일상의 삶에서는 예의가 바르고 점잖았다.

149

☆523 **novel**
[návəl]

adj. not like anything known before; new and perhaps clever; original
SYN fresh, new, innovative

In her novel, the author took a _____ look at nineteenth-century history.

☆524 **novelty**
[návəlti]

n. newness, originality, or innovation, or something that displays those qualities; a small, inexpensive manufactured product intended to amuse people
SYN newness, originality

The _____ of the idea interested people who were tired of old, familiar things.

☆525 **novice**
[návis]

n. someone who has just arrived or is starting to learn or to do something
SYN beginner, newcomer

Starting as a _____ in his craft, he learned quickly, and soon he was a skilled craftsman.

☆526 **nuance**
[njú:ɑːns]

n. a subtle difference in meaning
SYN shade, hue, dimension, aspect

The word she chose to use gave her sentence a _____ of anger and impatience.

☆527 **nullify**
[nʌ́ləfài]

v. to reduce to zero or nothingness; to cancel or neutralize in degree, effect, or influence
SYN negate, cancel, neutralize

To _____ noise from outside, the room had a computerized system that canceled sound.

☆528 **nurture**
[nə́ːrtʃər]

v. to protect and encourage development, especially during the early stages of growth
SYN encourage, feed, protect, support

The university's English Department _____ the early careers of several famous writers.

☆529 **oasis**
[ouéisis]

n. a place of refuge, rest, support, and refreshment; a place in the desert where water may be had

SYN haven, refuge

The library was an _____ of calm in the midst of the noisy city.

☆530 **obdurate**
[ábdʒurit]

adj. very resistant or difficult to work with

SYN hard, tough, resistant, stubborn

Granite is a much more _____ stone than marble and is harder to carve.

☆531 **objective**
[əbdʒéktiv]

adj. not biased or prejudiced

SYN impartial, unbiased

We called in a consultant from outside our company to provide an _____ evaluation of our work.

☆532 **objective**
[əbdʒéktiv]

n. a goal or purpose for doing something

SYN aim, goal, mission, purpose

The _____ of our study was to find out how many fish were left in the river.

☆533 **obliterate**
[əblítərèit]

v. to remove or erase completely; to destroy without leaving a trace

SYN erase, delete, remove, destroy, annihilate

An attack from the air _____ the enemy's positions in this area.

☆534 **oblivion**
[əblíviən]

n. a condition of not existing or not being recognized; complete forgetfulness or unawareness

SYN nonexistence, obscurity, forgetfulness

After his business failed, he spent a few years in _____ before he started another company.

DAY 18

529 오아시스, 휴식처, 피난처   도서관은 시끄러운 도시 가운데 있는 고요한 휴식처oasis였다.
530 완고한, 고집 센, 완강한   화강암은 대리석보다 더 단단한obdurate 암석이며, 조각하기가 더 힘들다.
531 객관적인, 편견이 없는   우리는 우리의 작업에 대해 객관적objective 평가를 제공하기 위해 회사 밖에서 고문을 초빙했다.
532 목적, 목표   우리 연구의 목표objective는 강에 얼마나 많은 물고기가 남아있는지를 알아내는 것이다.
533 지우다, 말살하다   공중 공격은 이 지역에 있는 적의 소재지의 흔적을 없애버렸다obliterated.
534 망각, 건망   그의 사업이 실패한 이후, 그는 새로운 회사를 시작하기 전에 수년을 망각oblivion 속에 살았다.

☆535 **obscure**
[əbskjúər]

adj. difficult to see, locate, or discern; not widely known; concealed
SYN hidden, unknown, unseen, uncertain, hard to find or detect

She was just another _____ writer before her work was rediscovered and she became famous.

☆536 **obstinate**
[ábstənit]

adj. uncooperative; hard to work with, move, or manipulate
SYN stubborn, recalcitrant, unyielding, uncooperative

An _____ animal, the mule stopped and refused to move any farther.

☆537 **odious**
[óudiəs]

adj. extremely disagreeable and disliked; hated and despised
SYN vile, despicable, loathsome, hateful, detestable

The dictator was hated because he used even the most _____ methods to keep himself in power.

☆538 **ominous**
[ámənəs]

adj. in the character of a warning; strongly indicative of danger or ultimate failure
SYN sinister, foreboding, unfavorable, discouraging

An _____ black cloud told us that a dangerous storm was approaching.

☆539 **opacity**
[oupǽsəti]

n. inability to transmit light or other radiation; obscurity, cloudiness, vagueness, or incomprehensibility
SYN cloudiness, darkness, obscurity, murkiness, turbidity

The _____ of this writer's prose prevents anyone from understanding what he writes.

☆540 **opaque**
[oupéik]

adj. unclear or obscure; impervious to light or other radiation; difficult to interpret or understand
SYN cloudy, dark, obscure, unclear

This glass is _____, so one cannot see through it.

SCAFFOLDING

535 어두운, 눈에 띄지 않는, 불명확한   그녀의 작품이 재발견되고 유명해지기 전까지 그녀는 단지 무명obscure작가에 불과했다.
536 고집 센, 완고한, 끈질긴   고집 센obstinate 동물인 노새는 멈춰 서서 더 이상 움직이는 것을 거부했다.
537 싫은, 혐오스러운   그 독재자는 권력을 유지하기 위해 심지어 가장 혐오스러운odious 방법을 사용했기 때문에 미움받았다.
538 불길한, 나쁜 징조의   위험한 폭풍이 근접하고 있음을 불길한ominous 검은 구름이 일러주었다.
539 불투명, 통하지 않음   이 작가의 불명료한opacity 신문은 그가 무엇을 썼는지 아무도 이해하지 못하도록 했다.
540 불투명한, 광택이 없는, 우둔한   이 유리는 불투명해서opaque, 누구도 이것을 통해 볼 수 없다.

152

SYNONYMS WORDS THAT MEAN THE SAME THING

511 The Romans commonly used **mosaics** to decorate the floors of their homes.

   ⓐ mobiles

   ⓑ visions

   ⓒ assemblages

   ⓓ paintings

512 The criminal's **motive** for robbing the museum was a desire to have a famous painting in his home.

   ⓐ inducement

   ⓑ discouragement

   ⓒ hindrance

   ⓓ handicap

513 These tools were meant for **mundane** uses such as cooking food or grinding grain.

   ⓐ divine

   ⓑ ordinary

   ⓒ jocular

   ⓓ cautious

514 Under the auspices of a **munificent** sovereign, this house was built for John Duke.

   ⓐ prosaic

   ⓑ selfish

   ⓒ generous

   ⓓ miserly

515 The outlaw was known for **nefarious** deeds such as robbing banks and stealing horses.

   ⓐ vile

   ⓑ famous

   ⓒ hidden

   ⓓ throbbing

516 This computer uses special software to **negate** the effects of electronic interference.

   ⓐ ignore

   ⓑ reprimand

   ⓒ nullify

   ⓓ renew

517 The court found that the company's **negligence** had caused the release of pollutants.

   ⓐ assiduity

   ⓑ constancy

   ⓒ persistence

   ⓓ carelessness

518 The farmer looked up and saw one of those **newfangled** flying machines overhead.

   ⓐ esoteric

   ⓑ opaque

   ⓒ innovative

   ⓓ precarious

519 She was extremely **nimble** on her feet.

   ⓐ clumsy

   ⓑ lethargic

   ⓒ spry

   ⓓ swift

520 The king appeared **nonchalant** about his people's suffering and did nothing to help them.

   ⓐ tense

   ⓑ involved

   ⓒ pensive

   ⓓ unconcerned

DAY 18

521 It is common for adults to feel nostalgia about their childhood, when they think life was happier.

ⓐ homesickness
ⓑ utopia
ⓒ ideality
ⓓ paradigm

522 Despite his notoriety as a robber, the outlaw was courteous and well-mannered in everyday life.

ⓐ honor
ⓑ disrepute
ⓒ remission
ⓓ homage

523 In her novel, the author took a novel look at nineteenth-century history.

ⓐ cacophonous
ⓑ elaborate
ⓒ ornate
ⓓ innovative

524 The novelty of the idea interested people who were tired of old, familiar things.

ⓐ malice
ⓑ reprehensibility
ⓒ originality
ⓓ vitality

525 Starting as a novice in his craft, he learned quickly, and soon he was a skilled craftsman.

ⓐ pacifist
ⓑ pariah
ⓒ newcomer
ⓓ monarch

526 The word she chose to use gave her sentence a nuance of anger and impatience.

ⓐ shade
ⓑ assertion
ⓒ remembrance
ⓓ distortion

527 To nullify noise from outside, the room had a computerized system that canceled sound.

ⓐ reprimand
ⓑ reform
ⓒ neutralize
ⓓ repulse

528 The university's English Department nurtured the early careers of several famous writers.

ⓐ supported
ⓑ disdained
ⓒ marred
ⓓ aggravated

529 The library was an oasis of calm in the midst of the noisy city.

ⓐ haven
ⓑ wasteland
ⓒ embassy
ⓓ dune

530 Granite is a much more obdurate stone than marble and is harder to carve.

ⓐ resistant
ⓑ munificent
ⓒ volatile
ⓓ insipid

531 We called in a consultant from outside our company to provide an **objective** evaluation of our work.

ⓐ unprejudiced

ⓑ vociferous

ⓒ feeble

ⓓ subjective

532 The **objective** of our study was to find out how many fish were left in the river.

ⓐ disinclination

ⓑ sloth

ⓒ volition

ⓓ goal

533 An attack from the air **obliterated** the enemy's positions in this area.

ⓐ wrenched

ⓑ squeezed

ⓒ destroyed

ⓓ preserved

534 After his business failed, he spent a few years in **oblivion** before he started another company.

ⓐ discord

ⓑ obscurity

ⓒ fame

ⓓ alertness

535 She was just another **obscure** writer before her work was rediscovered and she became famous.

ⓐ lurid

ⓑ diffuse

ⓒ unknown

ⓓ laughable

536 An **obstinate** animal, the mule stopped and refused to move any farther.

ⓐ recalcitrant

ⓑ cooperative

ⓒ illicit

ⓓ annoying

537 The dictator was hated because he used even the most **odious** methods to keep himself in power.

ⓐ explicit

ⓑ loathsome

ⓒ exacting

ⓓ appealing

538 An **ominous** black cloud told us that a dangerous storm was approaching.

ⓐ foreboding

ⓑ lucid

ⓒ infamous

ⓓ auspicious

539 The **opacity** of this writer's prose prevents anyone from understanding what he writes.

ⓐ clearness

ⓑ potential

ⓒ cloudiness

ⓓ flatness

540 This glass is **opaque**, so one cannot see through it.

ⓐ fuzzy

ⓑ plain

ⓒ threadbare

ⓓ obscure

Answers

511-515 ⓒⓐⓑⓒⓐ	526-530 ⓐⓒⓐⓐⓐ
516-520 ⓒⓓⓒⓒⓓ	531-535 ⓐⓓⓒⓑⓒ
521-525 ⓐⓑⓓⓒⓒ	536-540 ⓐⓑⓐⓒⓓ

DAY 19

☆541 **opposition**
[àpəzíʃən]

n. the act of opposing or resisting
SYN antagonism, hostility, resistance

Our plan encountered strong _____ from other people in the community, but we proceeded anyway.

☆542 **optimism**
[áptəmìzəm]

n. a tendency to expect a favorable outcome
SYN confidence, hopefulness

Her natural _____ led her to think she would be successful in business.

☆543 **optimist**
[áptəmist]

n. someone who tends to expect a favorable outcome or view everything in a positive context
SYN Pollyanna, Little Mary Sunshine (slang expressions)

An _____ by nature, my father thought everything would turn out for the best.

☆544 **opulence**
[ápjuləns]

n. great wealth; affluence; prosperity
SYN affluence, wealth

The size and elegance of the palace showed the _____ of the royal family's lifestyle.

☆545 **orator**
[ɔ́(ː)rətər]

n. someone who delivers speeches in public
SYN speaker, speechmaker

One of Rome's great _____ complained about the morals of people during his time.

☆546 **ornate**
[ɔːrnéit]

adj. embellished to an extreme; elaborately decorated
SYN elaborate, embellished

The door was decorated with _____ carvings.

SCAFFOLDING

541 반대, 대립, 적대   우리의 계획은 공동체 내의 다른 사람들로부터 강한 반대opposition에 직면했지만, 우리는 계속 진척시켰다.
542 낙천주의, 낙관, 무사태평   그녀의 천성적인 낙천주의optimism는 그녀가 사업에서 성공할 것이라는 생각으로 이어졌다.
543 낙천주의자   천성적으로 낙천주의자인optimist 아버지는 모든 것이 최상으로 될 것이라 생각했다.
544 풍부, 부유   궁전의 크기와 우아함은 왕실 가족의 생활방식의 풍요로움opulence을 보여주었다.
545 연설자, 웅변가   로마의 최고 웅변가orators 중 한 명이 당시대의 사람들의 도덕상을 한탄했다.
546 잘 꾸민, 화려한   그 문은 화려한ornate 조각으로 장식돼 있었다.

156

☆547	**orthodox** [ɔ́ːrθədὰks]	*adj.* correct; right; approved; done according to custom or tradition **SYN** correct, approved, customary, traditional *We used the _____ method of solving this problem because we knew it would work.*

☆547 **orthodox** [ɔ́ːrθədὰks]
adj. correct; right; approved; done according to custom or tradition
SYN correct, approved, customary, traditional

We used the _____ method of solving this problem because we knew it would work.

☆548 **ostentatious** [ὰstentéiʃəs]
adj. done for show or to impress others; outstanding in a garish, loud, or tasteless way
SYN grandiose, showy

Automobiles in the 1950s had _____ features such as big tail fins.

☆549 **pacifist** [pǽsəfist]
n. someone who favors and works for peace and is opposed to war
SYN conscientious objector, passive resister

_____ may find themselves unpopular in times of war.

☆550 **palatable** [pǽlətəbəl]
adj. having a pleasant or acceptable taste
SYN appetizing, delectable, luscious, mouth-watering, agreeable

Some of the dialogue has been changed to make it more _____ to an American audience.

☆551 **paltry** [pɔ́ːltri]
adj. very small in extent, number, or degree; unimportant in the extreme
SYN insignificant, mere, trivial

The man's pocket held a single _____ dollar.

☆552 **paradigm** [pǽrədὰim]
n. something that is worth imitating or following; a model to be followed
SYN example, model, pattern, standard

When the old model of the solar system could no longer be used, a new _____ was needed.

☆553 **pariah**
[pəráiə]

n. someone cast out and rejected by the rest of society

SYN outcast, undesirable

His unethical conduct made him a _____ in his profession, and he lost his license to practice.

☆554 **parody**
[pǽrədi]

n. a mocking or satirical imitation of another work, such as a novel or motion picture

SYN mockery, satire, spoof, takeoff

This humor magazine specializes in _____ of motion pictures and television shows.

☆555 **parsimony**
[pá:rsəmòuni]

n. extreme thrift; stinginess; unwillingness to spend or give money

SYN stinginess, tight-fistedness

The old miser's _____ made him reluctant to spend even a few cents for a newspaper.

☆556 **partisan**
[pá:rtəzən]

n. an enthusiastic supporter of a particular party, group, plan, etc.

SYN backer, defender, supporter

The policy had a strong and articulate group of _____ who promoted it with vigor.

☆557 **paucity**
[pó:səti]

n. a deficiency, insufficiency, or scarcity of something; a short supply

SYN dearth, lack, shortage

In English, the word "orange" has a _____ of one-word rhymes.

☆558 **peculiar**
[pikjú:ljər]

adj. strange; odd

SYN characteristic, distinctive, idiosyncratic, unique

There is something _____ about him.

553 천민, 추방당한 사람, 부랑자   그의 비윤리적 행동으로 하여금 그는 직업에서 추방당했고pariah, 그는 개업자격증을 상실했다.

554 모방, 흉내   이 유머 잡지는 영화와 TV쇼의 모방parodies을 전문으로 하고 있다.

555 인색, 극도의 절약   늙은 구두쇠의 인색함parsimony은 신문에 몇 센트 쓰는 것도 주저하게 만들었다.

556 열성적 지지자, 당파심이 강한 사람   그 정책을 활기차게 지지했던 강력하고 명백한 당원들partisans의 무리가 있었다.

557 소수, 소량, 결핍   영어로 "오렌지"라는 단어는 한 단어 압운이 없다paucity.

558 독특한, 기교한, 특별한   그는 어딘가 특이한peculiar 구석이 있다.

☆559 **pedestrian**
[pədéstriən]

n. someone who travels on foot rather than in a vehicle, especially in the city

SYN walker, hiker

_____ *have the right of way over automobiles in a crosswalk.*

☆560 **pedestrian**
[pədéstriən]

adj. lackluster; commonplace; lacking in interest or color

SYN everyday, banal, commonplace

The author wrote such _____ prose that people found his work boring.

☆561 **penury**
[pénjuri]

n. poverty; a lack of money

SYN poverty, destitution, indigence

The loss of a worker's job can cast a whole family into _____ .

☆562 **perfunctory**
[pəːrfʌ́ŋktəri]

adj. done automatically, indifferently, or unconcernedly

SYN careless, uninterested, indifferent, superficial

Critics gave the book only short, _____ reviews, so it did not get much attention.

☆563 **peripheral**
[pərífərəl]

adj. on the extreme boundary or fringe of something; not of principal interest or importance

SYN incidental, marginal, outermost

Arteries carry blood from the heart to the _____ parts of the body.

☆564 **pernicious**
[pəːrníʃəs]

adj. capable of doing great harm

SYN destructive, harmful, hurtful

Some say Western culture has had a _____ influence on Asia by encouraging crime and decadence.

☆565 **perpetuate**
[pə(:)rpétʃuèit]

v. to keep in operation or existence; to extend the lifetime of something

SYN continue, maintain, preserve, prolong

The university's policy is to _____ the goals and ideals of its founder.

☆566 **pervasive**
[pərvéisiv]

adj. present everywhere; spread throughout

SYN common, extensive, widespread

A _____ aroma of olive oil and spices gave the restaurant a delightful atmosphere.

☆567 **pessimism**
[pésəmìzəm]

n. a tendency to expect the worst possible result

SYN gloom, negativity

His _____ led him to prepare for failure even as everyone else expected to succeed.

☆568 **phenomena**
[finámənə]

n. all things that happen and can be observed

SYN events, happenings, occurrences

Some _____ are so rare that they occur only once in a hundred years.

☆569 **philanthropist**
[filǽnθrəpist]

n. someone who gives money to help improve society or advance the arts and sciences

SYN donor, contributor, supporter, patron, backer

With the support of a _____ who loved music, the orchestra toured the world.

☆570 **philanthropy**
[filǽnθrəpi]

n. charitable contributions; financial support from individuals for worthy causes

SYN donations, contributions, support, patronage, backing

The foundation focused its _____ on cultivating promising writers and artists.

SCAFFOLDING

565 영속시키다
대학의 정책은 설립자의 목표와 이상들을 영속시키는 것을perpetuate 목표로 한다.

566 퍼지는, 널리 스미는, 스며드는
널리 퍼지는pervasive 올리브유와 향신료의 향은 식당을 유쾌한 분위기로 만들었다.

567 비관, 염세관
그의 염세주의pessimism는 그로 하여금. 다른 모든 이들이 성공을 기대하는 와중에도 실패에 준비하게끔 했다.

568 현상, 사건
어떤 현상들phenomena은 매우 희귀해서 백년에 오직 한 번씩 발생한다.

569 박애가, 자선가
음악을 사랑했던 박애주의자philanthropist의 지지로. 그 오케스트라는 세계를 순회했다.

570 박애, 인자, 자선행위
그 재단은 자선행위philanthropy를 유망한 작가와 예술가들을 발굴하는데 집중했다.

SYNONYMS WORDS THAT MEAN THE SAME THING

541 Our plan encountered strong **opposition** from other people in the community, but we proceeded anyway.

ⓐ degradation

ⓑ hostility

ⓒ support

ⓓ ally

542 Her natural **optimism** led her to think she would be successful in business.

ⓐ cynicism

ⓑ hopefulness

ⓒ regard

ⓓ suspicion

543 An **optimist** by nature, my father thought everything would turn out for the best.

ⓐ green hand

ⓑ Mr. Right

ⓒ Little Mary Sunshine

ⓓ red herring

544 The size and elegance of the palace showed the **opulence** of the royal family's lifestyle.

ⓐ scarcity

ⓑ poverty

ⓒ wealth

ⓓ plainness

545 One of Rome's great **orators** complained about the morals of people during his time.

ⓐ citizens

ⓑ speakers

ⓒ villains

ⓓ churls

546 The door was decorated with **ornate** carvings.

ⓐ industrial

ⓑ stale

ⓒ elaborate

ⓓ spartan

547 We used the **orthodox** method of solving this problem because we knew it would work.

ⓐ radical

ⓑ liberal

ⓒ customary

ⓓ playful

548 Automobiles in the 1950s had **ostentatious** features such as big tail fins.

ⓐ obscure

ⓑ boisterous

ⓒ voluminous

ⓓ showy

549 **Pacifists** may find themselves unpopular in times of war.

ⓐ philanthropists

ⓑ outcasts

ⓒ novices

ⓓ conscientious objector

550 Some of the dialogue has been changed to make it more **palatable** to an American audience.

ⓐ repulsive

ⓑ understandable

ⓒ agreeable

ⓓ throbbing

551 The man's pocket held a single **paltry** dollar.

ⓐ moral

ⓑ cognizant

ⓒ insignificant

ⓓ shabby

552 When the old model of the solar system could no longer be used, a new **paradigm** was needed.

ⓐ pattern

ⓑ sample

ⓒ instance

ⓓ segment

553 His unethical conduct made him a **pariah** in his profession, and he lost his license to practice.

ⓐ refugee

ⓑ immigrant

ⓒ outcast

ⓓ alien

554 This humor magazine specializes in **parodies** of motion pictures and television shows.

ⓐ admiration

ⓑ esteem

ⓒ mockeries

ⓓ praises

555 The old miser's **parsimony** made him reluctant to spend even a few cents for a newspaper.

ⓐ elation

ⓑ extravagance

ⓒ tight-fistedness

ⓓ waste

556 The policy had a strong and articulate group of **partisans** who promoted it with vigor.

ⓐ antagonists

ⓑ churls

ⓒ backers

ⓓ pedestrians

557 In English, the word "orange" has a **paucity** of one-word rhymes.

ⓐ surplus

ⓑ balance

ⓒ shortage

ⓓ glut

558 There is something **peculiar** about him.

ⓐ mercurial

ⓑ grum

ⓒ strange

ⓓ average

559 **Pedestrians** have the right of way over automobiles in a crosswalk.

ⓐ hiker

ⓑ walkers

ⓒ recalcitrant

ⓓ man on the street

560 The author wrote such **pedestrian** prose that people found his work boring.

ⓐ banal

ⓑ detrimental

ⓒ novel

ⓓ expansive

561 The loss of a worker's job can cast a whole family into **penury**.

ⓐ surfeit

ⓑ poverty

ⓒ abundance

ⓓ profusion

562 Critics gave the book only short, **perfunctory** reviews, so it did not get much attention.

ⓐ conjectural

ⓑ peevish

ⓒ superficial

ⓓ parsimonious

563 Arteries carry blood from the heart to the **peripheral** parts of the body.

   ⓐ central

   ⓑ major

   ⓒ frivolous

   ⓓ incidental

564 Some say Western culture has had a **pernicious** influence on Asia by encouraging crime and decadence.

   ⓐ harmful

   ⓑ healthful

   ⓒ overt

   ⓓ propitious

565 The university's policy is to **perpetuate** the goals and ideals of its founder.

   ⓐ embody

   ⓑ lapse

   ⓒ continue

   ⓓ abolish

566 A **pervasive** aroma of olive oil and spices gave the restaurant a delightful atmosphere.

   ⓐ fuzzy

   ⓑ restricted

   ⓒ restrained

   ⓓ extensive

567 His **pessimism** led him to prepare for failure even as everyone else expected to succeed.

   ⓐ negativity

   ⓑ faith

   ⓒ trust

   ⓓ creed

568 Some **phenomena** are so rare that they occur only once in a hundred years.

   ⓐ occurrences

   ⓑ evolution

   ⓒ revamps

   ⓓ effervescence

569 With the support of a **philanthropist** who loved music, the orchestra toured the world.

   ⓐ misanthropy

   ⓑ contributor

   ⓒ prattle

   ⓓ critic

570 The foundation focused its **philanthropy** on cultivating promising writers and artists.

   ⓐ opposition

   ⓑ jabber

   ⓒ decoy

   ⓓ patronage

DAY 19

Answers

541-545 ⓑⓑⓒⓒⓑ	556-560 ⓒⓒⓒⓑⓐ
546-550 ⓒⓒⓓⓓⓒ	561-565 ⓑⓒⓓⓐⓒ
551-555 ⓒⓐⓒⓒⓒ	566-570 ⓓⓐⓐⓑⓓ

☆571 **piety**

[páiəti]

n. close attention to religious duties or beliefs

SYN devotion, religiosity

Noted for her _____, the old lady was seen at religious services every morning.

☆572 **pious**

[páiəs]

adj. devoted to religious duties or beliefs

SYN religious, reverent

A few _____ individuals continued to attend religious services despite being persecuted.

☆573 **pitfall**

[pítfɔ̀:l]

n. a hidden trap, hazard, or danger

SYN hazard, danger, trap

This business is filled with _____ for the unwary.

☆574 **pithy**

[píθi]

adj. brief, vigorous, and effective in expression

SYN terse, forceful

The book became popular because of its _____, witty observations on life and society.

☆575 **pivotal**

[pívətl]

adj. of great importance

SYN critical, vital, important

The general's decision to advance proved a _____ moment in the war.

☆576 **placate**

[pléikeit]

v. to calm, reassure, or pacify; to restore tranquillity after a crisis

SYN appease, pacify, calm

To _____ his angry wife, he brought home a bouquet of flowers.

SCAFFOLDING

571 경건, 신앙심, 충성심 | 신앙심piety으로 알려진 그녀는 매일 아침 종교예배에 모습을 드러냈다.

572 신앙심 깊은, 경건한, 종교적인 | 몇몇 독실한pious 개인들은 박해에도 불구하고 종교적 예배에 계속해서 참석했다.

573 함정, 마수, 유혹 | 이 사업은 부주의한 자들에겐 함정들pitfalls로 가득하다.

574 골이 있는, 함축성 있는, 간결한 | 이 책은 그것의 삶과 사회에 대한 함축성 있고pithy, 재치있는 관찰로 유명해졌다.

575 주축의, 중요한 | 그 장군의 전진 결정은 그 전쟁에서 중요한pivotal 순간임을 입증해주었다.

576 달래다, 화해하다 | 화난 아내를 달래기placate 위해, 그는 꽃 한다발을 집에 가져왔다.

☆577 **plausible**
[plɔ́:zəbəl]

adj. believable; credible; realistic; consistent with reality; likely to work
SYN reasonable, believable, realistic

The scientist's hypothesis provided a _____ explanation for some mysterious observations.

☆578 **polemical**
[pəlémikəl]

adj. related to, or meant to provoke, controversy; often used to describe partisan political tracts
SYN controversial, argumentative

An openly _____ work, the book tried to increase public support for social change.

☆579 **pomposity**
[pɑmpásəti]

n. a stuffy and self-important manner; bombast; exaggerated pretension
SYN bombast, self-importance

The comedian mocked the _____ of public figures.

☆580 **pompous**
[pámpəs]

adj. characterized by false dignity, pretension, or self-importance
SYN pretentious, stuffy, bombastic

Though the politician meant well, he was disliked because of his _____ manner and pretentious language.

☆581 **ponder**
[pándər]

v. to think very carefully and seriously about something
SYN contemplate, weigh, evaluate, consider

The psychologist's advice gave his clients much to _____.

☆582 **ponderous**
[pándərəs]

adj. very heavy and difficult to wield or maneuver; long, weighty, and uninteresting (used to describe an especially long and boring book, for example)
SYN heavy, weighty, massive, unwieldy, lengthy, boring

His doctoral dissertation was a _____ work more than 1,000 pages long.

DAY 20

SCAFFOLDING

577 그럴듯한, 정말 같은 　　　　　 그 과학자의 가설은 몇몇 미스터리한 관측에 그럴듯한plausible 설명을 제공한다.

578 논쟁의, 논쟁을 좋아하는 　　　　 공공연한 논쟁적인polemical 작품인 그 책은 사회 변화에 대한 대중적 지지를 높이기 위해 노력했다.

579 거만, 건방짐, 과장됨 　　　　　 그 코미디언은 공인들의 거만함pomposity을 조롱했다.

580 거만한, 건방진, 호화로운, 성대한 　 그 정치인은 호의적이었으나, 그의 거만한pompous 태도와 우쭐한 언사로 미움을 샀다.

581 숙고하다, 깊이 생각하다, 신중히 고려하다 　그 심리학자의 충고는 그의 고객들이 숙고해야 할ponder 많은 것들을 주었다.

582 대단히 무거운, 묵직한, 지루한 　　　 그의 박사논문은 1,000쪽이 넘는 방대한ponderous 작업이었다.

165

☆583 **pragmatic**
[prægmǽtik]

adj. having a practical, realistic attitude toward the world

SYN practical, realistic, effective

The prime minister had a highly _____ approach to solving problems and showed little concern for moral issues.

☆584 **prattle**
[prǽtl]

n. seemingly endless talk about unimportant matters

SYN chatter, jabber, rattling

Her ceaseless _____ about movies she had seen made her annoying as a co-worker.

☆585 **precarious**
[prikɛ́əriəs]

adj. uncertain; unstable; easily disrupted by outside influences; dependent on someone else's wishes

SYN insecure, uncertain, unstable

Our CEO's departure left our project in a _____ position because we did not know if the new CEO would favor it.

☆586 **preclude**
[priklú:d]

v. to prevent something from happening

SYN prevent, forestall, block

A lack of funding _____ our doing any research on this phenomenon.

☆587 **precocious**
[prikóuʃəs]

adj. advanced in development at an early age

SYN advanced, early, premature

A _____ child, the musician began composing symphonies at age ten.

☆588 **predator**
[prédətər]

n. a hunter, killer, or destroyer; one who hunts or preys actively upon another

SYN hunter, killer

One could tell this animal was a _____ by looking at its long, sharp teeth.

SCAFFOLDING

583 실용적인, 실제적인 　 그 수상은 문제 해결에 고도로 실제적인pragmatic 접근법을 가지고 있었지만 도덕 문제에는 거의 관심을 보이지 않았다.

584 허짤배기 소리, 실없는 소리 　 그녀가 보았던 영화에 대한 멈추지 않는 수다prattle는 직장 동료로서 그녀를 성가시게 만들었다.

585 불확실한, 믿을 수 없는, 불안정한 　 우리 CEO의 이탈로 우리의 프로젝트는 불안정한precarious 위치로 전락하였는데, 새 CEO가 이를 선호할지 모르기 때문이었다.

586 제외하다, 방해하다, 막다 　 자본의 부족은 이 현상에 대한 어떠한 연구도 못하게 하였다precluded.

587 조숙한, 어른다운 　 조숙한precocious 아이였던 그 음악가는 열살의 나이에 교향곡을 작곡하기 시작했다.

588 약탈자, 육식동물 　 이 동물은 길고, 날카로운 이빨로 봤을 때 육식동물predator이었다고 할 수 있다.

166

☆589 **predecessor**
[prédisèsər]

n. an earlier individual in a series; an ancestor; the previous occupant of an office or position

SYN ancestor, forefather, foremother

My _____ in this job was a good administrator and gave me a good model to follow.

☆590 **predicament**
[pridíkəmənt]

n. a troubling situation, difficult to resolve

SYN crisis, difficulty, dilemma

Big cuts in our budget left our department in a horrible _____.

☆591 **preposterous**
[pripástərəs]

adj. absurd in the extreme

SYN absurd, ludicrous

In the 18th century, building a bridge across the bay would have seemed a _____ proposal.

☆592 **presumptuous**
[prizΛmptʃuəs]

adj. disrespectfully or offensively bold

SYN arrogant, brash, brazen, disrespectful, rude

For his _____ behavior in class, the student got a reprimand from his teacher.

☆593 **pretentious**
[priténʃəs]

adj. done only for show; full of pretension and desire to impress others

SYN pompous, showy, ostentatious

Though the artist's early work was _____, it began to acquire substance later.

☆594 **prevalent**
[prévələnt]

adj. in widespread or common use

SYN common, widespread, extensive, usual

The _____ wind direction here is from the northwest.

DAY 20

SCAFFOLDING

589 전임자, 선배 | 이 직업의 내 선임predecessor은 훌륭한 관리자였고, 내가 따를 훌륭한 모델을 내게 남겼다.
590 곤경, 궁지 | 우리 예산에 대한 큰 삭감으로 우리 부서는 끔찍한 궁지predicament에 몰렸다.
591 앞뒤가 바뀐, 터무니없는, 어리석은 | 18세기에 만을 가로질러 다리를 건설하는 것은 어리석은preposterous 제안으로 보였을 것이다.
592 주제넘은, 뻔뻔한, 건방진 | 교실에서의 그의 건방진presumptuous 태도로, 그 학생은 선생님에게 징계를 받았다.
593 자부하는, 우쭐하는, 과장된 | 예술가의 초기 작품은 과장되었지만pretentious, 이 후에 본질을 얻기 시작했다.
594 보급된, 널리 행해지는, 유행하는, 유력한 | 이 곳의 일반적인prevalent 바람의 방향은 북서풍이다.

167

☆595 **prevaricate**
[privǽrəkèit]

n. prevarication
[privæ̀rikéiʃ(ə)n]

v. to deceive or mislead with false or evasive statements
SYN evade, misstate, mislead, lie

The ambassador's remarks were seen as _____ and an attempt to hide his country's aggression.

☆596 **primeval**
[praimí:vəl]

adj. relating or belonging to the Earth's beginnings
SYN prehistoric, primitive

Their _____ emotion and irrationality get in the way of their aspirations.

☆597 **proclaim**
[proukléim]

v. to announce in public
SYN announce, broadcast, declare

The king _____ that the following day would be a holiday.

☆598 **prodigal**
[prɑ́digəl]

adj. characterized by extravagant spending or self-indulgence; wasteful to an extreme
SYN extravagant, profligate, wasteful, lavish

The young man's _____ lifestyle left him bankrupt at the age of twenty-five.

☆599 **prodigious**
[prədídʒəs]

adj. extraordinary in some way
SYN abnormal, excessive, monstrous, prodigious, wonderful, amazing

The man's _____ strength allowed him to lift heavy loads easily.

☆600 **profane**
[prəféin]

adj. not holy, revered, or consecrated; in poor taste; worldly as opposed to religious
SYN irreverent, vulgar, secular

The ship's captain was known for his _____ language.

595 얼버무려 넘기다, 발뺌하다, 거짓말하다   대사의 발언은 거짓말prevarications과 국가의 침략을 감추기 위한 노력으로 비춰졌다.

596 초기의, 원시의, 태고의   그들의 초기primeval 감정과 불합리가 그들의 큰 뜻에 방해가 되고 있다.

597 포고하다, 선포하다, 성명하다   왕은 다음날이 휴일이 될거라고 선포했다proclaimed.

598 낭비하는, 방탕한, 아낌없이 주는   젊은 남자의 낭비하는prodigal 생활양식으로 그는 나이 스물다섯에 파산했다.

599 거대한, 막대한, 비범한, 이상한   그 남자의 비범한prodigious 힘은 무거운 짐도 쉽게 옮길 수 있게 했다.

600 모독적인, 불경스런, 이교적인   그 선박의 선장은 그의 불경스런profane 언사로 알려져 있다.

SYNONYMS WORDS THAT MEAN THE SAME THING

571 Noted for her **piety**, the old lady was seen at religious services every morning.

ⓐ delusion
ⓑ devotion
ⓒ quandary
ⓓ misconception

572 A few **pious** individuals continued to attend religious services despite being persecuted.

ⓐ stale
ⓑ religious
ⓒ forceful
ⓓ humble

573 This business is filled with **pitfalls** for the unwary.

ⓐ traps
ⓑ labyrinths
ⓒ tangles
ⓓ opportunities

574 The book became popular because of its **pithy**, witty observations on life and society.

ⓐ superficial
ⓑ rambling
ⓒ terse
ⓓ conceptual

575 The general's decision to advance proved a **pivotal** moment in the war.

ⓐ critical
ⓑ intricate
ⓒ frivolous
ⓓ minor

576 To **placate** his angry wife, he brought home a bouquet of flowers.

ⓐ innocuous
ⓑ calm
ⓒ warm
ⓓ diffuse

577 The scientist's hypothesis provided a **plausible** explanation for some mysterious observations.

ⓐ impossible
ⓑ condensed
ⓒ extensive
ⓓ reasonable

578 An openly **polemical** work, the book tried to increase public support for social change.

ⓐ profuse
ⓑ indisputable
ⓒ argumentative
ⓓ agreeable

579 The comedian mocked the **pomposity** of public figures.

ⓐ humility
ⓑ bombast
ⓒ courtesy
ⓓ submissiveness

580 Though the politician meant well, he was disliked because of his **pompous** manner and pretentious language.

ⓐ humble
ⓑ perplexing
ⓒ stuffy
ⓓ robust

DAY 20

581 The psychologist's advice gave his clients much to **ponder**.

  ⓐ undo

  ⓑ elicit

  ⓒ clarify

  ⓓ contemplate

582 His doctoral dissertation was a **ponderous** work more than 1,000 pages long.

  ⓐ attentive

  ⓑ heavy

  ⓒ light

  ⓓ absorbing

583 The prime minister had a highly **pragmatic** approach to solving problems and showed little concern for moral issues.

  ⓐ feasible

  ⓑ practical

  ⓒ noxious

  ⓓ errant

584 Her ceaseless **prattle** about movies she had seen made her annoying as a co-worker.

  ⓐ jabber

  ⓑ condolence

  ⓒ elegy

  ⓓ endurance

585 Our CEO's departure left our project in a **precarious** position because we did not know if the new CEO would favor it.

  ⓐ ephemeral

  ⓑ unstable

  ⓒ erudite

  ⓓ rotund

586 A lack of funding **precluded** our doing any research on this phenomenon.

  ⓐ forestalled

  ⓑ winced

  ⓒ redirected

  ⓓ facilitated

587 A **precocious** child, the musician began composing symphonies at age ten.

  ⓐ advanced

  ⓑ precautionary

  ⓒ vague

  ⓓ slow

588 One could tell this animal was a **predator** by looking at its long, sharp teeth.

  ⓐ pawn

  ⓑ alien

  ⓒ killer

  ⓓ vegetarian

589 My **predecessor** in this job was a good administrator and gave me a good model to follow.

  ⓐ partner

  ⓑ ancestor

  ⓒ supervisor

  ⓓ researcher

590 Big cuts in our budget left our department in a horrible **predicament**.

  ⓐ harassment

  ⓑ depravity

  ⓒ crisis

  ⓓ solution

591 In the 18th century, building a bridge across the bay would have seemed a **preposterous** proposal.

   ⓐ gargantuan

   ⓑ logical

   ⓒ ludicrous

   ⓓ coherent

592 For his **presumptuous** behavior in class, the student got a reprimand from his teacher.

   ⓐ brash

   ⓑ lucid

   ⓒ humble

   ⓓ lazy

593 Though the artist's early work was **pretentious**, it began to acquire substance later.

   ⓐ slothful

   ⓑ ostentatious

   ⓒ modest

   ⓓ sincere

594 The **prevalent** wind direction here is from the northwest.

   ⓐ usual

   ⓑ equivalent

   ⓒ tedious

   ⓓ retentive

595 The ambassador's remarks were seen as **prevarications** and an attempt to hide his country's aggression.

   ⓐ knacks

   ⓑ deceits

   ⓒ vindications

   ⓓ evasions

596 Their **primeval** emotion and irrationality get in the way of their aspirations.

   ⓐ esoteric

   ⓑ uncouth

   ⓒ illiterate

   ⓓ primitive

597 The king **proclaimed** that the following day would be a holiday.

   ⓐ undermined

   ⓑ announced

   ⓒ estimated

   ⓓ satiated

598 The young man's **prodigal** lifestyle left him bankrupt at the age of twenty-five.

   ⓐ extravagant

   ⓑ lofty

   ⓒ frugal

   ⓓ suspended

599 The man's **prodigious** strength allowed him to lift heavy loads easily.

   ⓐ monstrous

   ⓑ fickle

   ⓒ archaic

   ⓓ fallow

600 The ship's captain was known for his **profane** language.

   ⓐ lithe

   ⓑ ardent

   ⓒ ornate

   ⓓ vulgar

DAY 20

Answers

571-575 ⓑⓑⓐⓒⓐ	586-590 ⓐⓐⓒⓑⓒ
576-580 ⓑⓓⓒⓑⓒ	591-595 ⓒⓐⓑⓐⓓ
581-585 ⓓⓑⓑⓐⓑ	596-600 ⓓⓑⓐⓐⓓ

DAY 21

☆601 **profanity**
[prəfǽnəti]

n. vulgar or obscene language; curses; swearing
SYN vulgarity, obscenity, swearing

_____ and expressions of hatred may not be broadcast on television or radio.

☆602 **profligate**
[prɑ́fligit]

adj. completely immoral, dissolute, and without shame
SYN dissipated, extravagant, immoral, prodigal, wild

A weakness for alcohol led him into _____ and self-destructive behavior.

☆603 **profound**
[prəfáund]

adj. characterized by extreme depth or deep understanding
SYN deep, penetrating

The professor's lectures reflected his _____ understanding of philosophy.

☆604 **profuse**
[prəfjúːs]

adj. used or given freely and in great quantities; extremely numerous or abundant
SYN abundant, copious, excessive, extravagant, lavish

A _____ use of adjectives made the writer's prose heavy and hard to understand.

☆605 **profusion**
[prəfjúːʒən]

n. a great, extravagant, or excessive occurrence or use of something
SYN abundance, proliferation, extravagance, outpouring

Flowers grew in _____ on the hillside.

☆606 **progressive**
[prəgrésiv]

adj. liberal in character or favoring a liberal agenda; proceeding by steps or increments
SYN liberal, incremental

The _____ income tax has critics who see it as a punishment for success.

☆607 **proliferate**
[prouílfərèit]

v. to multiply, increase in number, and spread
SYN increase, multiply, reproduce, spread

After rabbits were brought to Australia, they _____ and became an ecological hazard.

☆608 **proliferation**
[prouìlfəréiʃən]

n. an increase in numbers through reproduction, division, imitation, or replication
SYN increase, multiplication, reproduction, spread

When the railroad started operating, it enabled the _____ of new towns along its route.

☆609 **prolific**
[prouílfik]

adj. able to produce large numbers of offspring or creative works; highly productive or fruitful
SYN abundant, fruitful, productive

A _____ author, he wrote more than 100 published books.

☆610 **prolong**
[prouló:ŋ]

v. to make longer; to increase in duration
SYN extend, lengthen, protract

This year, warmer weather _____ the growing season for crops by two weeks.

☆611 **propriety**
[prəpráiəti]

n. conformity to standards of correct behavior or fashion
SYN correctness, decency, modesty, rightness

Standards of _____ change slightly every few years to reflect shifts in opinion, taste, and style.

☆612 **prosaic**
[prouzéiik]

adj. ordinary; uninteresting; unremarkable
SYN boring, commonplace, everyday, ordinary, plain, unexceptional

The short story was so _____ that not even small magazines would publish it.

DAY 21

☆613 **prose**
[prouz]

n. ordinary speech or written language distinct from verse
SYN essay, story

To explain his meaning clearly, the poet shifted from verse into

_____ .

☆614 **prosperous**
[práspərəs]

adj. successful; comfortable; financially secure
SYN successful, wealthy

Hard work and good business ability made the merchant

_____ .

☆615 **protrude**
[proutrú:d]

v. to project; to thrust outward or forward
SYN bulge, project, swell

*Below the water line, a large dome _____ from the ship's
bow.*

☆616 **provincial**
[prəvínʃəl]

adj. of or pertaining to rural or provincial areas; rustic; narrowly
informed; not sophisticated or cosmopolitan
SYN rural, rustic, unsophisticated, narrow

*The family's rustic manners and _____ language concealed
their cleverness and keen understanding of human behavior.*

☆617 **provocative**
[prəvákətiv]

adj. meant to stimulate, irritate, or provoke a response
SYN irritating, stimulating

The student's _____ question made the teacher angry.

☆618 **proximity**
[prɑksíməti]

n. a degree of nearness
SYN closeness, nearness

*Its _____ to the ocean made the town prosperous through
trade by sea.*

613 산문, 단조로운 이야기　　그의 의미를 명확하게 설명하기 위해, 그 시인은 운문을 산문prose으로 변환시켰다.

614 번영하는, 성공한, 부유한　　열심히 일하고, 좋은 사업 수완으로 인해 그 상인은 부유해졌다prosperous.

615 불쑥 튀어나오다　　해수면 아래로 뱃머리로부터 큰 돔형이 불쑥 나왔다protruded.

616 지방의, 시골의, 옹졸한　　그 가족의 교양없는 태도와 시골풍provincial 언어로 그들의 기민함과 인간 행동에 대한 날카로운 이해가 가려졌다.

617 성나게 하는, 도발적인, 자극적인　　학생들의 도발적인provocative 질문은 선생님을 화나게 했다.

618 근접, 가까움　　대양으로부터의 근접성proximity으로 인해 그 도시는 해상무역으로 부유해졌다.

☆619 **prudent**
[prú:dənt]

adj. careful or cautious; mindful of the future and prepared for it

SYN careful, cautious, discreet

Because a storm is approaching, it would be _____ for you to stay indoors.

☆620 **prudish**
[prú:diʃ]

n. prude
[pru:d]

adj. overly concerned with propriety

SYN strict, straight-laced, stuffy

The Victorians were known for their _____ attitude toward children's behavior.

☆621 **pushover**
[púʃòuvər]

n. something very easy, with a guaranteed result

SYN breeze, cinch, snap, cakewalk

The boxer thought his opponent would be a _____ but was mistaken.

☆622 **quagmire**
[kwǽgmàiər]

n. a seemingly insoluble dilemma; a trap with no easy way out (often used in reference to failed military campaigns)

SYN predicament, trap

The invasion and occupation of the country became a _____ for the invaders.

☆623 **qualified**
[kwáləfàid]

adj. competent to perform a job; restricted and conditional in applicability

SYN able, competent, restricted, conditional

1. *The company had trouble finding _____ workers to fill jobs.*
2. *This promise is so heavily _____ that it is hardly a promise at all.*

☆624 **qualify**
[kwáləfài]

v. to meet certain standards or expectations; to place conditions, limitations, or restrictions on something

SYN enable, prepare, limit, modify, restrict

1. *The athlete _____ to play on the team.*
2. *The speaker _____ his statements, saying that they did not apply in every case.*

SCAFFOLDING

619 신중한, 세심한, 총명한 폭풍이 다가오고 있기 때문에, 실내에 있는 것이 현명하다prudent.

620 엄격한, 케케묵은 빅토리아 시대의 사람들은 아이들의 행동에 대한 엄격한prudish 태도로 알려져 있었다.

621 식은 죽 먹기, 약한 상대 그 권투선수는 그의 상대편이 식은죽 먹기pushover일 것이라 생각했지만 이는 착오였다.

622 곤경, 진구렁 그 국가의 침략과 점령으로 침략자들은 곤경quagmire에 빠졌다.

623 자격있는, 제한된, 조건부의 1. 그 회사는 직업에 맞는 역량있는qualified 직원들을 찾는데 어려움을 겪었다.

2. 이 약속은 너무 심하게 제한되어 있어서qualified 약속이라고 보기 어렵다.

624 자격을 주다, 제한하다 1. 그 운동선수는 팀에서 경기를 하는데 충분한 자격이 되었다qualified.

2. 연설자는 그들이 모든 경우에 해당하는 것은 아니라며 그의 성명을 제한했다qualified.

175

☆625 **quandary**
[kwándəri]

n. a state of indecision or uncertainty

SYN dilemma, impasse, problem, puzzle

The difficulty of their situation put the family in a _____ about how to proceed.

☆626 **quell**
[kwel]

v. to subdue or put down; often used in reference to suppressing rebellion or dissent

SYN subdue, suppress, extinguish

The king sent soldiers to _____ the rebellion in the provinces.

☆627 **querulous**
[kwérjuləs]

adj. discontented; irritable; inclined to complain

SYN discontented, peevish, petulant, testy

Illness made the old lady so _____ that she complained about everything.

☆628 **quiescent**
[kwaiésənt]

adj. at rest; peaceful; unmoving

SYN inactive, motionless, quiet, still

The volcano was once active but is _____ now.

☆629 **ramble**
[rǽmbəl]

v. to walk, talk, or write in an aimless manner

SYN digress, stray, wander

His speech was hard to follow because he _____ on about many different topics.

☆630 **rancor**
[rǽŋkər]

n. lasting resentment, bitterness, or hostility

SYN resentment, bitterness

The meeting was so filled with _____ that everyone accused everyone else of wrongdoing.

SCAFFOLDING

625 곤혹, 당혹, 곤경   어려운 상황으로 가족들이 어떻게 계속해 나가야 할지 곤경quandary에 빠졌다.

626 억누르다, 소멸시키다   그 왕은 지방의 반란을 진압하기quell 위해 군을 파병했다.

627 불평을 하는, 성을 잘 내는   병은 그 노(老)부인을 까탈스럽게querulous 만들어서 그녀는 모든 것에 대해 불평했다.

628 정지한, 무활동의, 침묵의   그 화산은 한때 활화산이었으나 이제는 활동을 멈추었다quiescent.

629 두서없이 이야기하다   그가 너무 많은 다른 주제들을 두서없이 이야기 해서rambled 그의 연설을 따라가기 어려웠다.

630 깊은 원한, 적의   그 회의는 적의rancor로 너무 가득 차 있어서 모두가 모두의 잘못된 점을 비난했다.

SYNONYMS WORDS THAT MEAN THE SAME THING

601 **Profanity** and expressions of hatred may not be broadcast on television or radio.

ⓐ vulgarity

ⓑ determination

ⓒ reverence

ⓓ homage

602 A weakness for alcohol led him into **profligate** and self-destructive behavior.

ⓐ lithe

ⓑ immoral

ⓒ proper

ⓓ assertive

603 The professor's lectures reflected his **profound** understanding of philosophy.

ⓐ shallow

ⓑ lofty

ⓒ archaic

ⓓ deep

604 A **profuse** use of adjectives made the writer's prose heavy and hard to understand.

ⓐ austere

ⓑ abundant

ⓒ appropriate

ⓓ adamant

605 Flowers grew in **profusion** on the hillside.

ⓐ indolence

ⓑ abundance

ⓒ scarcity

ⓓ shortage

606 The **progressive** income tax has critics who see it as a punishment for success.

ⓐ fecund

ⓑ stolid

ⓒ morose

ⓓ incremental

607 After rabbits were brought to Australia, they **proliferated** and became an ecological hazard.

ⓐ deprecated

ⓑ decreased

ⓒ reproduced

ⓓ relapsed

608 When the railroad started operating, it enabled the **proliferation** of new towns along its route.

ⓐ resolution

ⓑ depletion

ⓒ spread

ⓓ affirmation

609 A **prolific** author, he wrote more than 100 published books.

ⓐ glum

ⓑ vicious

ⓒ lucid

ⓓ productive

610 This year, warmer weather **prolonged** the growing season for crops by two weeks.

ⓐ placated

ⓑ forced

ⓒ extended

ⓓ lingered

611 Standards of propriety change slightly every few years to reflect shifts in opinion, taste, and style.

ⓐ decency

ⓑ vacancy

ⓒ uproar

ⓓ misconduct

612 The short story was so prosaic that not even small magazines would publish it.

ⓐ productive

ⓑ commonplace

ⓒ ardent

ⓓ poetic

613 To explain his meaning clearly, the poet shifted from verse into prose.

ⓐ mosaic

ⓑ decoy

ⓒ stimulant

ⓓ story

614 Hard work and good business ability made the merchant prosperous.

ⓐ reachable

ⓑ invisible

ⓒ successful

ⓓ florid

615 Below the water line, a large dome protruded from the ship's bow.

ⓐ invited

ⓑ knocked

ⓒ bulged

ⓓ conceded

616 The family's rustic manners and provincial language concealed their cleverness and keen understanding of human behavior.

ⓐ hilarious

ⓑ foreign

ⓒ rustic

ⓓ urbane

617 The student's provocative question made the teacher angry.

ⓐ superlative

ⓑ dazzling

ⓒ mutual

ⓓ irritating

618 Its proximity to the ocean made the town prosperous through trade by sea.

ⓐ interval

ⓑ closeness

ⓒ estimator

ⓓ gauge

619 Because a storm is approaching, it would be prudent for you to stay indoors.

ⓐ derivative

ⓑ extravagant

ⓒ careful

ⓓ intrinsic

620 The Victorians were known for their prudish attitude toward children's behavior.

ⓐ miscellaneous

ⓑ fitful

ⓒ resplendent

ⓓ strict

621 The boxer thought his opponent would be a pushover but was mistaken.

ⓐ wrap
ⓑ understanding
ⓒ breeze
ⓓ predicament

622 The invasion and occupation of the country became a quagmire for the invaders.

ⓐ predicament
ⓑ ordering
ⓒ fervor
ⓓ tenacity

623 The company had trouble finding qualified workers to fill jobs.

ⓐ inept
ⓑ imbued
ⓒ competent
ⓓ prodigal

624 The speaker qualified his statements, saying that they did not apply in every case.

ⓐ bereaved
ⓑ bequeathed
ⓒ limited
ⓓ filed

625 The difficulty of their situation put the family in a quandary about how to proceed.

ⓐ dilemma
ⓑ trivial
ⓒ quackery
ⓓ intriguing

626 The king sent soldiers to quell the rebellion in the provinces.

ⓐ defy
ⓑ wander
ⓒ debunk
ⓓ subdue

627 Illness made the old lady so querulous that she complained about everything.

ⓐ precious
ⓑ conceptual
ⓒ peevish
ⓓ ominous

628 The volcano was once active but is quiescent now.

ⓐ redundant
ⓑ inactive
ⓒ relentless
ⓓ pivotal

629 His speech was hard to follow because he rambled on about many different topics.

ⓐ wrangled
ⓑ digressed
ⓒ converged
ⓓ mentioned

630 The meeting was so filled with rancor that everyone accused everyone else of wrongdoing.

ⓐ friendship
ⓑ ingenuity
ⓒ goodwill
ⓓ resentment

DAY 21

☆631 **rant**
[rænt]

v. to speak loudly and at length; especially in an insulting or hostile manner
SYN berate, declaim, rave

The host of the radio show _____ about society's problems in a very annoying way.

☆632 **ratify**
[rǽtəfài]

v. to accept or approve on an official basis
SYN affirm, approve, endorse, validate

A certain number of states must _____ an amendment to the U.S. Constitution before it can become law.

☆633 **raucous**
[rɔ́:kəs]

adj. noisy; undisciplined; discordant; often applied to music or arguments
SYN loud, noisy, rough, unruly

The bird's _____ cry awakened sleepers early in the morning.

☆634 **ravenous**
[rǽvənəs]

adj. very hungry
SYN greedy, voracious

The animal has a _____ appetite and can eat its own weight in food every day.

☆635 **raze**
[reiz]

v. to destroy completely; to level to the ground (usually used in reference to destroying buildings)
SYN demolish, destroy, level

The city must _____ several old buildings before it can build a new civic center.

☆636 **rebuff**
[ribʌ́f]

v. to reject, turn down, or turn away
SYN reject, snub, spurn

The landowner _____ all offers to buy his land because he wanted it to remain undeveloped.

631 폭언하다, 고함치다 — 라디오 쇼의 진행자는 매우 짜증섞인 방식으로 사회의 문제에 대해 폭언을 했다ranted.

632 비준하다, 실증하다 — 일정 수의 주들은 미 국회 수정안들이 법이 되기 전에 비준해야ratify 한다.

633 무질서하고 소란한, 쉰 목소리의 — 그 새의 소란한raucous 울음소리가 아침 일찍 자고 있는 사람들을 깨웠다.

634 탐욕스러운, 몹시 굶주린 — 그 동물은 탐욕스러운ravenous 식욕을 가지고 있으며 매일 자신의 무게에 해당하는 만큼 먹을 수 있다.

635 지우다, 없애다, 무너뜨리다 — 그 도시는 새 시민회관을 짓기 전에 몇몇 오래된 건물들을 무너뜨려야raze 한다.

636 거절하다, 저지하다 — 그 지주는 자신의 땅이 미개발지역으로 남아있길 원해서 땅을 사겠다는 모든 제안을 거절했다rebuffed.

☆637 **rebuttal**

[ribʌ́tl]

n. a reply made against an opponent's argument; usually used in reference to formal debates

SYN rejoinder, refutation

The candidate's _____ to her opponent's argument was so effective that she won the debate.

☆638 **recalcitrant**

[rikǽlsətrənt]

adj. resistant; hard to work or manage

SYN resistant, stubborn

Though the stone was a _____ medium for sculpture, the sculptor used it brilliantly.

☆639 **recant**

[rikǽnt]

v. to withdraw or retract a statement or opinion

SYN disavow, retract, withdraw

Under pressure, the mayor _____ his prior statement of support for the project.

☆640 **recluse**

[réklu:s]

n. someone who lives in solitude; a hermit or solitary

SYN hermit

In her final years, my grandmother became a _____ and never left her house.

☆641 **recount**

[rikáunt]

v. to convey information in words; to describe or report something; to tell a story

SYN relate, report, tell

The sailor _____ the story of a voyage in his sailboat.

☆642 **rectify**

[réktəfài]

v. to correct, cure, or set right

SYN amend, correct, fix, repair

The patch was designed to _____ a flaw in the software.

DAY 22

☆643 **redundant**
[ridʌ́ndənt]

adj. using too many words; repetitious; duplicated (as in "redundant systems")

SYN repetitious, superfluous, surplus

For safety, the spaceship used _____ systems to make sure that everything worked properly.

☆644 **reform**
[riːfɔ́ːrm]

v. to amend, correct, or rectify; to form again or to reshape

SYN amend, correct, rectify, repair, restore

Though corrupt, the court system made no attempt to _____ itself.

☆645 **refute**
[rifjúːt]

v. to argue or demonstrate that something is untrue

SYN disprove, rebut

In this book, the professor tries to _____ the claims of his critics.

☆646 **rejuvenate**
[ridʒúːvənèit]

v. to make young again; to refresh, renew, or reinvigorate

SYN regenerate, revive

Bringing in new, young employees is supposed to _____ the company.

☆647 **relegate**
[réləgèit]

v. to send, assign, or consign, usually to a lower status, rank, or position

SYN assign, banish, commit, consign

He was _____ to a low-paying job with none of his former status or privileges.

☆648 **relevant**
[réləvənt]

adj. having some connection with, or applicability to, the matter at hand

SYN applicable, appropriate, fitting, pertinent, suitable

Nothing he said in his speech was _____ to the problems we face.

SCAFFOLDING

643 여분의, 과다한, 중복되는
안전을 위해, 그 우주선은 모든 것이 적절히 작동하고 있다는 것을 확인하기 위한 여분의redundant 시스템을 사용하였다.

644 개혁하다, 교정하다
비록 부패했지만, 그 법정 체계는 스스로 개혁할reform 노력을 하지 않았다.

645 논박하다, 이의를 제기하다
이 책에서 교수는 그에 대한 비평가들의 주장들을 반박하려refute 하고 있다.

646 도로 젊어지게 하다, 활기를 띠게 하다
새롭고 젊은 고용인들을 데려오는 것은 회사에 활기를 띠게rejuvenate 해주게끔 되어있다.

647 추방하다, 지위를 떨어뜨리다, 이관하다
그는 그의 기존의 지위, 혹은 명예 없이 저임금의 직업으로 보내졌다relegated.

648 관련된, 적절한
그가 연설에서 말한 어떤 것도 우리가 직면한 문제와 관련되지relevant 않았다.

☆649 **relieve**
[rilíːv]

v. to free from some unpleasant condition; to replace on duty
SYN alleviate, ease, reduce, release

This medication is widely used to _____ the pain of headaches.

☆650 **remission**
[rimíʃən]

n. an abatement, diminution, or retreat; often used in reference to cancer
SYN lessening, reduction, relaxation

We are pleased to report that our mother's cancer is in _____.

☆651 **remorse**
[rimɔ́ːrs]

n. regret for having done something wrong
SYN compunction, contrition, regret

The thief felt _____ for the crime he had committed and returned the stolen property.

☆652 **remote**
[rimóut]

adj. in a distant or isolated location; unconcerned and emotionally unresponsive
SYN apart, distant, faraway, unconcerned, uninvolved

1. *The observatory was built on a _____ mountaintop to provide the best viewing conditions.*
2. *The children's stepmother was so _____ that she rarely saw them at all.*

☆653 **renounce**
[rináuns]

v. to give up, put away, or throw away
SYN abandon, disavow, disclaim, disown, repudiate

For medical reasons, the patient had to _____ eating rich foods.

☆654 **repel**
[ripél]

v. to ward off; to fend off; to drive away; to repel
SYN oppose, rebuff, repulse

There are various ways to _____ mosquitoes.

☆655 **replete**
[riplíːt]

adj. completely filled; abundantly applied

SYN filled, full, packed, stuffed

This book is long because it is _____ with footnotes and appendices.

☆656 **repletion**
[riplíːʃən]

n. eating until excessively full

SYN fullness, oversupply, satiation

After a heavy dinner, she felt full to _____.

☆657 **reprehensible**
[rèprihénsəbəl]

adj. deserving of blame or condemnation

SYN blameworthy, culpable

The criminal's life was a long record of _____ deeds.

☆658 **repress**
[riprés]

v. to keep under control; often used in the sense of controlling dissent or rebellion

SYN check, control, suppress

The government used many means to _____ dissent and to discourage opposition.

☆659 **reprimand**
[réprəmænd]

v. to reprove someone for misbehavior

SYN censure, rebuke

The teacher _____ the students for misbehavior in class.

☆660 **reprimand**
[réprəmænd]

n. censure or reproof for misbehavior

SYN condemnation, reproof

The school issued a strong _____ to the students for misbehaving.

SCAFFOLDING

655 가득 찬, 충분한
656 충만, 포식, 만복
657 비난할 만한, 괘씸한
658 억누르다, 진압하다
659 견책하다, 호되게 꾸짖다
660 견책, 징계, 비난, 질책

이 책은 각주와 부록들로 가득 차서replete 길다.
배부른 저녁식사 후에, 그녀는 포만감repletion을 느꼈다.
그 범죄자의 삶은 괘씸한reprehensible 행동들의 기나긴 기록이었다.
정부는 반대자들을 억누르고 야당을 저지하기repress 위해 많은 방법을 사용하였다.
선생님은 학생들을 교실에서의 나쁜 행실로 호되게 꾸짖었다reprimanded.
학교는 학생들의 나쁜 행실로 강한 징계reprimand를 내렸다.

184

SYNONYMS WORDS THAT MEAN THE SAME THING

631 The host of the radio show ranted about society's problems in a very annoying way.

ⓐ raved

ⓑ revamped

ⓒ patched

ⓓ devoted

632 A certain number of states must ratify an amendment to the U.S. Constitution before it can become law.

ⓐ condone

ⓑ acknowledge

ⓒ change

ⓓ vary

633 The bird's raucous cry awakened sleepers early in the morning.

ⓐ mellow

ⓑ loud

ⓒ fallow

ⓓ robust

634 The animal has a ravenous appetite and can eat its own weight in food every day.

ⓐ satiated

ⓑ reluctant

ⓒ voracious

ⓓ favorable

635 The city must raze several old buildings before it can build a new civic center.

ⓐ accomplish

ⓑ intend

ⓒ oust

ⓓ demolish

636 The landowner rebuffed all offers to buy his land because he wanted it to remain undeveloped.

ⓐ turned

ⓑ rejected

ⓒ cleared

ⓓ released

637 The candidate's rebuttal to her opponent's argument was so effective that she won the debate.

ⓐ equanimity

ⓑ knack

ⓒ apathy

ⓓ refutation

638 Though the stone was a recalcitrant medium for sculpture, the sculptor used it brilliantly.

ⓐ impregnable

ⓑ gaunt

ⓒ stubborn

ⓓ unconscious

639 Under pressure, the mayor recanted his prior statement of support for the project.

ⓐ disavowed

ⓑ confirmed

ⓒ authenticated

ⓓ corroborated

640 In her final years, my grandmother became a recluse and never left her house.

ⓐ predicament

ⓑ hermit

ⓒ socialite

ⓓ clamor

DAY 22

185

641 The sailor recounted the story of a voyage in his sailboat.

ⓐ wavered
ⓑ related
ⓒ venerated
ⓓ portrayed

642 The patch was designed to rectify a flaw in the software.

ⓐ damage
ⓑ transgress
ⓒ mock
ⓓ amend

643 For safety, the spaceship used redundant systems to make sure that everything worked properly.

ⓐ incessant
ⓑ superfluous
ⓒ pertinent
ⓓ supercilious

644 Though corrupt, the court system made no attempt to reform itself.

ⓐ appease
ⓑ soar
ⓒ correct
ⓓ conserve

645 In this book, the professor tries to refute the claims of his critics.

ⓐ rebut
ⓑ spur
ⓒ oust
ⓓ preclude

646 Bringing in new, young employees is supposed to rejuvenate the company.

ⓐ supply
ⓑ finance
ⓒ regenerate
ⓓ restructure

647 He was relegated to a low-paying job with none of his former status or privileges.

ⓐ invigorated
ⓑ assigned
ⓒ detained
ⓓ opined

648 Nothing he said in his speech was relevant to the problems we face.

ⓐ whimsical
ⓑ applicable
ⓒ flawless
ⓓ infamous

649 This medication is widely used to relieve the pain of headaches.

ⓐ intensify
ⓑ attune
ⓒ abandon
ⓓ ease

650 We are pleased to report that our mother's cancer is in remission.

ⓐ relaxation
ⓑ subsidy
ⓒ regression
ⓓ calamity

651 The thief felt remorse for the crime he had committed and returned the stolen property.

ⓐ quirky
ⓑ apocryphal
ⓒ serene
ⓓ compunction

652 The children's stepmother was so remote that she rarely saw them at all.

ⓐ munificent
ⓑ vacant
ⓒ distant
ⓓ pertinent

653 For medical reasons, the patient had to **renounce** eating rich foods.

ⓐ assert

ⓑ develop

ⓒ claim

ⓓ disown

654 There are various ways to **repel** mosquitoes.

ⓐ welcome

ⓑ repulse

ⓒ placate

ⓓ detect

655 This book is long because it is **replete** with footnotes and appendices.

ⓐ abstruse

ⓑ erudite

ⓒ abundant

ⓓ incessant

656 After a heavy dinner, she felt full to **repletion**.

ⓐ quirk

ⓑ oblivion

ⓒ satiation

ⓓ penchant

657 The criminal's life was a long record of **reprehensible** deeds.

ⓐ blameworthy

ⓑ deceitful

ⓒ peculiar

ⓓ ornate

658 The government used many means to **repress** dissent and to discourage opposition.

ⓐ release

ⓑ soothe

ⓒ suppress

ⓓ incite

659 The teacher **reprimanded** the students for misbehavior in class.

ⓐ provoked

ⓑ lauded

ⓒ added

ⓓ censured

660 The school issued a strong **reprimand** to the students for misbehaving.

ⓐ mystery

ⓑ condemnation

ⓒ vivacity

ⓓ equivocation

DAY 22

Answers

631-635 ⓐⓑⓑⓒⓓ	646-650 ⓒⓑⓑⓓⓐ
636-640 ⓑⓓⓒⓐⓑ	651-655 ⓓⓒⓓⓑⓒ
641-645 ⓑⓓⓑⓒⓐ	656-660 ⓒⓐⓒⓓⓑ

☆661 **reproach**
[ripróutʃ]

v. to criticize or rebuke someone for wrongdoing
SYN blame, condemn, criticize, upbraid

Their parents _____ the boys for getting poor grades in school.

☆662 **reproach**
[ripróutʃ]

n. a rebuke or reproof for wrongdoing
SYN reproof, rebuke

The parents issued a strong _____ to their children for getting poor grades.

☆663 **reprove**
[riprú:v]

v. to criticize someone (in many cases, mildly, in order to correct misbehavior)
SYN censure, correct, criticize

The prime minister _____ the legislature for failing to pass the important legislation.

☆664 **repudiate**
[ripjú:dièit]

v. to reject strongly, with condemnation
SYN disavow, reject, renounce

Late in life, the author _____ his early work as worthless.

☆665 **repugnant**
[ripʌ́gnənt]

adj. offensive; strongly opposed to prevailing standards of good taste or correct behavior
SYN distasteful, disgusting, offensive

Visitors to the country were sometimes shocked by what they considered its _____ customs.

☆666 **repulse**
[ripʌ́ls]

v. to drive back
SYN rebuff, repel

The country had _____ many invasions and had never been conquered.

SCAFFOLDING

661 비난하다, 나무라다, 꾸짖다   부모님은 학교에서 나쁜 성적을 받아 아이들을 꾸짖었다reproached.

662 비난, 질책, 치욕   부모님은 자식들이 나쁜 성적을 받은 것에 대해 강한 질책reproach을 했다.

663 꾸짖다, 훈계하다   수상은 중요한 법령을 통과시키지 못한 입법부를 꾸짖었다reproved.

664 거부하다, 부인하다   늘그막에, 그 작가는 그의 초기 작품을 무가치하다며 부인했다repudiated.

665 비위에 거슬리는, 반대의, 모순된   그 국가의 방문객들은 때때로 그들이 유쾌하지 못한repugnant 풍습이라 여겼던 것들로 인해 충격을 받았다.

666 격퇴하다, 논박하다   그 국가는 많은 침략을 격퇴하였고repulsed 절대 정복되는 일이 없었다.

☆667 **rescind**
[risínd]

v. to annul; to say that something is no longer valid or in effect
SYN annul, invalidate, revoke, repeal, retract

The state government _____ sales taxes on food and clothing.

☆668 **reserve**
[rizə́:rv]

v. to set aside for later use; to keep in storage
SYN hold, keep, store

The farmers _____ a part of their corn harvest to use as seed the following year.

☆669 **reserved**
[rizə́:rvd]

adj. very quiet and restrained in behavior and manner
SYN cold, distant, withdrawn

Our parents are very _____ and quiet in public but are warm and friendly at home.

☆670 **residual**
[rizídʒuəl]

adj. remaining after an operation or process has taken place
SYN extra, leftover, remaining, surplus

After the patient exhaled, there was still some _____ air in his lungs.

☆671 **resignation**
[rèzignéiʃən]

n. a formal statement of giving up an office or position; an attitude of quiet acceptance and patience toward something unwanted or unpleasant
SYN abdication, acceptance, acquiescence, patience

1. The chairman submitted his _____ to the committee, and then a new chairman was chosen.
2. The young man's parents viewed his choice of career with quiet _____.

☆672 **resigned**
[rizáind]

adj. acquiescent or patient toward something unwelcome or unpleasant
SYN acquiescent, submissive

The team appeared _____ to having the match postponed because of rain.

667 폐지하다, 무효로 하다, 취소하다   주 정부는 식품과 의복에 대한 판매세를 폐지했다rescinded.

668 떼어두다, 비축하다   농부들은 그들의 옥수수 수확의 일부를 내년에 씨앗으로 사용하기 위해 비축해 두었다reserved.

669 보류된, 수줍어하는, 말없는   우리 부모님은 사람들 앞에서는 매우 말이 없고reserved 조용하지만 집에서는 따뜻하고 친절하다.

670 나머지의, 잔류의   환자가 숨을 내쉰 후에도 여전히 그의 폐에는 공기가 남아있었다residual.

671 사직, 단념, 묵인, 인내   1. 그 의장이 위원회에 사표resignation를 제출하자 새로운 의장이 선출되었다.

    2. 그 젊은이의 부모는 그의 직업 선택을 인내resignation를 두고 보았다.

672 체념한, 복종하고 있는   그 팀은 비로 인해 경기가 연기되자 체념한 듯resigned 보였다.

☆673 **resolute**
[rézəlùːt]

adj. fixed in purpose, intention, or opinion

SYN determined, firm, steadfast, unshakeable, unwavering

The mayor knew that his plan would encounter _____ opposition from the city council.

☆674 **resolution**
[rèzəlúːʃən]

n. firmness of intention, opinion, or plan; a formal expression of opinion by a group, usually following a vote

SYN determination, fortitude, strength

1. *The general was famous for his _____ in the face of opposition.*
2. *The legislature passed a _____, but it did not have the force of law.*

☆675 **resolve**
[rizálv]

v. to decide or commit oneself

SYN decide, determine

The detective _____ to find the criminal no matter how long the hunt would take.

☆676 **resolve**
[rizálv]

n. determination or commitment

SYN commitment, dedication, determination

The detective showed an unshakeable _____ to find the criminal and bring him to justice.

☆677 **resourceful**
[risɔ́ːrsfəl]

adj. able to deal successfully with the unexpected

SYN able, adaptable, imaginative, inventive

Because conditions change so quickly, this position requires a _____, energetic person.

☆678 **respite**
[réspit]

n. temporary relief, delay, or suspension

SYN hiatus, recess, pause, postponement

A thunderstorm cooled the air and brought a _____ from the heat.

☆679	**resplendent**	*adj.* extremely brilliant or impressive in appearance
	[rispléndənt]	**SYN** dazzling, magnificent, splendid
		The princess wore a _____ dress to the ceremony.

☆680	**responsive**	*adj.* sensitive and responding promptly to appeals or appearances of need
	[rispánsiv]	**SYN** receptive, sensitive, understanding, helpful
		The charity was _____ to requests from the poor for help.

☆681	**restraint**	*n.* the act of holding something back or preventing it from moving
	[ri:stréint]	**SYN** check, curb, stop, limitation, restriction
		The law provided a _____ on the government's ability to act in some situations.

☆682	**retaliation**	*n.* something done in return for an offense or injury; harm exchanged for harm
	[ritæliéiʃən]	**SYN** reprisal, punishment
		The missiles allowed for immediate _____ if the country were attacked.

☆683	**reticence**	*n.* the ability to remain silent
	[rétəsəns]	**SYN** reserve, self-control, silence, taciturnity
		Her natural _____ prevented her from taking part in the discussion.

☆684	**reticent**	*adj.* quiet by nature; reluctant to speak
	[rétəsənt]	**SYN** reserved, self-controlled, silent, taciturn
		During the discussion, she was too _____ to say anything.

DAY 23

☆685 **retract**

[ritrǽkt]

v. to withdraw; to draw back; to take back

SYN withdraw, deny, disavow

The candidate had to _____ his statement when he learned that he was mistaken.

☆686 **revelation**

[rèvəléiʃən]

n. the act of revealing something

SYN disclosure, divulgence, exposure

The book included a _____ about a major crime.

☆687 **reverent**

[révərənt]

adj. characterized by reverence

SYN devout, pious

The worshippers at the cathedral had a highly _____ attitude.

☆688 **revere**

[rivíər]

v. to hold in high honor or esteem

SYN respect, honor

After the singer died, many fans _____ his memory.

☆689 **revive**

[riváiv]

v. to set in motion or operation again

SYN reactivate, refresh, revitalize

The artists _____ old artistic traditions that many people had forgotten.

☆690 **rhetorical**

[ritɔ́(:)rikəl]

adj. of or pertaining to rhetoric; sometimes used in a negative sense, to describe speech or writing that is elegant but meaningless

SYN verbal

The author used every _____ device he knew to make his book interesting.

SCAFFOLDING

685 끌어넣다, 최소/철회하다   그가 실수했다는 것을 알았을 때 그 후보자는 그의 성명을 철회해야retract 했다.

686 폭로, 누설, 발각   그 책은 주요 범죄에 대한 폭로revelation를 담고 있었다.

687 경건한, 공손한   성당의 예배자들은 극도로 경건한reverent 태도를 가졌다.

688 존경하다, 숭배하다   그 가수가 죽자, 많은 팬들이 그의 유물을 숭배했다revered.

689 소생하게 하다, 부흥시키다   예술가들은 많은 사람들이 잊어왔던 오래된 예술적 전통을 부흥시켰다revived.

690 수사적인, 화려한, 과장적인   작가는 그가 아는 모든 수사적인rhetorical 도구를 써서 그의 책을 재미있게 만들었다.

SYNONYMS WORDS THAT MEAN THE SAME THING

661 Their parents **reproached** the boys for getting poor grades in school.

ⓐ upbraided

ⓑ annulled

ⓒ expelled

ⓓ discharged

662 The parents issued a strong **reproach** to their children for getting poor grades.

ⓐ evasion

ⓑ compliment

ⓒ rebuke

ⓓ credit

663 The prime minister **reproved** the legislature for failing to pass the important legislation.

ⓐ vindicated

ⓑ criticized

ⓒ prevaricated

ⓓ praised

664 Late in life, the author **repudiated** his early work as worthless.

ⓐ accepted

ⓑ authorized

ⓒ confined

ⓓ rejected

665 Visitors to the country were sometimes shocked by what they considered its **repugnant** customs.

ⓐ stolid

ⓑ mercurial

ⓒ distasteful

ⓓ ardent

666 The country had **repulsed** many invasions and had never been conquered.

ⓐ welcomed

ⓑ enticed

ⓒ rebuffed

ⓓ encouraged

667 The state government **rescinded** sales taxes on food and clothing.

ⓐ inclined

ⓑ annulled

ⓒ boasted

ⓓ soared

668 The farmers **reserved** a part of their corn harvest to use as seed the following year.

ⓐ stored

ⓑ squandered

ⓒ abandoned

ⓓ restricted

669 Our parents are very **reserved** and quiet in public but are warm and friendly at home.

ⓐ booked

ⓑ withdrawn

ⓒ friendly

ⓓ cautious

670 After the patient exhaled, there was still some **residual** air in his lungs.

ⓐ stale

ⓑ attentive

ⓒ surplus

ⓓ polluted

671 The chairman submitted his **resignation** to the committee, and then a new chairman was chosen.

ⓐ inauguration

ⓑ abdication

ⓒ harassment

ⓓ resistance

DAY 23

672 The team appeared **resigned** to having the match postponed because of rain.

  ⓐ insolent

  ⓑ acquiescent

  ⓒ cheerful

  ⓓ insipid

673 The mayor knew that his plan would encounter **resolute** opposition from the city council.

  ⓐ coward

  ⓑ vacillating

  ⓒ wavering

  ⓓ determined

674 The general was famous for his **resolution** in the face of opposition.

  ⓐ determination

  ⓑ proliferation

  ⓒ depletion

  ⓓ indecision

675 The detective **resolved** to find the criminal no matter how long the hunt would take.

  ⓐ began

  ⓑ hesitated

  ⓒ determined

  ⓓ halted

676 The detective showed an unshakeable **resolve** to find the criminal and bring him to justice.

  ⓐ scheme

  ⓑ paradigm

  ⓒ pitfall

  ⓓ commitment

677 Because conditions change so quickly, this position requires a **resourceful**, energetic person.

  ⓐ formal

  ⓑ inventive

  ⓒ esoteric

  ⓓ customary

678 A thunderstorm cooled the air and brought a **respite** from the heat.

  ⓐ fervor

  ⓑ hiatus

  ⓒ patronage

  ⓓ decoy

679 The princess wore a **resplendent** dress to the ceremony.

  ⓐ reckless

  ⓑ expensive

  ⓒ dazzling

  ⓓ laughable

680 The charity was **responsive** to requests from the poor for help.

  ⓐ receptive

  ⓑ esoteric

  ⓒ cold

  ⓓ deceptive

681 The law provided a **restraint** on the government's ability to act in some situations.

  ⓐ disrepute

  ⓑ freedom

  ⓒ curb

  ⓓ warmth

682 The missiles allowed for immediate **retaliation** if the country were attacked.

ⓐ forgiveness

ⓑ pomposity

ⓒ remission

ⓓ reprisal

683 Her natural **reticence** prevented her from taking part in the discussion.

ⓐ outgoing

ⓑ silence

ⓒ attribute

ⓓ commiseration

684 During the discussion, she was too **reticent** to say anything.

ⓐ talkative

ⓑ epistemic

ⓒ taciturn

ⓓ effusive

685 The candidate had to **retract** his statement when he learned that he was mistaken.

ⓐ fluctuate

ⓑ withdraw

ⓒ accept

ⓓ maintain

686 The book included a **revelation** about a major crime.

ⓐ disposition

ⓑ turbulence

ⓒ divulgence

ⓓ tranquility

687 The worshippers at the cathedral had a highly **reverent** attitude.

ⓐ odious

ⓑ disrespectful

ⓒ pious

ⓓ impertinent

688 After the singer died, many fans **revered** his memory.

ⓐ intimidated

ⓑ slandered

ⓒ sanctioned

ⓓ honored

689 The artists **revived** old artistic traditions that many people had forgotten.

ⓐ thrived

ⓑ revitalized

ⓒ languished

ⓓ vindicated

690 The author used every **rhetorical** device he knew to make his book interesting.

ⓐ written

ⓑ theoretic

ⓒ verbal

ⓓ epistemic

Answers

661-665 ⓐⓒⓑⓓⓒ	676-680 ⓓⓑⓑⓒⓐ
666-670 ⓒⓑⓐⓑⓒ	681-685 ⓒⓓⓑⓒⓑ
671-675 ⓑⓑⓓⓐⓒ	686-690 ⓒⓒⓓⓑⓒ

DAY 24

☆691 **rigidity**
[ridʒídəti]

n. rigidity; resistance to bending
SYN **stiffness, firmness, inflexibility**

The _____ of its shell protects the lobster from injury.

☆692 **rigor**
[rígər]

n. inflexibility; rigidity; strictness; often used to describe strict intellectual or bodily discipline
SYN **inflexibility, strictness**

After the _____ of military duty, the soldiers returned to a less disciplined life as civilians.

☆693 **rigorous**
[rígərəs]

adj. very intense, demanding, hard, or difficult; often used to describe strict discipline in thinking or physical training
SYN **inflexible, strict, hard, scrupulous, severe**

Critics subjected the professor's argument to _____ analysis.

☆694 **robust**
[roubʌ́st]

adj. very healthy and strong
SYN **strong, powerful, healthy, hardy**

My brother enjoys _____ health and rarely has to visit the doctor.

☆695 **rotund**
[routʌ́nd]

adj. round; fully fleshed; overweight
SYN **fat, round, plump, portly, stout**

A lifetime of eating fatty foods made him _____ and unhealthy.

☆696 **ruffle**
[rʌ́fəl]

v. to upset someone's composure or peace of mind
SYN **aggravate, annoy, bother, disturb, perturb, unsettle**

The old lady was so calm that it seemed nothing could _____ her.

☆697 **rupture**

[rʌ́ptʃər]

n. a breach; a breaking or bursting

SYN breakage, fracture, rip

The talk between management and labor came to a _____ .

☆698 **saccharine**

[sǽkərin]

adj. overly sweet and sentimental; often used to describe a person's manner or the tone of a drama

SYN cloying, sugary, sweet

Television showed cartoons so _____ that young viewers could not tolerate them.

☆699 **sage**

[seidʒ]

adj. wise; learned; philosophical; a person who displays wisdom

SYN judicious, wise

The philosopher's book was full of _____ advice which many people followed.

☆700 **salutary**

[sǽljutèri]

adj. conducive to good health or well-being

SYN healthful, salubrious, wholesome

A well-balanced, nutritious diet has _____ effects on the body.

☆701 **sanction**

[sǽŋkʃən]

n. official approval or permission to do something

SYN approval, permission

The security measures received official _____ and were put into effect immediately.

☆702 **satirical**

[sətírikəl]

adj. of or about satire

SYN biting, cutting, sardonic, taunting

The monthly _____ magazine subjected human behavior to ridicule.

DAY 24

☆703 **saturate**
[sǽtʃərèit]

v. to fill something to its greatest possible capacity

SYN imbue, fill, soak

Water _____ the soil and made it impossible to build houses there.

☆704 **savor**
[séivər]

v. to appreciate or enjoy, especially through the senses of smell and taste

SYN excite, interest, relish, taste, enjoy

The travelers _____ the hot meal after their long journey.

☆705 **savory**
[séivəri]

adj. pleasant or enjoyable, especially through the senses of smell and taste

SYN attractive, delicious, enjoyable, luscious, pleasant

From the kitchen came the aroma of some _____ food.

☆706 **scale**
[skeil]

v. to remove the outer layer of something

SYN pare, peel, skin, strip

The cook had to _____ the fish before cooking it.

☆707 **scanty**
[skǽnti]

adj. inadequate in volume, area, number, or extent

SYN inadequate, meager, sparse, thin

The soil was so dry that only a _____ covering of grass grew on it.

☆708 **scrupulous**
[skrúːpjuləs]

adj. painstaking; very mindful of rules

SYN careful, conscientious, detail-oriented, painstaking

The editor was _____ in her attention to grammar.

SCAFFOLDING

703 삼투시키다, 포화시키다   물이 흙을 흠뻑 적시는saturated 바람에 그 곳에 집을 지을 수 없게 했다.
704 맛 보다   여행자들은 오랜 여행 후에 따뜻한 식사를 맛보았다savored.
705 풍미좋은, 맛좋은, 향기좋은   부엌에서 맛좋은savory 음식의 향이 났다.
706 비늘을 벗기다, 껍질을 까다   요리사는 요리하기 전에 생선의 비늘을 벗겨야 했다scale.
707 부족한, 얼마 안되는, 불충분한   토양이 너무 건조해서 그 위를 덮는 얼마 안되는scanty 잔디가 자랄 뿐이었다.
708 빈틈없는, 면밀한, 양심적인   그 편집자는 문법에 대한 주의가 빈틈없었다scrupulous.

198

☆709	**scrutinize** [skrú:tənàiz]	*v.* to look at or review carefully **SYN** analyze, check, examine *Historians _____ the old map for clues to the city's location.*
☆710	**seclusion** [siklúːʒən]	*n.* a voluntary withdrawal from society; a condition of being alone by one's own choice **SYN** solitude, privacy *The grieving woman went into _____ after the death of her husband.*
☆711	**sedentary** [sédəntèri]	*adj.* in a seated position; commonly used to describe the lifestyle of persons who get little exercise **SYN** stationary, seated, sitting *The _____ lifestyles of people in developed countries harm their health in many ways.*
☆712	**serene** [səríːn] *n.* serenity [sərénəti]	*adj.* not excited or uneasy; calm and collected **SYN** calm, composed, peaceful, placid, undisturbed, unruffled *Despite the turmoil around him, the philosopher remained _____ and quiet.*
☆713	**servile** [sə́ːrvil]	*adj.* concerning, or in the role of, a servant or slave **SYN** menial, slavish, subservient *Though in a _____ position, the young woman was treated well and never harmed.*
☆714	**severe** [sivíər]	*adj.* intense; extreme; highly onerous; unpleasant; challenging **SYN** harsh, extreme, intense *A _____ storm destroyed several buildings in the town and damaged many others.*

DAY 24

709 자세히 조사하다, 음미하다   역사가들은 도시의 위치에 대한 단서를 찾기 위해 오랜 지도를 자세히 조사했다scrutinized.

710 격리, 은퇴, 은둔   비탄에 젖은 여자는 남편의 죽음 이후에 속세에서 멀리 떨어져 지냈다seclusion.

711 앉은 채 있는, 정주하는   선진국 사람들의 앉아서 일하는sedentary 생활방식은 여러 방면으로 그들의 건강을 해친다.

712 고요한, 침착한, 맑게 갠   그 주변의 소란에도 불구하고, 그 철학자는 침착하고serene 조용하게 있었다.

713 노예의, 비굴한, 자주성이 없는   노예의servile 지위에서도 그 젊은 여성은 잘 대우 받았고 절대 해를 입지 않았다.

714 엄한, 가혹한, 맹렬한   맹렬한severe 폭풍이 마을의 몇몇 건물을 파괴했고, 다른 많은 것들을 손상시켰다.

☆715 **shrine**
[ʃrain]

n. a consecrated structure; in a very broad sense, any place set aside to honor the memory of a deceased and famous person

SYN temple

One of the deceased singer's fans turned her home into a _____ to him.

☆716 **sinister**
[sínistər]

adj. threatening, with a component of evil

SYN dire, frightening, grim, menacing

The villain appeared on stage in a _____ black costume.

☆717 **skeptic**
[sképtik]

n. one who questions widely accepted beliefs

SYN doubter

A _____ by nature, she questioned the widely accepted explanation of the phenomenon.

☆718 **skeptical**
[sképtikəl]

adj. inclined to doubt or question widely accepted beliefs

SYN doubting, critical, unbelieving

She was _____ about the widely accepted explanation of the phenomenon and openly questioned it.

☆719 **slander**
[slǽndər]

n. speaking harmful, false, and malicious statements about someone

SYN calumny, defamation

After insulting someone publicly on a radio show, he was sued for _____.

☆720 **slight**
[slait]

adj. very little; weak; unimportant

SYN insignificant, nominal, trivial

The instruments showed a _____ increase in temperature, but it was not cause for concern.

715 성체용기, 성당, 사당　　죽은 가수의 팬 중 한 명이 그녀의 집을 그의 사당shrine으로 변환시켰다.
716 불길한, 재난의, 못된　　악역이 불길한sinister 검은색 복장을 입고 무대에 나타났다.
717 회의론자, 무신론자　　천성적으로 회의론자skeptic인 그녀는 현상에 대해 널리 받아들여진 설명에도 의문을 가졌다.
718 의심 많은, 회의적인　　그녀는 현상에 대해 널리 받아들여진 설명에 대해서 회의적이었으며skeptical 공공연히 의문을 가졌다.
719 중상, 명예훼손　　라디오에서 어떤 사람을 공개적으로 모욕하고 난 후, 그는 명예훼손slander으로 고소당했다.
720 약간의, 근소한　　그 기기들은 약간의slight 온도 증가를 보였지만, 이는 걱정할 만한 것이 아니었다.

SYNONYMS WORDS THAT MEAN THE SAME THING

691 The **rigidity** of its shell protects the lobster from injury.

  ⓐ prevarication

  ⓑ foaminess

  ⓒ firmness

  ⓓ treachery

692 After the **rigor** of military duty, the soldiers returned to a less disciplined life as civilians.

  ⓐ lenience

  ⓑ ease

  ⓒ carelessness

  ⓓ strictness

693 Critics subjected the professor's argument to **rigorous** analysis.

  ⓐ industrial

  ⓑ scrupulous

  ⓒ lax

  ⓓ negligent

694 My brother enjoys **robust** health and rarely has to visit the doctor.

  ⓐ hardy

  ⓑ weak

  ⓒ expansive

  ⓓ quiet

695 A lifetime of eating fatty foods made him **rotund** and unhealthy.

  ⓐ gaunt

  ⓑ impressive

  ⓒ angular

  ⓓ stout

696 The old lady was so calm that it seemed nothing could **ruffle** her.

  ⓐ smooth

  ⓑ calm

  ⓒ placate

  ⓓ unsettle

697 The talk between management and labor came to a **rupture**.

  ⓐ breakage

  ⓑ juncture

  ⓒ mend

  ⓓ leverage

698 Television showed cartoons so **saccharine** that young viewers could not tolerate them.

  ⓐ supercilious

  ⓑ cloying

  ⓒ titillative

  ⓓ tempting

699 The philosopher's book was full of **sage** advice which many people followed.

  ⓐ stupid

  ⓑ wise

  ⓒ epistemic

  ⓓ tragic

700 A well-balanced, nutritious diet has **salutary** effects on the body.

  ⓐ stale

  ⓑ tranquil

  ⓒ preposterous

  ⓓ healthful

701 The security measures received official **sanction** and were put into effect immediately.

  ⓐ objection

  ⓑ depravity

  ⓒ approval

  ⓓ contempt

DAY 24

702 The monthly **satirical** magazine subjected human behavior to ridicule.

ⓐ gentle
ⓑ considerate
ⓒ biting
ⓓ meek

703 Water **saturated** the soil and made it impossible to build houses there.

ⓐ dehydrated
ⓑ deprived
ⓒ imbued
ⓓ divested

704 The travelers **savored** the hot meal after their long journey.

ⓐ condensed
ⓑ acquiesced
ⓒ enjoyed
ⓓ pacified

705 From the kitchen came the aroma of some **savory** food.

ⓐ brash
ⓑ delicious
ⓒ fickle
ⓓ invigorated

706 The cook had to **scale** the fish before cooking it.

ⓐ fish
ⓑ feed
ⓒ temperate
ⓓ skin

707 The soil was so dry that only a **scanty** covering of grass grew on it.

ⓐ plentiful
ⓑ sparse
ⓒ defensive
ⓓ protruding

708 The editor was **scrupulous** in her attention to grammar.

ⓐ careless
ⓑ corrupt
ⓒ painstaking
ⓓ lax

709 Historians **scrutinized** the old map for clues to the city's location.

ⓐ derided
ⓑ examined
ⓒ appeased
ⓓ skimmed

710 The grieving woman went into **seclusion** after the death of her husband.

ⓐ agitation
ⓑ loophole
ⓒ penchant
ⓓ solitude

711 The **sedentary** lifestyles of people in developed countries harm their health in many ways.

ⓐ stationary
ⓑ energetic
ⓒ rambling
ⓓ dynamic

712 Despite the turmoil around him, the philosopher remained **serene** and quiet.

ⓐ stormy
ⓑ moody
ⓒ peaceful
ⓓ animated

713 Though in a servile position, the young woman was treated well and never harmed.

ⓐ commanding

ⓑ monarchic

ⓒ omnipotent

ⓓ menial

714 A severe storm destroyed several buildings in the town and damaged many others.

ⓐ intense

ⓑ trivial

ⓒ incautious

ⓓ tranquil

715 One of the deceased singer's fans turned her home into a shrine to him.

ⓐ statue

ⓑ donation

ⓒ temple

ⓓ cremation

716 The villain appeared on stage in a sinister black costume.

ⓐ frivolous

ⓑ throbbing

ⓒ grim

ⓓ vulgar

717 A skeptic by nature, she questioned the widely accepted explanation of the phenomenon.

ⓐ drone

ⓑ vulgarian

ⓒ doubter

ⓓ slaughter

718 She was skeptical about the widely accepted explanation of the phenomenon and openly questioned it.

ⓐ garrulous

ⓑ prodigal

ⓒ unbelieving

ⓓ rustic

719 After insulting someone publicly on a radio show, he was sued for slander.

ⓐ remission

ⓑ rupture

ⓒ defamation

ⓓ evasion

720 The instruments showed a slight increase in temperature, but it was not cause for concern.

ⓐ insignificant

ⓑ pious

ⓒ sturdy

ⓓ intricate

Answers

691-695 ⓒⓓⓑⓐⓓ	706-710 ⓓⓑⓒⓑⓓ
696-700 ⓓⓐⓑⓑⓓ	711-715 ⓐⓒⓓⓐⓒ
701-705 ⓒⓒⓒⓒⓑ	716-720 ⓒⓒⓒⓒⓐ

☆721 **slight**
[slait]

n. a mild insult; a snub

SYN snub

The innocent mistake was interpreted as a _____ and made the woman angry.

☆722 **sluggard**
[slʌ́ɡərd]

n. a lazy or slothful person

SYN idler, drone, lazybones (slang)

The man was criticized as a _____ because he made no effort to find a job.

☆723 **sluggish**
[slʌ́ɡiʃ]

adj. slow; lazy; lacking in energy

SYN slow, slack, indolent

The flow of water in the canal was so _____ that it barely moved at all.

☆724 **sobriety**
[soubráiəti]

n. temperance (especially in the use of alcoholic drinks); a solemn, grave, or serious demeanor

SYN temperance, moderation, solemnity, seriousness

adj. sober
[sóubər]

The man's natural _____ of manner was sometimes mistaken for dislike.

☆725 **solemn**
[sáləm]

adj. very serious; completely lacking in humor or cheer

SYN grave, humorless, solemn

In a _____ ceremony, the prime minister recognized the soldiers who had fallen in battle.

☆726 **solicit**
[səlísit]

v. to seek, entreat, or petition respectfully for something

SYN ask, seek, entreat

The city _____ help from the state government in solving its problems.

SCAFFOLDING

721 경멸, 모욕, 냉대   단순한 실수가 모욕slight으로 이해되었고 그 여자를 화나게 했다.

722 게으름쟁이, 나태자   그 남자는 직업을 찾기 위해 아무런 노력도 하지 않았기 때문에 나태자sluggard로 비난을 받았다.

723 게으른, 굼뜬, 부진한   운하내의 물의 흐름이 느려sluggish 거의 움직이지를 않았다.

724 절제, 냉엄, 침착   그 남자의 천성적인 침착한sobriety 태도는 때때로 싫어하는 것으로 오해된다.

725 엄숙한, 근엄한   근엄한solemn 의식에서, 수상은 전사한 군인들을 표창했다.

726 간청하다, 구하다   그 도시는 자신의 문제들을 해결하는데 주 정부에 도움을 요청했다solicited.

☆727 **solitary**
[sálitèri]

adj. alone; completely removed from the company of others

SYN alone, isolated

At the end of the road stood a _____ house surrounded by empty land.

☆728 **somber**
[sámbər]

adj. dark; depressing; joyless; sad

SYN depressed, gloomy, glum, sad

The funeral was a _____ occasion with many people in attendance.

☆729 **soothe**
[su:ð]

v. to calm, comfort, or relieve someone

SYN alleviate, ease, relieve

An hour of rest in a quiet room _____ her distress and made her calm again.

☆730 **soporific**
[sàpərífik]

adj. leading to or causing sleepiness; exhibiting sleepiness

SYN drowsy, sleepy, sleep-inducing

The orchestra's performance was so _____ that several people in the audience fell asleep.

☆731 **spacious**
[spéiʃəs]

adj. having ample room inside

SYN big, capacious, roomy, voluminous

My parents' home has a _____ living room which can accommodate many guests.

☆732 **splinter**
[splíntər]

n. a small fragment of a shattered object

SYN fragment, shard

Working with wood left her with a _____ in her finger.

SCAFFOLDING

727 고독한, 외딴 길의 끝머리에 빈 땅으로 둘러싸인 외딴solitary 집 하나가 서있었다.
728 어두침침한, 칙칙한, 우울한 그 장례식은 많은 사람들이 참석한 음침한somber 행사였다.
729 달래다, 위로하다, 완화시키다 조용한 방안에서의 한 시간이 그녀의 심통을 달래주었고soothed 그녀를 다시 차분하게 해주었다.
730 최면성의, 졸린 그 오케스트라의 연주는 너무 졸려서soporific 청중의 몇몇 사람들이 잠들었다.
731 넓은, 광범위한 내 부모님의 집에는 많은 손님들을 수용할 수 있는 넓은spacious 거실이 있다.
732 (나무, 대나무 따위의) 가시, 파편 나무로 일을 하여 그녀의 손가락에 가시splinter가 남았다.

☆733 **splinter**
[splíntər]

v. to fragment or shatter into small pieces
SYN fragment, shatter

The glass fell on the floor and _____ into tiny pieces.

☆734 **spontaneous**
[spɑntéiniəs]

adj. occurring or performed without command, planning, or prior intent
SYN impulsive, involuntary, unbidden, unplanned, sudden

n. spontaneity
[spɑ̀ntəníːəti]

There was _____ applause from the audience when the musician played a beloved song.

☆735 **sporadic**
[spərǽdik]

adj. infrequent in occurrence
SYN intermittent, occasional

This area has _____ small earthquakes but nothing regular or dangerous.

☆736 **spurious**
[spjúəriəs]

adj. intentionally false; intended and arranged to deceive
SYN counterfeit, fake, false, fraudulent, phony

His university degree was _____ and had been purchased by mail for a few dollars.

☆737 **spurn**
[spəːrn]

v. to reject or treat with disdain
SYN refuse, reject

The book collector _____ all offers to buy his library and gave it to a college instead.

☆738 **squander**
[skwɑ́ndər]

v. to waste, dissipate, or spend lavishly and recklessly
SYN misspend, waste

My friend had great ability as a writer but _____ it on writing cheap novels for money.

☆739 **stagnant**
[stǽgnənt]

adj. motionless; not flowing; stale because of inactivity

SYN sluggish, stale, unchanging

Pollution accumulated in the _____ water and began to smell bad.

☆740 **stagnation**
[stǽgnéiʃən]

n. inactivity; a stale condition resulting from inactivity

SYN inactivity

The government hoped its new policies would help businesses and end the _____ of the economy.

☆741 **stalemate**
[stéilmèit]

n. a situation where progress or action is impossible

SYN deadlock, draw, impasse, standoff, standstill

Negotiations between the company and the union have reached a _____, and progress is unlikely.

☆742 **stanza**
[stǽnzə]

n. a division of a poem, usually having a regular number of lines

SYN strophe, verse

The first _____ of this poem contains one of the most famous quotations in English literature.

☆743 **static**
[stǽtik]

adj. fixed in one place; motionless

SYN fixed, stationary, unmoving

The _____ characterizations made the novel uninteresting.

☆744 **static**
[stǽtik]

n. radio interference caused by electricity in the atmosphere

SYN interference, noise

There was so much _____ on the radio that listeners could hardly hear the program.

SCAFFOLDING

739 정체된, 썩은   정체된stagnant 물에 오염이 축적되었고 나쁜 냄새가 나기 시작했다.

740 침체, 불황   정부는 새로운 정책들이 기업체를 도와 경제 침체stagnation를 끝내길 희망했다.

741 수의 막힘, 교착상태   회사측과 노조간 협상은 교착상태stalemate에 빠졌고, 발전 가능성이 없어 보인다.

742 (시의) 연   이 시의 첫번째 연stanza은 영문학에서 가장 유명한 인용구중 하나를 포함하고 있다.

743 정적인   정적인static 인물설정이 소설을 재미없게 만들었다.

744 공전, 잡음   라디오에 너무 많은 잡음static이 있어서 청취자들이 그 프로그램을 거의 들을 수 없었다.

☆745 **steadfast**
[stédfæst]

adj. fixed and steady in purpose or allegiance

SYN faithful, firm, loyal, steady, unwavering

The army was _____ in its allegiance to the king.

☆746 **stilts**
[stílts]

n. tall, slender posts used to elevate buildings off the ground; tall wooden poles that let users walk at some height above the ground

SYN pillars, poles, posts

The beach house was elevated on _____ to keep it above the level of the tide.

☆747 **stoic**
[stóuik]

adj. seemingly unaffected by pain, pleasure, or emotions in general

SYN impassive

The captain remained _____ even after he had lost his ship.

☆748 **stolid**
[stálid]

adj. not given to emotional response

SYN impassive, unemotional

The most _____ man we knew, he never smiled or frowned at anything.

☆749 **stratagem**
[strǽtədʒəm]

n. a plan or scheme used to deceive an enemy

SYN plan, ruse, scheme, trick

The enemy's _____ was to send false radio messages.

☆750 **stratum**
[stréitəm]

v. stratify
[strǽtəfài]

n. a distinct layer or level; usually used to describe layers in the crust of the earth

SYN layer, level, tier

Between these two _____ of rocks, you can see a layer of sandstone.

SYNONYMS WORDS THAT MEAN THE SAME THING

721 The innocent mistake was interpreted as a **slight** and made the woman angry.

ⓐ snub
ⓑ compliment
ⓒ peril
ⓓ accolade

722 The man was criticized as a **sluggard** because he made no effort to find a job.

ⓐ sycophant
ⓑ sophist
ⓒ lazybones
ⓓ skeptic

723 The flow of water in the canal was so **sluggish** that it barely moved at all.

ⓐ luxuriant
ⓑ putrid
ⓒ arable
ⓓ slack

724 The man's natural **sobriety** of manner was sometimes mistaken for dislike.

ⓐ adulation
ⓑ seclusion
ⓒ seriousness
ⓓ persecution

725 In a **solemn** ceremony, the prime minister recognized the soldiers who had fallen in battle.

ⓐ laudable
ⓑ furtive
ⓒ intrinsic
ⓓ serious

726 The city **solicited** help from the state government in solving its problems.

ⓐ reprimanded
ⓑ lingered
ⓒ entreated
ⓓ misconstrued

727 At the end of the road stood a **solitary** house surrounded by empty land.

ⓐ recurred
ⓑ gathered
ⓒ grouped
ⓓ isolated

728 The funeral was a **somber** occasion with many people in attendance.

ⓐ optimistic
ⓑ fuzzy
ⓒ glum
ⓓ laughable

729 An hour of rest in a quiet room **soothed** her distress and made her calm again.

ⓐ impaired
ⓑ relieved
ⓒ denounced
ⓓ redirected

730 The orchestra's performance was so **soporific** that several people in the audience fell asleep.

ⓐ ardent
ⓑ lethargic
ⓒ intricate
ⓓ sleep-inducing

731 My parents' home has a **spacious** living room which can accommodate many guests.

ⓐ lithe
ⓑ capacious
ⓒ plausible
ⓓ rustic

732 Working with wood left her with a **splinter** in her finger.

   ⓐ fragment

   ⓑ loophole

   ⓒ foe

   ⓓ difficulty

733 The glass fell on the floor and **splintered** into tiny pieces.

   ⓐ heeded

   ⓑ reverted

   ⓒ shattered

   ⓓ mended

734 There was **spontaneous** applause from the audience when the musician played a beloved song.

   ⓐ exacting

   ⓑ extravagant

   ⓒ impulsive

   ⓓ erudite

735 This area has **sporadic** small earthquakes but nothing regular or dangerous.

   ⓐ munificent

   ⓑ intermittent

   ⓒ erroneous

   ⓓ archaic

736 His university degree was **spurious** and had been purchased by mail for a few dollars.

   ⓐ acrid

   ⓑ counterfeit

   ⓒ obsolete

   ⓓ fretful

737 The book collector **spurned** all offers to buy his library and gave it to a college instead.

   ⓐ improvised

   ⓑ scorned

   ⓒ rejected

   ⓓ curtailed

738 My friend had great ability as a writer but **squandered** it on writing cheap novels for money.

   ⓐ soared

   ⓑ misspent

   ⓒ provided

   ⓓ aimed

739 Pollution accumulated in the **stagnant** water and began to smell bad.

   ⓐ vile

   ⓑ indignant

   ⓒ ephemeral

   ⓓ stale

740 The government hoped its new policies would help businesses and end the **stagnation** of the economy.

   ⓐ quality

   ⓑ pomposity

   ⓒ oblivion

   ⓓ inactivity

741 Negotiations between the company and the union have reached a **stalemate**, and progress is unlikely.

   ⓐ affirmation

   ⓑ chaos

   ⓒ agreement

   ⓓ deadlock

742　The first **stanza** of this poem contains one of the most famous quotations in English literature.

　ⓐ verse

　ⓑ aesthetic

　ⓒ atrophy

　ⓓ verb

743　The **static** characterizations made the novel uninteresting.

　ⓐ stationary

　ⓑ hardy

　ⓒ valid

　ⓓ austere

744　There was so much **static** on the radio that listeners could hardly hear the program.

　ⓐ attribute

　ⓑ omission

　ⓒ noise

　ⓓ distaste

745　The army was **steadfast** in its allegiance to the king.

　ⓐ contemptible

　ⓑ ominous

　ⓒ odious

　ⓓ loyal

746　The beach house was elevated on **stilts** to keep it above the level of the tide.

　ⓐ walls

　ⓑ pillars

　ⓒ labyrinth

　ⓓ bastion

747　The captain remained **stoic** even after he had lost his ship.

　ⓐ attentive

　ⓑ gaunt

　ⓒ impassive

　ⓓ glacial

748　The most **stolid** man we knew, he never smiled or frowned at anything.

　ⓐ unemotional

　ⓑ passionate

　ⓒ forgetful

　ⓓ fervid

749　The enemy's **stratagem** was to send false radio messages.

　ⓐ stronghold

　ⓑ trait

　ⓒ scheme

　ⓓ stopgap measure

750　Between these two **strata** of rocks, you can see a layer of sandstone.

　ⓐ hiatus

　ⓑ combinations

　ⓒ statues

　ⓓ tiers

Answers

721-725	ⓐⓒⓓⓒⓓ	736-740	ⓑⓒⓑⓓⓓ
726-730	ⓒⓓⓒⓑⓓ	741-745	ⓓⓐⓐⓒⓓ
731-735	ⓑⓐⓒⓒⓑ	746-750	ⓑⓒⓐⓒⓓ

☆751 **strident**

[stráidənt]

adj. loud and unpleasant to hear

SYN loud, noisy, raucous, shrill

Her _____ voice made listening to her speech very unpleasant.

☆752 **stringent**

[stríndʒənt]

adj. rigorous; severe; strict

SYN inflexible, restrictive, rigid, strict

The company adopted _____ measures to improve its quality control.

☆753 **strut**

[strʌt]

v. to walk in an extremely proud or pompous manner

SYN swagger

The rooster _____ about the yard as if he owned the property.

☆754 **stupefy**

[stjú:pəfài]

v. to stun; to render insensible

SYN astonish, astound, overwhelm, stun

The light display was meant to _____ viewers with brilliant flashes of light.

☆755 **stupor**

[stjú:pər]

n. a state of insensibility

SYN apathy, daze, insensibility

A night of drinking left him in a _____.

☆756 **stymie**

[stáimi]

v. to hinder or prevent someone from doing something

SYN block, hinder

The weather _____ all our attempts to work outdoors.

☆757 **subjugate**
[sʌ́bdʒugèit]

v. to conquer or enslave; to bring under total control

SYN conquer, enslave

The Romans _____ many other peoples while building their empire.

☆758 **submissive**
[səbmísiv]

adj. obedient; unresisting

SYN compliant, obedient, subservient, tame

The servants all were highly _____ and carried out their duties obediently.

☆759 **subordinate**
[səbɔ́:rdənit]

adj. lower in rank, importance, etc.; secondary

SYN inferior, lower-ranking, secondary

In the army, a lieutenant is _____ in rank to a colonel.

☆760 **subside**
[səbsáid]

v. to drop or sink to a lower level or intensity

SYN diminish, drop, ebb, lessen, sink, wane

When the floodwaters _____, they left behind much debris and wreckage.

☆761 **substantiate**
[səbstǽnʃièit]

v. to affirm as correct, significant, or substantial; to confirm or verify

SYN confirm, verify

Investigators tried to _____ the report that a new species of bird had been discovered.

☆762 **subtle**
[sʌ́tl]

adj. very delicate; requiring keen perception to discern

SYN delicate, faint, slight

The spice added a _____ but important flavor to the food.

DAY 26

SCAFFOLDING

757 정복하다, 복종시키다   로마인들은 그들의 제국을 건설하면서 많은 다른 민족들을 복종시켰다subjugated.

758 순종하는, 온순한   그 하인들은 모두가 극도로 순종적이었고submissive 고분고분하게 그들의 임무를 수행했다.

759 하위의, 아래의   육군에서 중위는 서열상 대령보다 하위에 있다subordinate.

760 침전하다, 꺼지다, 주저앉다   홍수의 물이 빠지면서subsided 많은 파편과 잔해를 남겼다.

761 실증하다, 입증하다   연구자들은 새로운 종류의 조류가 발견되었다는 보고서를 입증하려substantiate 했다.

762 미묘한, 난해한   그 양념은 음식에 미묘하지만subtle 중요한 향을 첨가했다.

213

☆763 **succinct**
[səksíŋkt]

adj. in very few words

SYN brief, concise, short, terse

In only paragraph, the author wrote a _____ summary of the book.

☆764 **sullen**
[sʌ́lən]

adj. gloomy or depressed, with a component of anger and resentment

SYN dismal, gloomy, ill-tempered, irritated, morose

The children were _____ after their parents punished them.

☆765 **summons**
[sʌ́mənz]

n. a demand by someone in authority; an official demand to appear in court

SYN call, command, demand, order

By _____, he was called to appear in court.

☆766 **supercilious**
[sù:pərsíliəs]

adj. arrogant or disdainful in manner

SYN arrogant, contemptuous, haughty

The woman's _____ attitude toward her poorer neighbors made her unpopular.

☆767 **superficial**
[sù:pərfíʃəl]

adj. at or on the surface of something

SYN apparent, external, obvious, outward, shallow, minor

The soldier's wound was _____, so he did not require hospitalization.

☆768 **superfluity**
[sù:pərflú:əti]

n. an excess, overflow, overabundance, or excessive quantity

SYN excess, overabundance, superabundance

Heavy rainfall caused a _____ of water in the reservoir.

☆769 **superfluous**

[su:pə́rfluəs]

adj. more than necessary

SYN extra, excess, redundant

The presence of two players made any more players _____, so the rest had to find another game.

☆770 **superlative**

[səpə́:rlətiv]

adj. of the best or highest kind, degree, or quality

SYN best, excellent

The food at the dinner was of _____ quality, and everyone was delighted.

☆771 **supplant**

[səplǽnt]

v. to take the place of someone or something else, in many cases by force or intrigue

SYN remove, replace, succeed

The clever duke found a way to remove the king and to _____ him as ruler.

☆772 **suppress**

[səprés]

v. to inhibit or put a stop to something

SYN curtail, inhibit, subdue

By force, the government _____ the rebellion.

☆773 **surfeit**

[sə́:rfit]

n. (usually a surfeit of something) an excess

SYN excess, overabundance, oversupply

A _____ of food and drink at dinner made the man ill.

☆774 **surfeit**

[sə́:rfit]

v. to eat or drink or excess

SYN glut, satiate

After _____ on food and drink at dinner, the man felt ill.

769 남는, 여분의, 불필요한 　　두 선수의 참석으로 더 이상의 선수가 불필요하였고superfluous, 나머지 선수들은 다른 게임을 찾아야 했다.

770 최상의, 과도한 　　저녁식사 음식은 최상급superlative이었으며, 모두는 기뻐했다.

771 밀어내다, 대신 들어앉다 　　그 기민한 공작은 왕을 제거할 방법을 찾아 그를 통치자의 자리에서 밀어냈다supplant.

772 억압하다, 진압하다 　　정부는 무력으로 폭동을 진압했다suppressed.

773 과다, 과식, 과음 　　저녁에 과음과 과식으로surfeit 그 남자는 아팠다.

774 과식하다, 과음하다 　　저녁에 음식과 음료수를 과하게 먹은 후surfeiting 그 남자는 아픔을 느꼈다.

☆775 **surmise**

[sərmáiz]

n. a conclusion drawn from the information available, especially when the information is incomplete or insubstantial

SYN conclusion, deduction, extrapolation, inference

The detective's _____ was that the criminal was both well-educated and extremely careful.

☆776 **surpass**

[sərpǽs]

v. to be better or greater than something or someone else

SYN exceed, excel, outdo

Because the company _____ all others in the quality of its products, it soon dominated the industry.

☆777 **surreptitious**

[sə̀:rəptíʃəs]

adj. done in secret or by stealth

SYN concealed, furtive, hidden, secret

The _____ movement of troops by night gave the army an advantage in the battle the next day.

☆778 **susceptible**

[səséptəbl]

adj. easily influenced or overcome; vulnerable; weak

SYN vulnerable, weak

His weakened immune system left the patient very _____ to infections.

☆779 **sustain**

[səstéin]

v. to support the weight of something

SYN bear, hold, support

The bridge must _____ the weight of hundreds of automobiles at once.

☆780 **swagger**

[swǽgər]

v. to walk with an arrogant or insolent manner

SYN strut

The athlete _____ after he had won a medal.

SYNONYMS WORDS THAT MEAN THE SAME THING

751 Her **strident** voice made listening to her speech very unpleasant.

ⓐ stuffy

ⓑ shrill

ⓒ resplendent

ⓓ lifeless

752 The company adopted **stringent** measures to improve its quality control.

ⓐ auspicious

ⓑ wintry

ⓒ rigid

ⓓ impulsive

753 The rooster **strutted** about the yard as if he owned the property.

ⓐ embodied

ⓑ acquiesced

ⓒ expanded

ⓓ swaggered

754 The light display was meant to **stupefy** viewers with brilliant flashes of light.

ⓐ uphold

ⓑ refute

ⓒ trick

ⓓ astound

755 A night of drinking left him in a **stupor**.

ⓐ buttress

ⓑ daze

ⓒ succinctness

ⓓ muscularity

756 The weather **stymied** all our attempts to work outdoors.

ⓐ rolled

ⓑ hindered

ⓒ reinforced

ⓓ droned

757 The Romans **subjugated** many other peoples while building their empire.

ⓐ enslaved

ⓑ attempted

ⓒ freed

ⓓ employed

758 The servants all were highly **submissive** and carried out their duties obediently.

ⓐ shallow

ⓑ impulsive

ⓒ tame

ⓓ rugged

759 In the army, a lieutenant is **subordinate** in rank to a colonel.

ⓐ hardy

ⓑ inferior

ⓒ vulgar

ⓓ incorrigible

760 When the floodwaters **subsided**, they left behind much debris and wreckage.

ⓐ waned

ⓑ ousted

ⓒ pled

ⓓ deigned

761 Investigators tried to **substantiate** the report that a new species of bird had been discovered.

ⓐ lament

ⓑ confirm

ⓒ contradict

ⓓ abhor

DAY 26

762 The spice added a **subtle** but important flavor to the food.

ⓐ faint

ⓑ cloying

ⓒ infamous

ⓓ blatant

763 In only one paragraph, the author wrote a **succinct** summary of the book.

ⓐ deceptive

ⓑ precise

ⓒ concise

ⓓ plain

764 The children were **sullen** after their parents punished them.

ⓐ remorse

ⓑ cheerful

ⓒ sorry

ⓓ morose

765 By **summons**, he was called to appear in court.

ⓐ clout

ⓑ hangar

ⓒ hue

ⓓ demand

766 The woman's **supercilious** attitude toward her poorer neighbors made her unpopular.

ⓐ contemptuous

ⓑ gracious

ⓒ profuse

ⓓ rustic

767 The soldier's wound was **superficial**, so he did not require hospitalization.

ⓐ menial

ⓑ central

ⓒ genuine

ⓓ minor

768 Heavy rainfall caused a **superfluity** of water in the reservoir.

ⓐ attribute

ⓑ superabundance

ⓒ agitation

ⓓ candor

769 The presence of two players made any more players **superfluous**, so the rest had to find another game.

ⓐ audacious

ⓑ obvious

ⓒ gaunt

ⓓ redundant

770 The food at the dinner was of **superlative** quality, and everyone was delighted.

ⓐ excellent

ⓑ extensive

ⓒ frivolous

ⓓ candid

771 The clever duke found a way to remove the king and to **supplant** him as ruler.

ⓐ display

ⓑ succeed

ⓒ subscribe

ⓓ imply

772 By force, the government **suppressed** the rebellion.

ⓐ incited

ⓑ promoted

ⓒ inhibited

ⓓ revealed

773 A **surfeit** of food and drink at dinner made the man ill.

ⓐ shortcoming

ⓑ dearth

ⓒ deficiency

ⓓ oversupply

774 After **surfeiting** on food and drink at dinner, the man felt ill.

ⓐ draining

ⓑ counterfeiting

ⓒ satiating

ⓓ exhausting

775 The detective's **surmise** was that the criminal was both well-educated and extremely careful.

ⓐ certainty

ⓑ vigor

ⓒ fact

ⓓ deduction

776 Because the company **surpassed** all others in the quality of its products, it soon dominated the industry.

ⓐ outdid

ⓑ retracted

ⓒ withdrew

ⓓ revoked

777 The **surreptitious** movement of troops by night gave the army an advantage in the battle the next day.

ⓐ shallow

ⓑ furtive

ⓒ intuitive

ⓓ contagious

778 His weakened immune system left the patient very **susceptible** to infections.

ⓐ ardent

ⓑ superficial

ⓒ vulnerable

ⓓ intermittent

779 The bridge must **sustain** the weight of hundreds of automobiles at once.

ⓐ sequester

ⓑ deter

ⓒ confine

ⓓ support

780 The athlete **swaggered** after he had won a medal.

ⓐ exaggerated

ⓑ swelled

ⓒ strutted

ⓓ sank

Answers

751-755 ⓑⓒⓓⓓⓑ	766-770 ⓐⓓⓑⓓⓐ
756-760 ⓑⓐⓒⓑⓐ	771-775 ⓑⓒⓓⓒⓓ
761-765 ⓑⓐⓒⓓⓓ	776-780 ⓐⓑⓒⓓⓒ

☆781 **swell**
[swel]

v. to grow in volume or extent
SYN expand, grow, inflate

The balloon _____ as we pumped air into it.

☆782 **swindler**
[swíndlə*r*]

n. someone who commits fraud
SYN crook, fraud

The _____ stole the savings of hundreds of families before he was caught.

☆783 **sycophant**
[síkəfənt]

n. someone who tries to advance himself by flattery
SYN flatterer, toady

At his palace, the king was surrounded by parasites and _____.

☆784 **symbolism**
[símbəlìzəm]

n. representing something by something else, often a figure, mark, or shape
SYN representation

The _____ of the sign made people stop, for it meant danger was ahead.

☆785 **sympathy**
[símpəθi]

n. the ability to share the feelings of someone who is in trouble or pain
SYN compassion, commiseration

After my father died, my mother received many cards expressing _____.

☆786 **synchronize**
[síŋkrənàiz]

v. to set watches to an identical time; to make things happen at the same time
SYN agree, coincide

The members of the team _____ their watches so that they all could act at the same moment.

---

781 부풀다, 솟아오르다   우리가 풍선 속에 펌프로 공기를 주입하자 부풀어 올랐다swelled.

782 사기꾼   그 사기꾼swindler은 잡히기 전에 수백의 가족들의 저축을 훔쳤다.

783 알랑쇠, 아첨꾼   그의 성에서 왕은 아첨꾼과 알랑쇠들sycophants에 둘러싸여 있었다.

784 상징, 부호체계   기호의 상징symbolism은 전방의 위험을 뜻했기 때문에 사람들을 멈추게 했다.

785 동정, 동감, 교감   아버지가 돌아가시고, 어머니는 많은 위문sympathy 카드를 받았다.

786 같은 시간으로 맞추다, 동시에 발생하다   그 팀의 구성원들은 동시에 모두가 행동할 수 있도록 시간을 똑같이 맞추었다synchronized.

☆787 **synopsis**

[sinápsis]

n. a brief summary or condensation of a novel, play, or other work

SYN abstract, condensation, summary

For readers who do not have time to read the whole book, a _____ is included.

☆788 **table**

[téibəl]

v. to put off until a later time

SYN defer, delay, postpone, shelve

The committee voted to _____ the legislation.

☆789 **taciturn**

[tǽsətə̀:rn]

adj. not given to speaking; close-mouthed; tight-lipped

SYN reticent, silent

He was such a _____ man that on some days he said nothing at all to anyone.

☆790 **tailor**

[téilər]

v. to make or modify something to meet certain specifications

SYN adapt, adjust, modify

We must _____ this product to meet the needs of our client.

☆791 **tangent**

[tǽndʒənt]

n. a digression or sudden change of subject

SYN aside, digression

After talking about the main subject for a few minutes, he suddenly went off on a _____ and started talking about something else.

☆792 **tangential**

[tændʒénʃəl]

adj. divergent; digressive; oblique; not strictly related to the subject under discussion

SYN digressive, parenthetical

This information is _____ to the subject under discussion, and we should ignore it for now.

SCAFFOLDING

787 개관, 개요　　　　책 전체를 읽을 시간이 없는 독자들을 위해, 개요synopsis가 포함되어 있다.

788 연기하다　　　　그 위원회는 법률제정을 연기하는table 쪽으로 가결했다.

789 말없는, 입이 무거운　그는 너무도 과묵한taciturn 남자라 어떤 날에는 누구에게도 아무 말을 하지 않았다.

790 짓다, 손질하다　　우리는 이 상품을 고객들의 요구에 맞추어 만들어야tailor 한다.

791 탈선, 여담　　　　얼마동안 주요 주제에 대해 이야기를 하고 난 후, 그는 느닷없이 방향을 바꾸어tangent 다른 것들을 이야기 하기 시작했다.

792 규준에서 벗어난, 이탈한　이 정보는 심의중인 주제에서 벗어나므로tangential, 지금으로선 이를 무시해야 한다.

☆793 **tangible**
[tǽndʒəbəl]

adj. capable of being touched and felt with the hands; real; actual; true; certain; definite

SYN palpable, real, definite

There are no _____ grounds for suspicion.

☆794 **tantamount**
[tǽntəmàunt]

adj. equivalent in effect, meaning, or value

SYN equal, equivalent

The king's statement was _____ to a declaration of war.

☆795 **tardy**
[táːrdi]

adj. late; behind schedule

SYN belated, dilatory, late, slack

The student was reprimanded for being _____ to school.

☆796 **tedious**
[tíːdiəs]

adj. so long or wordy as to make one feel tired

SYN boring, tiresome

The journey by road was so long and _____ that many travelers preferred to go by ship.

☆797 **temper**
[témpər]

n. a disposition; a state of mind; an emotional condition

SYN mood, personality, disposition

My mother was of an even _____ and seldom got angry.

☆798 **temper**
[témpər]

v. to mitigate or bring to a desirable state or temperature by mixing in something else

SYN mitigate, moderate, soften

The judge felt the need to _____ justice with compassion.

SCAFFOLDING

793 실체적인, 확실한, 명백한   의심할 만한 확실한tangible 근거는 없었다.

794 동등한, 상당하는   그 왕의 말은 전쟁의 선포와도 같았다tantamount.

795 느린, 완만한, 더딘   학생들은 학교에 지각하여tardy 꾸지람을 들었다.

796 지루한, 장황한   가도 여행은 너무 길고 지루해tedious 많은 여행가들은 선박 여행을 선호했다.

797 기질, 기분, 평정   어머니는 성미가 차분했고temper 거의 노하지 않았다.

798 진정시키다, 조화시키다   그 판사는 동정심과 정의를 조화시켜야temper 할 필요성을 느꼈다.

☆799 **temperate**
[témpərit]

adj. moderate or self-controlled; not extreme or given to extreme behavior
SYN moderate, restrained

My father was a man of _____ behavior and tried to avoid extremes in everything.

☆800 **tenacious**
[tənéiʃəs]

adj. firm; persistent; tough; hard to break or overcome
SYN firm, obstinate, persistent, retentive, stubborn, tight

The cat held the bird in a _____ grip.

☆801 **tenacity**
[tənǽsəti]

n. strong resistance to being broken or overcome
SYN firmness, obstinacy, persistence

The _____ of the man's smoking habit made the addiction hard to defeat.

☆802 **tentative**
[téntətiv]

adj. in the nature of an attempt or trial
SYN proposed, provisional, temporary

Korea and China reached a _____ agreement on the Koguryo issue.

☆803 **terrestrial**
[təréstriəl]

adj. of or pertaining to the earth or to dry land
SYN earthly, mundane, worldly

_____ ecosystems are very different from aquatic ecosystems.

☆804 **terse**
[tə:rs]

adj. expressed in very few words
SYN brief, concise

His e-mails were always _____ and seldom more than two short sentences in length.

SCAFFOLDING

799 온화한, 절제하는   아버지는 행실이 온건했고temperate 모든 것에서 극단을 피하려고 했다.

800 완강한, 집요한   그 고양이는 새를 꼭 잡고tenacious 놓지 않았다.

801 고집, 끈기, 집요   그 남자의 흡연 습관에 대한 집요함tenacity은 중독을 극복하기 어렵게 했다.

802 시험적인, 임시의, 모호한   한국과 중국은 고구려 문제에 대해 임시tentative 합의를 하였다.

803 지구상의, 지상의   지상의Terrestrial 생태계는 수상 생태계와 매우 상이하다.

804 간결한, 간명한   그의 이메일은 언제나 간결했고terse 길이는 짧은 두 문장을 거의 넘지 않았다.

DAY 27

☆805 **theoretical**
[θìːərétikəl]

adj. in or related to theory; speculative

SYN abstract, conjectural, ideal

Inventors soon turned the professor's _____ work into practical inventions.

☆806 **threadbare**
[θrédbὲər]

adj. worn; frayed; heavily used; scanty; in poor condition

SYN shabby, used, worn

The beggar wore a _____ coat that offered little protection against the cold wind.

☆807 **thrive**
[θraiv]

v. to grow vigorously; to prosper

SYN boom, burgeon, flourish, prosper

In this rich soil, crops will _____.

☆808 **tightfisted**
[tàitfístid]

adj. very reluctant to spend money; thrifty to an extreme

SYN parsimonious, stingy, ungenerous

The old man in the story was so _____ that he never spent a penny more than necessary.

☆809 **tirade**
[táireid]

n. a long and bitter denunciation

SYN diatribe, harangue

In her speech, the doctor delivered a _____ against smoking.

☆810 **tonic**
[tánik]

n. a stimulating or energizing drink; anything stimulating or restorative

SYN stimulant, pickup

The drink was advertised as a _____ that would improve the user's health.

SCAFFOLDING

805 이론상, 이론적으로   발명가들은 곧 그 교수의 이론상theoretical 작업을 실용적인 발명품으로 만들었다.
806 초라한, 오래 입은, 낡은   그 거지는 차가운 바람으로부터 거의 보호를 해주지 못하는 낡은threadbare 코트를 입었다.
807 번창하다, 번영하다   이 비옥한 토양에서 농작물이 잘 자랄 것이다thrive.
808 인색한, 검소한   이야기 속의 그 늙은 남자는 너무도 인색해서tightfisted 절대 필요이상의 돈을 쓰지 않았다.
809 장광설, 격론   그녀의 연설에서 그 의사는 흡연에 대해 통렬한 비난tirade을 했다.
810 강장제   그 음료수는 사용자의 건강을 증진시켜줄 강장제tonic로 선전되었다.

224

SYNONYMS WORDS THAT MEAN THE SAME THING

781 The balloon swelled as we pumped air into it.

ⓐ declined
ⓑ meddled
ⓒ inflated
ⓓ crashed

782 The swindler stole the savings of hundreds of families before he was caught.

ⓐ crook
ⓑ banker
ⓒ visitor
ⓓ director

783 At his palace, the king was surrounded by parasites and sycophants.

ⓐ analysts
ⓑ critics
ⓒ faultfinders
ⓓ toadies

784 The symbolism of the sign made people stop, for it meant danger was ahead.

ⓐ modernism
ⓑ representation
ⓒ pomposity
ⓓ fanaticism

785 After my father died, my mother received many cards expressing sympathy.

ⓐ commiseration
ⓑ seclusion
ⓒ rigidity
ⓓ equanimity

786 The members of the team synchronized their watches so that they all could act at the same moment.

ⓐ diverged
ⓑ elucidated
ⓒ marked
ⓓ coincided

787 For readers who do not have time to read the whole book, a synopsis is included.

ⓐ repulse
ⓑ condensation
ⓒ critic
ⓓ compensation

788 The committee voted to table the legislation.

ⓐ postpone
ⓑ book
ⓒ reserve
ⓓ sanction

789 He was such a taciturn man that on some days he said nothing at all to anyone.

ⓐ fastidious
ⓑ solitary
ⓒ tame
ⓓ reticent

790 We must tailor this product to meet the needs of our client.

ⓐ condescend
ⓑ confine
ⓒ modify
ⓓ allay

791 After talking about the main subject for a few minutes, he suddenly went off on a **tangent** and started talking about something else.

ⓐ valid

ⓑ digression

ⓒ superfluity

ⓓ largess

792 This information is **tangential** to the subject under discussion, and we should ignore it for now.

ⓐ unshakeable

ⓑ digressive

ⓒ esoteric

ⓓ carping

793 There are no **tangible** grounds for suspicion.

ⓐ composite

ⓑ amicable

ⓒ baneful

ⓓ definite

794 The king's statement was **tantamount** to a declaration of war.

ⓐ miscellaneous

ⓑ equivalent

ⓒ nascent

ⓓ fetid

795 The student was reprimanded for being **tardy** to school.

ⓐ fiery

ⓑ nagging

ⓒ serene

ⓓ late

796 The journey by road was so long and **tedious** that many travelers preferred to go by ship.

ⓐ boring

ⓑ sarcastic

ⓒ nasty

ⓓ biting

797 My mother was of an even **temper** and seldom got angry.

ⓐ disposition

ⓑ lassitude

ⓒ fringe

ⓓ charlatan

798 The judge felt the need to **temper** justice with compassion.

ⓐ misrepresent

ⓑ reproach

ⓒ mitigate

ⓓ upbraid

799 My father was a man of **temperate** behavior and tried to avoid extremes in everything.

ⓐ marred

ⓑ irksome

ⓒ restrained

ⓓ petulant

800 The cat held the bird in a **tenacious** grip.

ⓐ firm

ⓑ iniquitous

ⓒ fleet

ⓓ veracious

801 The **tenacity** of the man's smoking habit made the addiction hard to defeat.

ⓐ foaminess

ⓑ exaggeration

ⓒ bragging

ⓓ obstinacy

802 Korea and China reached a **tentative** agreement on the Koguryo issue.

ⓐ prehistoric

ⓑ antiquated

ⓒ temporary

ⓓ quaint

803 **Terrestrial** ecosystems are very different from aquatic ecosystems.

ⓐ worldly

ⓑ earthly

ⓒ celestial

ⓓ aquatic

804 His e-mails were always **terse** and seldom more than two short sentences in length.

ⓐ laughable

ⓑ officious

ⓒ laconic

ⓓ concise

805 Inventors soon turned the professor's **theoretical** work into practical inventions.

ⓐ confidential

ⓑ radical

ⓒ arrogant

ⓓ conjectural

806 The beggar wore a **threadbare** coat that offered little protection against the cold wind.

ⓐ shabby

ⓑ evasive

ⓒ germane

ⓓ grandiloquent

807 In this rich soil, crops will **thrive**.

ⓐ languish

ⓑ extirpate

ⓒ burgeon

ⓓ deplore

808 The old man in the story was so **tightfisted** that he never spent a penny more than necessary.

ⓐ ungenerous

ⓑ whimsical

ⓒ congruous

ⓓ attentive

809 In her speech, the doctor delivered a **tirade** against smoking.

ⓐ inertia

ⓑ knack

ⓒ reticence

ⓓ harangue

810 The drink was advertised as a **tonic** that would improve the user's health.

ⓐ stimulant

ⓑ peril

ⓒ loophole

ⓓ knot

DAY 27

Answers

781-785 ⓒⓐⓓⓑⓐ	796-800 ⓐⓐⓒⓒⓐ
786-790 ⓓⓑⓐⓓⓒ	801-805 ⓓⓒⓑⓓⓓ
791-795 ⓑⓑⓓⓑⓓ	806-810 ⓐⓒⓐⓓⓐ

☆811 **torpor**
[tɔ́ːrpər]

n. a state of apathy and inactivity

SYN apathy, inactivity, inertia, lethargy

During cold months, some animals spend their lives in a temporary _____ to conserve energy.

☆812 **torso**
[tɔ́ːrsou]

n. the trunk of the human body, excepting the limbs and head

SYN trunk

The body armor fits around the _____ of the body to protect the heart, lungs, and other important organs.

☆813 **tragic**
[trǽdʒik]

adj. extremely sad or sorrowful

SYN dreadful, melancholy, mournful, sad

A _____ event, the collapse of the bridge killed five people.

☆814 **trait**
[treit]

n. a distinguishing mark, characteristic, attribute, property, or quality

SYN attribute, characteristic, property

A distinctive _____ of this bird is its loud, harsh cry.

☆815 **tranquil**
[trǽŋkwil]

adj. calm; undisturbed; restful; relaxing; serene

SYN calm, peaceful, quiet

Deep in the woods was a _____ lake with clean water.

☆816 **tranquility**
[træŋkwíləti]

n. a tranquil, calm, peaceful state or condition

SYN calmness, quiet, serenity

The _____ of the place made him drowsy, so he went to sleep.

SCAFFOLDING

811 마비, 무감각, 휴면   추운 계절에 몇몇 동물들은 에너지를 보존하기 위해 일시적 휴면torpor으로 생을 보낸다.
812 몸통, 미완성 작품   방탄복은 몸통torso 주위를 둘러싸서 심장, 폐, 그리고 다른 중요한 기관들을 보호한다.
813 비극의, 비통한   다리 붕괴라는 비극적tragic 사건으로 다섯명이 죽었다.
814 특색, 특성   이 새의 독특한 특징trait은 크고 거친 울음소리이다.
815 조용한, 평온한   숲 깊숙이 깨끗한 물을 가진 조용한tranquil 호수가 있다.
816 고요함, 평온함   그 장소의 평온함tranquility이 그를 졸리게 만들어, 그는 잠들었다.

☆817 **transcribe**
[trænskráib]

v. to make a written or typewritten copy of spoken information
SYN copy, record, reproduce

A typist _____ the doctor's lecture for patients to read.

☆818 **transient**
[trǽnʃənt]

adj. lasting only a brief time; impermanent; short-lived
SYN brief, evanescent, fleeting, impermanent, short-lived, temporary, transitory

The phases of the moon are well-known examples of _____ phenomena.

☆819 **transparent**
[trænspɛ́ərənt]

adj. easily seen through
SYN clear, limpid

Through the _____ lens, we saw images of things far away.

☆820 **treachery**
[trétʃəri]

n. a violation of trust or faith
SYN betrayal, disloyalty, perfidy

The play is about the villain's act of _____ against his country.

☆821 **trepidation**
[trèpidéiʃən]

n. a state or condition of fearfulness or great unease
SYN agitation, alarm, fear, fright

The thought of climbing the mountain was so frightening that it filled us with _____.

☆822 **trespass**
[tréspəs]

v. to commit an offense against someone
SYN offend, sin, transgress, violate

We are told to forgive others when they _____ against us.

DAY 28

817 복사하다, 번역하다, 문자화하다   타자수는 그 의사의 강의를 환자들이 읽게 하기 위해 문자화했다transcribed.

818 일시적인, 무상한   달의 위상(位相)은 잘 알려진 일시적transient 현상의 예이다.

819 투명한, 명료한   투명한transparent 렌즈를 통해 우리는 저 멀리의 형상을 보았다.

820 배반, 반역   그 연극은 악역의 자국에 대한 배반treachery행위에 대한 것이다.

821 공포, 전율   산을 오르는 생각이 너무도 두려워 우리는 공포trepidation로 떨었다.

822 침해하다, 죄를 짓다   우리는 다른 사람들이 우리에게 지은 죄를trespass 용서하라고 가르침을 받는다.

☆823 **trifling**
[tráifliŋ]

adj. of little or no worth, value, or importance
SYN insignificant, worthless

It costs only a _____ amount of money to send a postcard.

☆824 **trite**
[trait]

adj. overly familiar; everyday; commonplace
SYN commonplace, ordinary, overused, stale

No one will pay attention to your essay if it is full of _____ expressions.

☆825 **trivial**
[tríviəl]

adj. without significance, importance, or value
SYN insignificant, unimportant, worthless

This information was so _____ that it was left out of the report.

☆826 **troupe**
[tru:p]

n. a group of performers, especially a traveling group of entertainers
SYN band, company, group

A _____ of actors visited the town and performed a play there.

☆827 **truncate**
[trʌ́ŋkeit]

v. to shorten by removing a part
SYN abbreviate, cut, shorten

The pier was _____ at the end, where a storm had removed a part of it.

☆828 **tumor**
[tjú:mər]

n. an abnormal, massive growth of cells in a tissue
SYN cancer, cyst

Surgeons removed a _____ from her lung.

823 하찮은, 시시한 · 엽서를 보내는데 소액의trifling 돈이 들 뿐이다.
824 흔해빠진, 진부한 · 진부한trite 표현으로 가득하다면 누구도 너의 에세이에 관심을 보이지 않을 것이다.
825 하찮은, 사소한 · 이 정보는 별로 대단하지 않아trivial 보고서에서 빠졌다.
826 일단, 한 패 · 일단troupe의 배우들이 마을을 방문해 거기서 연극을 했다.
827 꼭대기를 자르다, 끊다 · 그 부두의 끝이 잘려나갔는데truncated, 그 끝의 일부가 폭풍으로 파손되었었다.
828 종기, 종양 · 외과의사들은 그녀의 폐에서 종양tumor을 제거했다.

☆829	**turbulence** [tɔ́:rbjuləns]	*n.* a disturbed or disordered state or condition **SYN** commotion, disorder, instability, unrest _____ in the atmosphere made the aircraft's flight unsteady.
☆830	**turbulent** [tɔ́:rbjulənt]	*adj.* disturbed; unsettled; tumultuous **SYN** disordered, tumultuous, unstable At the base of the waterfall, the water is very _____.
☆831	**turmoil** [tɔ́:rmɔil]	*n.* a disordered or tumultuous state or condition; great unrest or agitation **SYN** agitation, commotion, disorder, disturbance, tumult, unrest After the _____ of a civil war, the country started to rebuild.
☆832	**turpitude** [tɔ́:rpitʃùːd]	*n.* very immoral conduct **SYN** depravity, vice In a frightening scene, the play showed the _____ of the villain.
☆833	**uncouth** [ʌnkúːθ]	*adj.* impolite; uncivil; discourteous **SYN** discourteous, impolite, rude The man's _____ behavior made him an embarrassment to his family.
☆834	**undermine** [ʌndərmáin]	*v.* to weaken by gradually removing the foundations of something **SYN** injure, undercut, weaken Erosion _____ the cliff until its top part was left unsupported and fell into the sea.

DAY 28

☆835 **uniform**
[júːnəfɔ̀ːrm]

adj. identical in character

SYN alike, homogeneous, identical, regular, same, unvarying

The layer of sand had a _____ thickness of one meter.

☆836 **uniformity**
[jùːnəfɔ́ːrməti]

n. the state or condition of being uniform

SYN homogeneity, regularity, sameness

The _____ of the products was such that any one could substitute for any other.

☆837 **unilateral**
[jùːnəlǽtərəl]

adj. having or involving only one side

SYN one-sided

The country would not agree to _____ disarmament, which would have left it defenseless.

☆838 **unkempt**
[ʌnkémpt]

adj. ill-groomed; untidy; untended; completely careless about one's appearance

SYN disheveled, ill-groomed, messy, untidy

An _____ beggar sat on the sidewalk while asking passersby for coins.

☆839 **unprecedented**
[ʌnprésədèntid]

adj. never witnessed before; without precedent; completely novel

SYN unique, extraordinary

The earthquake in our county was _____, for the earth there had always been quiet before.

☆840 **unruly**
[ʌnrúːli]

adj. not obedient; submissive; or easily managed

SYN disobedient, disorderly

The teacher had to deal with a class of _____ children who hated discipline.

SCAFFOLDING

835 한결같은, 균일한
모래의 층은 1미터의 균일한uniform 두께로 되어있다.

836 한결같음, 획일, 단조
상품의 단조성uniformity으로 인해 누구든지 다른 어떤 것으로든지 대체할 수 있었다.

837 일방의, 단독적인
국가는 자국을 무방비하게 만들 일방적인unilateral 무장해제에 동의하지 않을 것이다.

838 난잡한, 세련되지 못한
난잡한unkempt 거지가 보도에 앉아 통행인들에게 동전을 구걸했다.

839 전례가 없는, 새로운
우리나라의 지진은 전례가 없는데unprecedented 그곳의 지층은 이때까지 조용했기 때문이다.

840 감당할 수 없는, 제멋대로 구는
그 선생님은 규율을 싫어하는 제어하기 어려운unruly 아이들 반을 상대해야 했다.

232

SYNONYMS WORDS THAT MEAN THE SAME THING

811 During cold months, some animals spend their lives in a temporary **torpor** to conserve energy.

ⓐ inactivity

ⓑ labyrinth

ⓒ knack

ⓓ rupture

812 The body armor fits around the **torso** of the body to protect the heart, lungs, and other important organs.

ⓐ lampoon

ⓑ trail

ⓒ trunk

ⓓ wake

813 A **tragic** event, the collapse of the bridge killed five people.

ⓐ dreadful

ⓑ inclusive

ⓒ spurious

ⓓ esoteric

814 A distinctive **trait** of this bird is its loud, harsh cry.

ⓐ fetter

ⓑ parcel

ⓒ zenith

ⓓ attribute

815 Deep in the woods was a **tranquil** lake with clean water.

ⓐ calm

ⓑ erudite

ⓒ prodigal

ⓓ germane

816 The **tranquility** of the place made him drowsy, so he went to sleep.

ⓐ freight

ⓑ proliferation

ⓒ pomposity

ⓓ serenity

817 A typist **transcribed** the doctor's lecture for patients to read.

ⓐ ruffled

ⓑ arraigned

ⓒ reproduced

ⓓ impaired

818 The phases of the moon are well-known examples of **transient** phenomena.

ⓐ throbbing

ⓑ fleeting

ⓒ sparing

ⓓ miscellaneous

819 Through the **transparent** lens, we saw images of things far away.

ⓐ indefatigable

ⓑ endemic

ⓒ condensed

ⓓ clear

820 The play is about the villain's act of **treachery** against his country.

ⓐ barge

ⓑ elegy

ⓒ exigency

ⓓ perfidy

821 The thought of climbing the mountain was so frightening that it filled us with **trepidation**.

ⓐ fluster

ⓑ oath

ⓒ commiseration

ⓓ agitation

DAY 28

233

822 We are told to forgive others when they **trespass** against us.

ⓐ pierce

ⓑ murmur

ⓒ transgress

ⓓ pry

823 It costs only a **trifling** amount of money to send a postcard.

ⓐ limpid

ⓑ saccharine

ⓒ insignificant

ⓓ voracious

824 No one will pay attention to your essay if it is full of **trite** expressions.

ⓐ stale

ⓑ fresh

ⓒ significant

ⓓ apprehensive

825 This information was so **trivial** that it was left out of the report.

ⓐ significant

ⓑ scrambled

ⓒ worthless

ⓓ impressive

826 A **troupe** of actors visited the town and performed a play there.

ⓐ entity

ⓑ band

ⓒ soul

ⓓ object

827 The pier was **truncated** at the end, where a storm had removed a part of it.

ⓐ inflated

ⓑ abbreviated

ⓒ jumbled

ⓓ devoured

828 Surgeons removed a **tumor** from her lung.

ⓐ cyst

ⓑ trickery

ⓒ guile

ⓓ radiance

829 **Turbulence** in the atmosphere made the aircraft's flight unsteady.

ⓐ wrath

ⓑ seclusion

ⓒ unrest

ⓓ rim

830 At the base of the waterfall, the water is very **turbulent**.

ⓐ esoteric

ⓑ disordered

ⓒ soporific

ⓓ nascent

831 After the **turmoil** of a civil war, the country started to rebuild.

ⓐ tumult

ⓑ resolution

ⓒ cease-fire

ⓓ candor

832 In a frightening scene, the play showed the **turpitude** of the villain.

ⓐ betray

ⓑ nadir

ⓒ incidence

ⓓ depravity

833 The man's **uncouth** behavior made him an embarrassment to his family.

ⓐ onerous

ⓑ disjointed

ⓒ discourteous

ⓓ gingerly

834 Erosion **undermined** the cliff until its top part was left unsupported and fell into the sea.

ⓐ undercut
ⓑ mesmerized
ⓒ quivered
ⓓ extended

835 The layer of sand had a **uniform** thickness of one meter.

ⓐ incongruous
ⓑ regular
ⓒ caprice
ⓓ erroneous

836 The **uniformity** of the products was such that anyone could substitute for any other.

ⓐ reflux
ⓑ span
ⓒ recession
ⓓ homogeneity

837 The country would not agree to **unilateral** disarmament, which would have left it defenseless.

ⓐ inconsequential
ⓑ one-sided
ⓒ reachable
ⓓ immobile

838 An **unkempt** beggar sat on the sidewalk while asking passersby for coins.

ⓐ incisive
ⓑ attentive
ⓒ disheveled
ⓓ obscene

839 The earthquake in our county was **unprecedented**, for the earth there had always been quiet before.

ⓐ dangled
ⓑ startled
ⓒ incidental
ⓓ extraordinary

840 The teacher had to deal with a class of **unruly** children who hated discipline.

ⓐ inapt
ⓑ casual
ⓒ hasty
ⓓ disorderly

Answers

811-815 ⓐⓒⓐⓓⓐ	826-830 ⓑⓑⓐⓒⓑ
816-820 ⓓⓒⓑⓓⓓ	831-835 ⓐⓓⓒⓐⓑ
821-825 ⓓⓒⓒⓐⓒ	836-840 ⓓⓑⓒⓓⓓ

DAY 29

☆841 **unsung**
[ʌ̀nsʌ́ŋ]

adj. not widely known, recognized, or celebrated (often used in the cliché "unsung hero," meaning a person who has given distinguished service without recognition)

SYN obscure, uncelebrated, unknown, unpublicized

The little-known soldier was finally recognized as an _____ hero of the war.

☆842 **unwarranted**
[ʌ̀nwɔ́(:)rəntid]

adj. without justification

SYN baseless, groundless, unjustified

The project failed because of _____ interference from outside.

☆843 **uphold**
[ʌphóuld]

v. to defend or give support to something

SYN defend, support

The court's decision _____ the city's plan to build a new stadium.

☆844 **uproar**
[ʌ́prɔ̀:r]

n. noisy disorder

SYN clamor, racket, tumult, turmoil

The controversial book generated an _____ of criticism among readers.

☆845 **usurp**
[juːsə́rp]

v. to seize wrongfully or without authority

SYN grab, seize, steal, supplant

The prince _____ the king's authority and unlawfully took control of the kingdom.

☆846 **utilize**
[júːtəlàiz]

v. to use or put into one's service

SYN employ, use

The craftsman _____ a sharp knife to cut the wood.

SCAFFOLDING

841 찬미되지 않는, 무명의   거의 알려지지 않은 그 군인은 마침내 전쟁의 칭송받지 못한unsung 영웅으로 표창받았다.

842 보증되지 않은, 공인되지 않은   그 프로젝트는 외부로부터의 공인되지 않은unwarranted 추론으로 실패했다.

843 떠받치다, 들어올리다   법원의 결정은 새로운 경기장을 지을 도시의 계획을 지지했다upheld.

844 소란, 소동, 소음   논쟁의 대상이 되는 이 책은 독자들 사이에서 비평의 소동uproar을 일으켰다.

845 빼앗다, 찬탈하다   왕자는 왕의 권위를 찬탈했고usurped 불법으로 그 왕국을 지배했다.

846 활용하다, 이용하다   장인은 나무를 잘라내기 위해 날카로운 칼을 이용했다utilized.

☆847 **utter**
[ʌ́tər]

v. to speak or give voice to something

(SYN) say, speak, voice

The sick man _____ a cry of pain.

☆848 **utter**
[ʌ́tər]

adj. absolute; complete; total

(SYN) complete, total

When the light went out, the room was in _____ darkness.

☆849 **vacillate**
[vǽsəlèit]

v. to change one's mind or opinion; to be indecisive or uncertain

(SYN) fluctuate, hesitate, oscillate, waffle, waver

Because the candidate has _____ on this issue, no one knows what he really believes.

☆850 **vague**
[veig]

adj. poorly defined; not made clear

(SYN) imprecise, indistinct, uncertain, unclear

The description of this person is so _____ that it might apply to almost anyone.

☆851 **valid**
[vǽlid]

adj. defensible; justifiable; legitimate; solid; well-founded

(SYN) authoritative, just, sound

There was no _____ reason to grant the request, so we said no.

☆852 **vaporize**
[véipəràiz]

v. to turn into vapor

(SYN) boil, evaporate

The laser beam _____ a small amount of the target.

DAY 29

SCAFFOLDING

847 발언하다, 털어놓다   병든 남자는 고통의 울음을 내뱉었다uttered.
848 전적인, 완전한   불이 나갔을 때, 방은 완전한utter 어둠 속이었다.
849 망설이다, 흔들거리다   후보자가 그 사안에 대해 망설였기 때문에vacillated 누구도 그가 무엇을 믿는지 알 수 없다.
850 어렴풋한, 막연한   이 사람의 묘사가 너무도 애매해서vague 거의 아무에게나 들어맞을 수 있다.
851 근거가 확실한, 정당한   우리가 요청을 승인해 줄 정당한valid 근거가 없어서 우리는 안 된다고 말했다.
852 증발시키다, 희박하게 하다   레이저 빔이 목표물의 소량을 기화시켰다vaporized.

237

☆853 **variable**
[vέəriəbəl]

adj. capable of changing

SYN changeable, inconstant, volatile

The temperature in this location is highly _____ and may change 50 degrees in an hour.

☆854 **variable**
[vέəriəbəl]

n. a factor with more than one possible quantity or value

SYN a changeable value or quantity

The _____ in this equation is temperature, which may change greatly.

☆855 **variegated**
[vέəriəgèitid]

adj. diverse in color

SYN diversified, diverse

This painting shows a _____ pattern of colors against a dark background.

☆856 **vehement**
[víːəmənt]

adj. strongly felt; impassioned

SYN earnest, fervent, passionate

Despite his _____ protest, he was sent to prison.

☆857 **venerate**
[vénərèit]

v. to treat reverently

SYN honor, revere

The school _____ the memory of its founder.

☆858 **vent**
[vent]

v. to release or expel

SYN expel, release

The engine _____ its exhaust through a pipe.

853 가변적인, 변덕스러운   이 지역의 온도는 극도로 변덕스럽고variable 한 시간에 화씨 50도가 변할 수 있다.
854 변화하기 쉬운 것, 변수   이 방정식에서 변수variable는 크게 변할 수도 있는 기온이다.
855 잡색의, 고르지 못한   이 그림은 어두운 배경에 대비해 다채로운variegated 색의 양상을 보여준다.
856 격렬한, 열심인   그의 격렬한vehement 항의에도 불구하고 그는 감옥에 보내졌다.
857 존경하다, 받들어 모시다   그 학교는 설립자에 대한 기억을 받들어 모셨다venerated.
858 구멍을 내다, 배출하다   엔진은 파이프를 통해 배기가스를 배출한다vents.

☆859 **vent**
[vent]

n. an opening for releasing or expelling something
SYN duct, escape, exit, opening

This is the _____ through which hot air is expelled.

☆860 **verbose**
[vəːrbóus]

adj. characterized by the use of too many words
SYN prolix, wordy

The speech was too _____ and should have been shortened.

☆861 **verify**
[vérəfài]

v. to see whether or not information is correct
SYN ascertain, authenticate, check, validate

The arms control agreement required both sides to _____ the number of each other's weapons.

☆862 **vertical**
[vɔ́ːrtikəl]

adj. perpendicular to the horizon; straight up
SYN perpendicular, upright

The rocket's _____ flight took it to a high altitude.

☆863 **vestige**
[véstidʒ]

adj. vestigial
[vestídʒiəl]

n. a very small piece of evidence; a trace or hint
SYN hint, suggestion, trace

Only a _____ of the building remained after a thousand years.

☆864 **viable**
[váiəbəl]

adj. capable of being done; feasible or practical
SYN feasible, practical

We thought the plan was _____, so we proceeded with it.

DAY 29

SCAFFOLDING

859 구멍, 배출구, 표출   이것이 뜨거운 공기가 빠져 나가는 배출구vent이다.
860 말이 많은, 장황한   그 연설은 너무도 장황했고verbose 줄였어야 했다.
861 입증하다, 확인하다   무기제한협정은 서로 각자의 무기의 수를 확인하는verify 것을 요했다.
862 수직의, 곧추선   로켓은 수직vertical 비행으로 고도에 도달했다.
863 자취, 흔적   천년 후 오직 건물의 자취vestige만이 남아있었다.
864 시행 가능한, 실용적인   우리는 그 계획이 실행 가능하다고viable 생각해서 이를 계속 진척시켰다.

☆865 **vigor**
[vígər]

n. energy or strength of growth or other activity

SYN force, intensity, strength, vitality

A healthy diet gave the patient _____ and stamina.

☆866 **vilify**
[víləfài]

v. to insult or speak ill of someone

SYN defame, insult, slander

In a speech, the politician _____ his opponent with harsh language.

☆867 **vindicate**
[víndəkèit]

v. to exonerate; to clear the name of an accused person

SYN exonerate, justify

The commission's investigation _____ the judge of all accusations against him.

☆868 **vindictive**
[vindíktiv]

adj. wishing to take revenge

SYN spiteful, unforgiving, vengeful

She had a _____ character and often imagined taking revenge on those who had wronged her.

☆869 **virtuoso**
[vè:rtʃuóusou]

adj. extremely skilled and brilliant in performance

SYN brilliant, consummate, masterly, skilled

This recording is a _____ performance of the concerto.

☆870 **virtuoso**
[vè:rtʃuóusou]

n. a brilliant or expert performer

SYN expert

This musician is a _____ known around the world.

SCAFFOLDING

865 활기, 체력
건강에 좋은 식이요법이 그 환자에게 활기vigor와 원기를 주었다.

866 비방하다, 헐뜯다
연설에서 그 정치가는 거친 언사로 그의 반대측을 비방했다vilified.

867 입증하다, 옹호하다, 지키다
위원회의 조사가 그에 대한 모든 고소에 대한 판단이 정당함을 입증했다vindicated.

868 원한을 품은, 보복의
그녀는 보복적vindictive 성격을 가지고 있으며 그녀에게 해를 끼친 사람들에게 복수하는 것을 종종 상상했다.

869 대가의, 거장의
이 녹음은 그 협주곡의 정통한 거장의virtuoso 연주이다.

870 예술의 거장, 대가
이 음악가는 세계적으로 알려진 거장virtuoso이다.

SYNONYMS WORDS THAT MEAN THE SAME THING

841 The little-known soldier was finally recognized as an **unsung** hero of the war.

ⓐ unpublicized
ⓑ fallacious
ⓒ serene
ⓓ pivotal

842 The project failed because of **unwarranted** interference from outside.

ⓐ wretched
ⓑ groundless
ⓒ detested
ⓓ relinquished

843 The court's decision **upheld** the city's plan to build a new stadium.

ⓐ begot
ⓑ rectified
ⓒ supported
ⓓ conceived

844 The controversial book generated an **uproar** of criticism among readers.

ⓐ throng
ⓑ clamor
ⓒ omission
ⓓ repletion

845 The prince **usurped** the king's authority and unlawfully took control of the kingdom.

ⓐ tapered
ⓑ gainsaid
ⓒ stole
ⓓ scoured

846 The craftsman **utilized** a sharp knife to cut the wood.

ⓐ wrangled
ⓑ used
ⓒ meddled
ⓓ strived

847 The sick man **uttered** a cry of pain.

ⓐ quoted
ⓑ assisted
ⓒ curbed
ⓓ said

848 When the light went out, the room was in **utter** darkness.

ⓐ torpid
ⓑ decisive
ⓒ complete
ⓓ voracious

849 Because the candidate has **vacillated** on this issue, no one knows what he really believes.

ⓐ toadied
ⓑ coveted
ⓒ waffled
ⓓ attuned

850 The description of this person is so **vague** that it might apply to almost anyone.

ⓐ synthetic
ⓑ imprecise
ⓒ slant
ⓓ esoteric

851 There was no **valid** reason to grant the request, so we said no.

ⓐ slavish
ⓑ fastidious
ⓒ sound
ⓓ industrious

DAY 29

852 The laser beam **vaporized** a small amount of the target.

    ⓐ deluged

    ⓑ befell

    ⓒ toiled

    ⓓ evaporated

853 The temperature in this location is highly **variable** and may change 50 degrees in an hour.

    ⓐ mercurial

    ⓑ fanatic

    ⓒ volatile

    ⓓ incorrigible

854 The **variable** in this equation is temperature, which may change greatly.

    ⓐ doctrine

    ⓑ factor

    ⓒ idiom

    ⓓ shade

855 This painting shows a **variegated** pattern of colors against a dark background.

    ⓐ implausible

    ⓑ resplendent

    ⓒ rendered

    ⓓ diverse

856 Despite his **vehement** protest, he was sent to prison.

    ⓐ earnest

    ⓑ furtive

    ⓒ glacial

    ⓓ impartial

857 The school **venerated** the memory of its founder.

    ⓐ revered

    ⓑ wavered

    ⓒ clarified

    ⓓ harnessed

858 The engine **vents** its exhaust through a pipe.

    ⓐ extricates

    ⓑ releases

    ⓒ facilitates

    ⓓ extirpates

859 This is the **vent** through which hot air is expelled.

    ⓐ votary

    ⓑ woe

    ⓒ duct

    ⓓ reflux

860 The speech was too **verbose** and should have been shortened.

    ⓐ subtle

    ⓑ ominous

    ⓒ prolix

    ⓓ infamous

861 The arms control agreement required both sides to **verify** the number of each other's weapons.

    ⓐ abridge

    ⓑ vary

    ⓒ refute

    ⓓ ascertain

862 The rocket's **vertical** flight took it to a high altitude.

    ⓐ abstract

    ⓑ perpendicular

    ⓒ horizontal

    ⓓ direct

863 Only a **vestige** of the building remained after a thousand years.

    ⓐ candor

    ⓑ fervor

    ⓒ trace

    ⓓ slab

864 We thought the plan was **viable**, so we proceeded with it.

ⓐ surreal

ⓑ insipid

ⓒ edible

ⓓ practical

865 A healthy diet gave the patient **vigor** and stamina.

ⓐ lodge

ⓑ barge

ⓒ parcel

ⓓ vitality

866 In a speech, the politician **vilified** his opponent with harsh language.

ⓐ fathomed

ⓑ abated

ⓒ defamed

ⓓ shivered

867 The commission's investigation **vindicated** the judge of all accusations against him.

ⓐ acquiesced

ⓑ shattered

ⓒ rendered

ⓓ exonerated

868 She had a **vindictive** character and often imagined taking revenge on those who had wronged her.

ⓐ imaginary

ⓑ spiteful

ⓒ forgiving

ⓓ capricious

869 This recording is a **virtuoso** performance of the concerto.

ⓐ fickle

ⓑ brilliant

ⓒ candid

ⓓ deft

870 This musician is a **virtuoso** known around the world.

ⓐ penchant

ⓑ craftsman

ⓒ artisan

ⓓ expert

DAY 29

Answers

841-845 ⓐⓑⓒⓑⓒ	856-860 ⓐⓐⓑⓒⓒ
846-850 ⓑⓓⓒⓒⓑ	861-865 ⓓⓑⓒⓓⓓ
851-855 ⓒⓓⓒⓑⓓ	866-870 ⓒⓓⓑⓑⓓ

243

DAY 30

☆871 **virtuous**
[vɔ́ːrtʃuəs]

adj. consistent with high moral or ethical standards
SYN principled, upright

It is much easier to praise _____ behavior than to practice it.

☆872 **virulent**
[vírʃulənt]

adj. highly infectious or poisonous; extremely bitter, hostile, or malicious
SYN infectious, infective, noxious, poisonous, bitter, hateful, hostile, malignant, venomous

The author's _____ attacks on other authors made him many enemies.

☆873 **vital**
[váitl]

adj. energetic; pertaining to life; essential or necessary
SYN energetic, strong, vigorous, critical, essential, necessary

1. An athlete, my sister is the most _____ person I know.
2. Respiration is a _____ function of the body.

☆874 **vitality**
[vaitǽləti]

n. great strength and energy
SYN energy, exuberance, force, power, strength, vigor

A man of great _____, he remained busy and productive until his death at age 80.

☆875 **vivid**
[vívi]

adj. extremely bright and distinct
SYN bright, colorful, intense

The warning sign was _____ red in color.

☆876 **vociferous**
[vousífərəs]

adj. highly vocal; very noisy and outspoken
SYN boisterous, loud, noisy

A _____ group of protesters showed up at city hall to oppose a planned highway project.

SCAFFOLDING

871 덕 있는, 고결한, 정숙한   덕망있는virtuous 행동은 실천하는 것보다 칭찬하는 것이 훨씬 더 쉽다.

872 유독한, 악의가 있는   그 작가는 다른 작가들에 대한 악의적virulent 공격으로 많은 적을 만들었다.

873 생기가 넘치는, 지극히 중요한, 치명적인   1. 육상선수인 내 여동생은 내가 아는 가장 생기 넘치는vital 사람이다.
     2. 호흡은 우리 몸에 지극히 중요한vital 기능이다.

874 생명력, 활력   생명력vitality이 왕성한 그는 그의 나이 80에 죽을 때까지 바쁘고 생산적으로 살았다.

875 생생한, 선명한   경고 표시는 선명한vivid 붉은 색이었다.

876 소란한, 시끄러운   시끄러운vociferous 항의자 단체가 계획된 고속도로 프로젝트에 반대하기 위해 시청에 모습을 드러냈다.

☆877 **void**
[vɔid]

adj. completely empty; of no effect or use

SYN devoid, empty, unoccupied, vacant, ineffective, inoperative, useless

1. This sentence is _____ of meaning.
2. This agreement is _____ and cannot be enforced.

☆878 **void**
[vɔid]

n. an empty space

SYN cavity, vacuum

The space between stars was once considered an empty
_____.

☆879 **volatile**
[válətil]

adj. quick to evaporate; very changeable in mood or disposition

SYN fleeting, transient, unstable

1. The _____ liquid evaporated quickly.
2. A man of _____ temperament, he was quick to get angry.

☆880 **volition**
[voulíʃən]

n. the act or power of will, choice, or decision

SYN choice, will

Did you act of your own _____, or were you forced to act by
others?

☆881 **voluble**
[váljubəl]

adj. able to speak easily and continuously, or given to doing so

SYN fluent, glib, loquacious, talkative

My aunt is such a _____ person that she seems never to
stop talking.

☆882 **voluminous**
[vəlú:mənəs]

adj. very large in volume or extent

SYN ample, big, extensive

A _____ work, this history is more than 2,000 pages long.

DAY 30

SCAFFOLDING

877 빈, 공허한, 무효의
    1. 이 문장은 의미가 없다void.
    2. 이 협정은 무효이며void 집행될 수 없다.
878 공허, 진공, 공간
    별들의 사이는 한때 빈 공간void으로 여겨졌다.
879 휘발성의, 변덕스러운
    1. 휘발성volatile 액체는 빨리 증발했다.
    2. 변덕스러운volatile 성미의 그 남자는 쉽게 화를 냈다.
880 의지, 결단력
    당신은 당신의 의지대로volition 행동을 했습니까 아니면 다른 사람들한테 떠밀려 했습니까?
881 수다스러운, 유창한
    내 이모는 매우 수다스러운voluble 사람이라 절대 말하는 것을 멈추는 법이 없는 듯 했다.
882 다작의, 방대한, 부피가 큰
    이 역사는 방대한voluminous 작업으로, 길이가 2,000페이지가 넘는다.

245

☆883 **voluntary**
[váləntèri]

adj. done or chosen of one's own free will

SYN deliberate, intended

_____ choices and actions carry with them certain responsibilities.

☆884 **vulgarian**
[vʌlgɛ́əriən]

n. a person of rude and uncultivated manners

SYN barbarian, churl

A _____, he offended everyone with his coarse manners and rude speech.

☆885 **vulnerable**
[vʌ́lnərəbəl]

adj. unprotected and therefore open to attack, damage, or capture

SYN defenseless, susceptible, weak

An unguarded approach left the fort _____ to attack.

☆886 **wake**
[weik]

n. a path or trail left by a moving object such as a ship; the aftermath or result of something

SYN path, trail

The ship left a long, white _____ behind it through the sea.

☆887 **warm**
[wɔ:rm]

adj. sincere and enthusiastic; moderately hot; heated

SYN enthusiastic, heated, hot

The entertainer got a _____ reception from her fans.

☆888 **wary**
[wɛ́əri]

adj. attentive; cautious; watchful

SYN careful, cautious, prudent

An unpleasant experience left him _____ of repeating it.

883 자발적인, 고의의   자발적인Voluntary 선택과 행동은 일정한 책임을 수반한다.
884 속물, 속인   속물vulgarian인 그는 조악한 태도와 무례한 연설로 모든 사람을 불쾌하게 했다.
885 상처입기 쉬운, 약한   요새는 무방비한 길로 인해 공격에 쉽게 노출됐다vulnerable.
886 항적, 배 떠나간 자국, 지나간 자국   배는 그 뒤로 바다 위에 길고도 하얀 항적wake을 남겼다.
887 따뜻한, 다정한, 더운   그 예능인은 그녀의 팬들로부터 열렬한warm 환영을 받았다.
888 경계하는, 주의 깊은   경험이 불쾌해서 그는 이를 반복하는데 신중했다wary.

☆889 **wayward**

[wéiwərd]

adj. unwilling to obey or conform

SYN errant, unpredictable, willful

A _____ child, he ran away from home at an early age and got into trouble.

☆890 **weary**

[wíəri]

adj. very tired and drained of energy.

SYN drained, exhausted, fatigued, overworked, tired

_____ after work, the man went home and went to sleep.

☆891 **weary**

[wíəri]

v. to annoy or make someone tired

SYN annoy, tire

Children sometimes _____ their parents with questions.

☆892 **weight**

[weit]

n. how much a thing weighs; the importance, significance, or relevance of something

SYN heaviness, mass, importance, significance

1. On Earth, this object has a _____ of 1 kilogram.
2. How much _____ should we give to this information when we make our decision?

☆893 **well-founded**

[wélfàundid]

adj. based on reliable information or sound judgment

SYN reasonable, sound, substantiated

Our suspicion of him was _____, for he turned out to be dishonest.

☆894 **whim**

[hwim]

n. an irrational, impulsive urge, decision, or action

SYN caprice, fancy, impulse

On a _____, she bought a book about travel to distant lands.

SCAFFOLDING

889 제멋대로 하는, 고집 센, 변덕스러운   제멋대로인wayward 그 아이는 어린 나이에 가출하여 말썽을 일으켰다.

890 피로한, 지쳐있는, 따분한, 실증 나는   일을 하고 난 뒤 지쳐서Weary 그 남자는 집에 가서 잠이 들었다.

891 지치게 하다, 싫증나게 하다   아이들은 가끔 질문들로 부모님들을 지치게 한다weary.

892 무게, 중요성, 비중   1. 이 물체는 지구에서 1kg 나간다weight.

     2. 우리가 결정을 할 때 이 정보에 얼마만큼의 비중weight을 둬야 합니까?

893 충분한 근거가 있는   그에 대한 우리의 의심은 충분히 근거가 있었다well-founded. 왜냐하면 그는 부정직하다고 판명되었기 때문이다.

894 변덕, 일시적 생각   일시적인 기분으로whim 그녀는 먼 지역으로의 여행에 대한 책을 샀다.

☆895 **whimsical**

[*h*wímzikəl]

adj. based on whim or fancy; often used to describe light humor

SYN fanciful, funny, playful

A _____ study of life in a big city, this book is full of funny stories.

☆896 **widespread**

[wàidspréd]

adj. covering a wide area; commonly practiced

SYN broad, common, extensive, general, large, popular, sweeping, wide-ranging

Drinking coffee is a _____ practice in many countries.

☆897 **willful**

[wílfəl]

adj. unwilling to obey, yield, or accept direction

SYN capricious, obstinate, stubborn

A _____ child, he was disobedient toward his parents and teachers.

☆898 **wince**

[wins]

v. to withdraw for reasons of fear, distaste, or disgust

SYN cringe, recoil, shrink

The movie was so full of violence that it made some viewers _____.

☆899 **zany**

[zéini]

adj. funny in an especially wild, extreme, or unpredictable way

SYN comical, funny

The comic actors became known for their _____ performances in movies.

☆900 **zealous**

[zéləs]

adj. very active, committed, or devoted

SYN ardent, enthusiastic

A _____ member of the group, he did all he could to help attain its goals.

SCAFFOLDING

895 마음이 잘 변하는, 별난 대도시에서의 삶에 대한 별난whimsical 연구를 담은 이 책은 재미있는 이야기들로 가득하다.

896 널리 보급된, 만연된 커피를 마시는 것은 많은 국가에서 널리 퍼진widespread 관행이다.

897 계획적인, 외고집의 제멋대로 구는willful 그 아이는 부모님이나 선생님들에게 순종하지 않았다.

898 주춤하다, 움츠리다 폭력장면으로 가득 찬 그 영화는 관객들로 하여금 움츠러들게wince 했다.

899 어릿광대 같은 그 코믹 연기자들은 영화에서의 우스꽝스러운zany 연기로 알려지게 되었다.

900 열심인, 열광적인 열정적인zealous 그룹의 멤버인 그는 목표를 성취하는데 그가 할 수 있는 모든 것을 하였다.

248

SYNONYMS WORDS THAT MEAN THE SAME THING

871 It is much easier to praise **virtuous** behavior than to practice it.

ⓐ officious
ⓑ upright
ⓒ vigilant
ⓓ voracious

872 The author's **virulent** attacks on other authors made him many enemies.

ⓐ serious
ⓑ constant
ⓒ noxious
ⓓ impetuous

873 Respiration is a **vital** function of the body.

ⓐ esoteric
ⓑ dull
ⓒ intensive
ⓓ essential

874 A man of great **vitality**, he remained busy and productive until his death at age 80.

ⓐ reprisal
ⓑ profanity
ⓒ strength
ⓓ mold

875 The warning sign was **vivid** red in color.

ⓐ slack
ⓑ intense
ⓒ infamous
ⓓ synthetic

876 A **vociferous** group of protesters showed up at city hall to oppose a planned highway project.

ⓐ transparent
ⓑ odious
ⓒ ethical
ⓓ boisterous

877 This agreement is **void** and cannot be enforced.

ⓐ prodigal
ⓑ inoperative
ⓒ vacant
ⓓ valid

878 The space between stars was once considered an empty **void**.

ⓐ euphony
ⓑ quagmire
ⓒ plight
ⓓ vacuum

879 The **volatile** liquid evaporated quickly.

ⓐ stable
ⓑ solid
ⓒ furtive
ⓓ transient

880 Did you act of your own **volition**, or were you forced to act by others?

ⓐ penchant
ⓑ will
ⓒ vengeance
ⓓ attempt

881 My aunt is such a **voluble** person that she seems never to stop talking.

ⓐ quiet
ⓑ noisy
ⓒ loquacious
ⓓ accessible

DAY 30

882 A **voluminous** work, this history is more than 2,000 pages long.

ⓐ sparse

ⓑ extensive

ⓒ erudite

ⓓ intensive

883 **Voluntary** choices and actions carry with them certain responsibilities.

ⓐ deliberate

ⓑ throbbing

ⓒ mandatory

ⓓ unconscious

884 A **vulgarian**, he offended everyone with his coarse manners and rude speech.

ⓐ mercenary

ⓑ extremist

ⓒ fanatic

ⓓ churl

885 An unguarded approach left the fort **vulnerable** to attack.

ⓐ fastidious

ⓑ voluntary

ⓒ susceptible

ⓓ impervious

886 The ship left a long, white **wake** behind it through the sea.

ⓐ peril

ⓑ trail

ⓒ penchant

ⓓ zest

887 The entertainer got a **warm** reception from her fans.

ⓐ desiccated

ⓑ mesmerized

ⓒ truncated

ⓓ sincere

888 An unpleasant experience left him **wary** of repeating it.

ⓐ reckless

ⓑ prodigal

ⓒ attentive

ⓓ heedless

889 A **wayward** child, he ran away from home at an early age and got into trouble.

ⓐ intuitive

ⓑ incorrigible

ⓒ errant

ⓓ obedient

890 **Weary** after work, the man went home and went to sleep.

ⓐ refreshed

ⓑ excited

ⓒ invigorated

ⓓ drained

891 Children sometimes **weary** their parents with questions.

ⓐ tire

ⓑ swell

ⓒ detect

ⓓ substantiate

892 How much **weight** should we give to this information when we make our decision?

ⓐ lampoon

ⓑ significance

ⓒ evasion

ⓓ proliferation

893 Our suspicion of him was **well-founded**, for he turned out to be dishonest.

ⓐ complimented

ⓑ facilitated

ⓒ substantiated

ⓓ embodied

894 On a whim, she bought a book about travel to distant lands.

ⓐ aversion

ⓑ misanthrope

ⓒ impulse

ⓓ apathy

895 A whimsical study of life in a big city, this book is full of funny stories.

ⓐ resplendent

ⓑ attentive

ⓒ playful

ⓓ unsung

896 Drinking coffee is a widespread practice in many countries.

ⓐ jovial

ⓑ mercurial

ⓒ cloying

ⓓ broad

897 A willful child, he was disobedient toward his parents and teachers.

ⓐ vulnerable

ⓑ intermittent

ⓒ reachable

ⓓ stubborn

898 The movie was so full of violence that it made some viewers wince.

ⓐ discern

ⓑ tire

ⓒ recoil

ⓓ applause

899 The comic actors became known for their zany performances in movies.

ⓐ unwarranted

ⓑ comical

ⓒ congenital

ⓓ condensed

900 A zealous member of the group, he did all he could to help attain its goals.

ⓐ susceptible

ⓑ ardent

ⓒ conceptual

ⓓ illusory

Answers

871-875 ⓑⓒⓓⓒⓑ	886-890 ⓑⓓⓒⓒⓓ
876-880 ⓑⓑⓓⓓⓑ	891-895 ⓐⓑⓒⓒⓒ
881-885 ⓒⓑⓐⓓⓒ	896-900 ⓓⓓⓒⓑⓑ